Disability and Technology

This edited collection brings together keynote articles from the journal *Disability & Society* to provide a comprehensive and thought-provoking exploration of the place of technology in disabled people's lives, documenting and analysing the growing impact of technology on disability and society over recent decades. The authors explore theoretical, empirical and moral dilemmas that arise with the changing relationship between technological change and the lives, aspirations and possibilities of disabled people. The volume is organised into three parts which consider early foundational work connecting disability and technology; key empirical studies related to the optimum use of technologies for independence and inclusion; and new moral and social dynamics thrown up by technological developments for disabled people's lives.

Alan Roulstone is Professor of Disability Studies at the University of Leeds, UK.

Alison Sheldon is a Teaching Fellow in Disability Studies at the University of Leeds, UK.

Jennifer Harris is Professor Emeritus in Social Work at the University of Dundee, UK.

Key Papers from Disability & Society
Editor: Professor Michele Moore

The *Key Papers from Disability & Society* series reflects a commitment to making significant papers that have been published in the journal over the years available to a wider audience in an easy-to-reach topic-based format. Each book in the series takes a retrospective look at the journal's contribution to understanding changing perspectives on a topic identified by the journal's Executive Editors as being of importance to the journal's readers. Executive Editors have worked back through all papers published on the topic in *Disability & Society* over the years to make a selection of material which offers the contemporary reader not only a historic overview of key developments in the field, but also a flavour of who the key researchers, theorists, and practitioners are in relation to the focal theme. The selection also highlights both the challenges which have been pursued, and those which lie ahead, in the struggle to promote the rights of disabled people. This struggle lies at the heart of the journal's core values. Each book in the series combines academic and activist perspectives, prioritising voices of disabled people, their families, and their representative organisations wherever possible, in order to give shape to the developments, debates, and change that inform our understanding of the relationship between disability and society.

Anyone new to the field of Disability Studies will find this series an essential resource, enabling rapid familiarity with the history of ideas which are relevant to students and researchers in the field, as well as to the ideas of activists and policy makers. Those familiar with the journal will find the series invaluable as it draws together contributions relating to a common issue and purpose, offering an efficient and stimulating repository of leading ideas. All books in the *Key Papers from Disability & Society* are highly recommended for reading lists and libraries.

In this Series:

Childhood and Disability
Key Papers from Disability & Society
Edited by Sarah Beazley and Val Williams
978-0-415-72923-9

Disability and Technology
Key Papers from Disability & Society
Edited by Alan Roulstone, Alison Sheldon and Jennifer Harris
978-1-138-93218-0

Disability and Technology

Key papers from *Disability & Society*

Edited by
Alan Roulstone, Alison Sheldon and Jennifer Harris

Routledge
Taylor & Francis Group

LONDON AND NEW YORK

First published 2016
by Routledge
2 Park Square, Milton Park, Abingdon, Oxon, OX14 4RN, UK

and by Routledge
711 Third Avenue, New York, NY 10017, USA

Routledge is an imprint of the Taylor & Francis Group, an informa business

© 2016 Taylor & Francis

British Library Cataloguing in Publication Data
A catalogue record for this book is available from the British Library

ISBN 13: 978-1-138-93218-0

Typeset in Times New Roman
by RefineCatch Limited, Bungay, Suffolk

Publisher's Note
The publisher accepts responsibility for any inconsistencies that may have
arisen during the conversion of this book from journal articles to book chapters,
namely the possible inclusion of journal terminology.

Disclaimer
Every effort has been made to contact copyright holders for their permission to
reprint material in this book. The publishers would be grateful to hear from any
copyright holder who is not here acknowledged and will undertake to rectify
any errors or omissions in future editions of this book.

Contents

CONTENTS

Part III: Moral and social tensions between disability and technology

Citation Information

The following chapters were originally published in *Disability & Society* (or in the same journal under its previous name of *Disability, Handicap & Society*). When citing this material, please use the original page numbering for each article, as follows:

Chapter 1
Communications Technology—empowerment or disempowerment?
Patricia Thornton
Disability, Handicap & Society, volume 8, issue 4 (1993) pp. 339–349

Chapter 2
In Whose Service? Technology, Care and Disabled People: the case for a disability politics perspective
Liz Johnson & Eileen Moxon
Disability & Society, volume 13, issue 2 (1998) pp. 241–258

Chapter 3
Information and Communication Technologies and the Opportunities of Disabled Persons in the Swedish Labour Market
Dimitris Michailakis
Disability & Society, volume 16, issue 4 (2001) pp. 477–500

Chapter 4
Enacting disability: how can science and technology studies inform disability studies?
Vasilis Galis
Disability & Society, volume 26, issue 7 (December 2011) pp. 825–838

Chapter 5
The use, role and application of advanced technology in the lives of disabled people in the UK
Jennifer Harris
Disability & Society, volume 25, issue 4 (June 2010) pp. 427–439

Chapter 6
A common open space or a digital divide? A social model perspective on the online disability community in China
Baorong Guo, John C. Bricout and Jin Huang
Disability & Society, volume 20, issue 1 (January 2005) pp. 49–66

Chapter 7
Increases in wheelchair use and perceptions of disablement
Bob Sapey, John Stewart and Glenis Donaldson
Disability & Society, volume 20, issue 5 (August 2005) pp. 489–505

Chapter 8
Back to the future, disability and the digital divide
Stephen J. Macdonald and John Clayton
Disability & Society, volume 28, issue 5 (August 2013) pp. 702–718

Chapter 9
Disability, identity and disclosure in the online dating environment
Natasha Saltes
Disability & Society, volume 28, issue 1 (January 2013) pp. 96–109

Chapter 10
'I know, I can, I will try': youths and adults with intellectual disabilities in Sweden using information and communication technology in their everyday life
Rebecka Näslund and Åsa Gardelli
Disability & Society, volume 28, issue 1 (January 2013) pp. 28–40

Chapter 11
Implants and ethnocide: learning from the cochlear implant controversy
Robert Sparrow
Disability & Society, volume 25, issue 4 (June 2010) pp. 455–466

Chapter 12
Cyborg anxiety: Oscar Pistorius and the boundaries of what it means to be human
Leslie Swartz and Brian Watermeyer
Disability & Society, volume 23, issue 2 (March 2008) pp. 187–190

For any permission-related enquiries please visit:
http://www.tandfonline.com/page/help/permissions

Notes on Contributors

John C. Bricout is Associate Dean in the School of Social Work at the University of Texas at Arlington, TX, USA. He studies the influence of social technologies, including Web-based and assistive technologies on the participation of people with disabilities in paid work, governance, and community life.

John Clayton is Senior Lecturer in Human Geography at Northumbria University, Newcastle, UK. His research interests lie primarily in social and urban geography, and the connections between geography, social identities, and inequalities. His research to date has focused on 'race' and racism, everyday urban multiculturalism, social class and Higher Education, digital inclusion/exclusion and the political discourses of austerity, localism, inclusion, and cohesion.

Glenis Donaldson is Senior Lecturer in the Department of Health Professions at Manchester Metropolitan University, UK. She has a clinical background in Paediatrics and worked as a senior clinician for 16 years in the north-west region. Her current research interests include disability – particularly the patient's experiences of health and social care, clinical gait analysis, and the use of lower limb orthotics in children.

Vasilis Galis is an Associate Professor in the Technologies in Practice Research Group at the IT University of Copenhagen, Denmark. His current research focuses on social movements and their use of digital media, radical politics, counter-information, internet activism, and lay expertise.

Åsa Gardelli is Associate Professor in the Department of Arts, Communication and Education at Luleå University of Technology, Sweden.

Baorong Guo is Associate Professor of Social Work at the University of Missouri – Saint Louis, MO, USA. Baorong's research interests include human service non-profits, socio-economic development, and asset-building among low-income families.

Jennifer Harris is Professor Emeritus in Social Work at the University of Dundee, UK.

Jin Huang is Assistant Professor of Social Work at Saint Louis University, Missouri, USA. He is interested in social policy that supports family and child well-being, with a particular focus on asset-based policy for disadvantaged children and children with disabilities.

Liz Johnson was based in the Community Care Division of the Nuffield Institute for Health, University of Leeds, UK.

Stephen J. Macdonald is Senior Lecturer and Programme Leader in the Centre for Applied Social Science at the University of Sunderland, UK. His research interests are in the area of learning disabilities and mental health. His theoretical interests are in criminology, disability studies, and medical sociology. He is the author of *Dyslexia and Crime: a social model approach* (2010), and *Towards a Sociology of Dyslexia: exploring links between dyslexia, disability and social class* (2009).

Dimitris Michailakis is Professor of Sociology at the University of Gävle, Sweden, and Chair Professor of Social Work at the University of Linköping, Sweden. He is the author of several reports for national and international organisations e.g. for the UN, WHO, The Swedish Ministry of Health and Social Affairs as well as the author of articles in journals with high reputation.

Michele Moore is Professor of Inclusive Education at Northumbria University, UK, and Editor-in-Chief of the journal *Disability & Society*.

Eileen Moxon was Head of the Department of Social Work at the University of Bradford, UK.

Rebecka Näslund is a Ph.D. student in the Department of Business Administration, Technology and Social Sciences at Luleå University, Sweden. Her current project aims to develop ways to study how ICT, agency and disability become constructed in a collective made up by actors such as humans (pupils with intellectual disabilities) and non-humans (computers, mobile phones, policy-documents).

Alan Roulstone is Professor of Disability Studies at the University of Leeds, UK.

Natasha Saltes is based in the Department of Sociology at Queen's University, Kingston, Ontario, Canada.

Bob Sapey was based in the Department of Applied Social Sciences at the University of Lancaster, UK. His current research is focused on voice hearing and the implications of social explanations for this experience for social work practice.

Alison Sheldon is a Teaching Fellow in Disability Studies at the University of Leeds, UK.

Robert Sparrow is Associate Professor in the Philosophy Department at Monash University, Melbourne, Australia. His research interests are bioethics, political philosophy and applied ethics, and philosophical arguments with real-world implications.

John Stewart was based in the Department of Applied Social Sciences at the University of Lancaster, UK.

Leslie Swartz is Professor of Psychology at Stellenbosch University, South Africa. His interests span the fields of mental health and disability studies, and he was central in establishing the Centre for Public Mental Health in collaboration with the University of Cape Town. His recent publications include *Disability and International Development* (co-edited with Mac MacLachlan, 2009), and *Able Bodied: scenes from a curious life* (2010).

Patricia Thornton worked in the Social Policy Research Unit at the University of York, UK, for 18 years, developing an international reputation for her comparative research on policies and practices to promote employment opportunities for disabled people. She left the SPRU in 2005 to work on a project for Voluntary Service Overseas in Papua New Guinea. She was piloting a survey in the Highlands region which was to become a foundation for a national survey.

Brian Watermeyer is a Research Fellow at Stellenbosch University, South Africa. He is a registered clinical psychologist, with extensive experience as a university academic and researcher, clinical trainer and supervisor, corporate and governmental consultant, psychotherapist, and in-service trainer. His field of research and training expertise is that of disability inequality and transformation.

Series Editor's Preface

Michele Moore

Over the past 30 years the increasing place of technology has had a huge and growing impact on disabled people's lives. This book, on *Disability and Technology* in the *Key Papers from Disability & Society* series, was first put together in our *Virtual Special Issues* series as part of an initiative to make significant papers published in the journal available to a wider audience in a topic-based format. Three of the journal's Executive Editors have taken a retrospective look at the journal's contribution over the past 30 years to understanding changing perspectives on the place of technology in disabled people's lives. Papers presented document the escalating and challenging impact of technology on disability and society over the decades.

Theoretical, philosophical and research articles have been collated to map changing technology, explore enabling application of new technologies and to promote understanding of potential new forms of disabling barriers which could, if treated uncritically, create unforeseen forms of oppression.

Readings included in this book signal the need for open and differing engagement with technological development. They keep in view controversies and contentions such as have been around since the invention of the telephone created new barriers to inclusion of deaf people, and which continue to intensify as technology perpetually both advances and problematizes inclusive responses to impairment issues. The Editors have chosen content to make explicit dilemmas posed by technology for disabled people such as the question of whether technology is reaching disabled people fast enough, global access issues and ways in which technology may liberate, but also limit us. The book highlights issues which will promote serious insider-led, activist and scholarly engagement with technology debates for the future.

I am grateful to all authors whose papers feature in this collection and to the Editorial Board of *Disability & Society* whose high-quality refereeing enables the journal to publish its influential work. Helen Oliver always provides invaluable, friendly and efficient administrative support which is much appreciated by journal friends across the world. Also our thanks are extended to the publishers who offer consistent support to the journal and its important ambitions for disabled people's rights.

Communications Technology—empowerment or disempowerment?

PATRICIA THORNTON

Social Policy Research Unit, University of York, Heslington, York, United Kingdom

ABSTTRACT   *Developments in communication technology can reduce dependence on others and facilitate independent living for disabled people. Recently developed telephone-based services allow users to call up help quickly, as and when they need it. But the dominant model of provision emphasises vulnerability, assumes a need for protection and imposes rules about appropriate use. The article identifies the influence of manufacturers and providers of communication alarms in perpetuating paternalistic approaches to services for older disabled people and limiting the potential for user determination of need. Emergent models which aim to facilitate user-control face low expectations among users, the entrenched attitudes of providers and the dominance of the market in influencing practice. The mixed economy of social care is likely to increase the gap between providers' interests and users' needs.*

Introduction

There is a growing consensus that people who need personal or practical help at home on a daily basis should be able to say when and by whom that help is given. It is increasingly recognised, too, that standard, routinely provided services cannot cater for fluctuating or unpredictable needs and can be as institutionalising as the institutional care that community care policies seek to avoid. We can now see pilot initiatives, such as the Haringey On-call Support Project (Zarb, 1991), which aim to facilitate control by disabled people over their care or support services at home. But, as yet, little attention has been given to the mechanisms needed to effect user-control over the nature and timing of support. In particular, how can users best make their non-routine or urgent needs known and be confident of a response to their wishes? What sort of communications system is needed to let users call up the help they want at times they themselves choose?

In this context new technology will have a central function. New telephone-based communication systems now offer people in their own homes a means of communicating with the providers of care services and are thought to be one of the few technological innovations to have had any impact on the range of home-based support services for older disabled people (Baldock, 1991). These systems, generically termed 'community alarms' in the UK, 'care phones' in Sweden and 'personal response systems' in the USA, overcome some of the limitations of the ordinary telephone: the technology includes a portable trigger and speech amplification so that the user can make a call without having to access the telephone; and calls are guaranteed an answer from staff at a central point who then arrange for someone to visit the user if required.

On the face of it, this type of technological innovation has the potential to fill the communication gap between a user who requires assistance and a source of help. Moreover, as the user takes the initiative in requesting a service, it may offer more scope for users themselves to define their needs and appropriate responses to them. But provision of the *means* of communication alone does not, as Harbert (1992) has claimed, necessarily place "a measure of power and control firmly in the hands of service users". The means is only one part of the communication system. Technology cannot be seen as standing alone, isolated from its cultural dimensions (Cornes, 1991). As I have argued elsewhere (Thornton with Mountain, 1992) at least three elements are necessary if communications technology is to have a part to play in offering users control over their services. First, the service user needs an accessible, reliable and easy to use means of communication between the home and those who will provide the assistance. Secondly, the people who provide the help must be acceptable and include a range of competencies, to meet diverse needs for assistance. Finally, the service system must let users themselves define need and legitimate use and not impose rules about its purpose.

Of these three elements the first has received most attention. Communications technology in recent years has become more reliable, accessible and easier to use. The equipment remains relatively standard, however, and although portable triggers have become lighter to carry and easier to manipulate they still depend on a degree of manual dexterity in the user. The second element—a pool of people available to respond to any request for help—is less well developed, for reasons which will be elaborated shortly. The third element, user-led definition of use is marked by its absence within the vast majority of 'community alarm' services. Most services which combine a means of communicating the request for help with an appropriate source of help are conceived and delivered within a narrow and restrictive set of rules about their purpose and function, effectively limiting the benefits to the users.

This article draws on evidence from a pluralistic study of the effectiveness of communication alarm services (Thornton with Mountain, 1992) carried out by the Social Policy Research Unit (SPRU) to report the experiences of older disabled users and to show how the dominant model of service provision fails to address the range of communication needs. I ask why, in contrast to the potential of new technology as an opportunity for user-control, communication alarm services typically operate within narrow definitions of their purpose and impose constraints on their use. The article outlines the evolution of the technology and identifies the influence of manufacturers and providers on the design and delivery of the service system as a whole. It draws on the research to show how constraints on use not only limit the effectiveness of the service but also perpetuate and reinforce paternalistic approaches to service delivery. I ask whether services dominated by manufacturer and provider interests can meet current expectations of user control and create more flexible and responsive support for people who wish to live independently but must rely on others for physical help.

Current Practice

Typically, communication alarm services are designed, promoted and delivered as emergency services for old people living alone. The operational priority is to provide a rapid response to physical injuries, often associated with falls, and to health emergencies where medically qualified attention is needed urgently. Although this article relates principally to provision in England and Wales, with, it is estimated, the largest proportion of alarm users in the population, this characterisation of typical services appears to be true worldwide. An overview of presentations at the first international symposium on personal response systems (PRS) noted that "across all countries primary users of PRS are women in their 70's and 80's, living alone, burdened with cardiac and musculoskeletal problems or subject to falls" (Dibner, 1991, p. 6).

Although the technology became available to people living outside grouped supported housing only in the last decade, most local authorities can now offer a communication alarm service. Services in England and Wales are run almost exclusively by housing departments, although a handful of social services departments run their own and some are jointly managed. Users get to have the service through a number of possible routes. They can subscribe directly to a service run by a housing department; or they can have provision arranged through a social services department, or, less commonly, a health authority. Home alarm equipment is not sold in shops but is available for purchase directly from some manufacturers for those users who are able to arrange and supervise their own team of supporters to respond when help is asked for. Because privately purchased equipment also links into operator centres run by public authorities private users find themselves subject the same philosophies and practices.

These communication services are set up to treat calls for help as potential life-threatening emergencies. They aim to eradicate fallibility in both the technology and in the staff who serve the system. Services either employ staff such as mobile wardens or call on a ready pool of individuals known to users. Ambulance services may be called on if other response services are unavailable. Some communication alarm services will respond to other kinds of call for assistance, providing their ability to respond to 'real emergencies' is not compromised. Staff will often act out of compassion to help people requiring personal care but it is unusual for the service to be viewed primarily as a means of assisting with personal care needs. Commonly, help with self care is considered to intrude on the remit of nursing or care staff employed by other departments. An independent scheme in Tower Hamlets appears to have had few emulators in its proclaimed purpose of filling the gap in out-of-hours and weekend care services, employing staff formally sanctioned to help people to bed or to use the lavatory (Pellow, 1987). A minority of services will communicate messages via the operator from users to other parts of the service system but this is usually an 'extra', rarely openly promoted.

Although the objectives and functions of communication alarm services are not often spelt out officially—because of the incremental and opportunistic way in which most have developed, as I will show below—most assume a taken-for-granted approach to operationalising the boundaries of their activities. Two assumptions dominate: potential users are older people living alone 'at risk' of injury, accident or sudden medical emergencies; and the role of the technology is to assuage their 'fear' of such events and to protect them against life-threatening consequences. The themes of fear, vulnerability and risk pervade promotional material directed by both manufacturers and providers at potential users; services commonly offer 'round the clock protection' or 'protection for people living alone'. One pamphlet, produced by a manufacturer for use by a local authority, calls a heart attack "the moment feared most by every elderly person—when, without help, they might be without hope".

Origins

The coincidence of manufacturers' interests and providers' organisational values has determined the shape of provision.

Communication alarm technology was not initially developed to meet the needs of people in the community. Needs and problems were not identified in advance of the search for appropriate technology (Shalinsky, 1989). The industry began with the introduction of communication systems within purpose built blocks or clusters of local authority housing intended primarily for elderly people. Once the idea of a communication link between occupants and a warden had been established, techno-logical methods of achieving that link became increasingly sophisticated. The rapid growth of sheltered housing provision in the 1960s and 1970s attracted manufac-turers in a competitive environment. The housing providers' interests were domi-nated by staffing considerations, rather than by tenants' needs; emphasis lay with increasing efficient use of the warden resource (Butler, 1989).

Further developments in technology meant that calls from several housing complexes could be routed to a single 'control centre', not merely to a site warden, via the telephone communication network. Equipping these offered a new opportu-nity for manufacturers. Although the basic equipment could be relatively simple and inexpensive, the drive to refine and improve upon communications technology led to increasing sophistication, including linked data bases holding details of callers, soft-ware for recording activity on the system, and multiple terminals to cope with antici-pated demand. Moreover, advances now meant that equipment installed in ordinary 'dispersed' housing, and not just in 'schemes', could be linked to central control stations. A new market in the community had opened up.

The establishment of central control systems added to providers' ability to make more efficient use of wardens who did not now need to be located within the housing complexes. The enormous capacity of the control centre technology meant that new users could be accommodated at little extra cost, especially where users nominated their relatives or neighbours to respond to their calls, instead of subscribing to the mobile warden service. The new dispersed technology also enabled housing depart-ments to expand their welfare role in a period of increasing pressure to justify a continuing and distinct role, as the traditional functions of local authority housing departments were squeezed by government policies. The Griffiths report (Griffiths, 1988) incited debate about who was best placed to run alarms schemes (Oldman, 1989) and proposals to reorganise local government also encouraged housing authorities to highlight their role as welfare providers.

Thus, communications technology did not become available to people living in ordinary housing in the community first and foremost as a response to their individual needs. Rather, manufacturers and housing providers were acting on generalised assumptions about the communality of need among older and disabled people. This 'special needs' view of the world is implicit in manufacturers' approach to the market: it assumes that if people suffer chronic ill-health, are old or disabled they 'need' an alarm service (Clapham & Smith, 1990; Thornton, 1992). It is, of course, in the inter-ests of the market to have as inclusive as possible a definition of 'need'. The attitude is deeply ingrained, leading to the invention of a phenomenon "denial of need" (Dibner, 1991) to explain the lack of demand for the technology. Housing departments, the principal providers of communication alarm services in England and Wales, tradition-ally have operated overtly within the special needs tradition, most notably in the provision of sheltered housing for elderly people and adapted accommodation for disabled people. As departments' ability to offer sheltered accommodation became constrained, alarm services meant that "one of the benefits of sheltered housing could be extended to people in their own homes" (Tinker, 1991, p. 21).

The policy of allocating services on the grounds of age or disability alone reinforces negative images of dependent populations and encourages the paternalistic practice of offering protection found in 'sheltered' housing and in alarm services. Local council traditions of 'looking after the elderly and disabled' remain strong, and services which demonstrate the care and protection provided retain their appeal for elected members (Butler, 1985). Indeed, local councils are still held publicly to account on those occasions when tenants in special category accommodation—and now those with an alarm service—are found dead. Protection is the business of the manufacturers too: they also make smoke alarms, intruder devices, door entry phones and, indeed, some alarms incorporate such features.

Consequences for Users

The previous sections have attempted to explain why communication alarm services promote the protection and reduction of risk of elderly people and why they aim to confine their uses to physical, life-endangering emergencies. I will turn now to consider the consequences for service users of this limited and narrow application of communications technology. Depth interviews with alarm service users in two case study services showed how narrow definitions of appropriate use limited the benefits to them of having the service. Interviews with workers in health, social services and voluntary services demonstrated how notions of appropriate users were perpetuated through the referral system. Yet close analysis of the sorts of use people *did* make of their alarm service showed how in reality the service was used more to sustain people in everyday living than to call up emergency treatment.

The rules for use are set by the providers and reinforced by social and health care workers in contact with users. Users are expected to comply in 'appropriate' use of the service, and not to 'abuse' it. Few services specify the sorts of circumstance in which the service might be used. Providers suppose a consensus as to what 'emergency' means and can be critical of users who try to cope without help even when injured. On the other hand they do not always accommodate users' own views of emergencies: one user interviewed was deterred by the attitude of the service providers who felt her urgent need to use the lavatory at night was not an 'emergency'.

The emergency-led stereotype made it difficult for users to consider employing the service for any purpose other than an event of a type they had already experienced. Users new to the service said "That's all you can use it for, falling. You can't use it for anything else". It did not occur to them that it could be used for reasons other than those they knew were permitted. Their reluctance to use the service other than in a physical emergency was shaped, too, by a concern about imposing on those whose role it was to respond. Even when physical help *was* urgently needed, some older people interviewed waited in discomfort until daylight before calling for help.

Assumptions about who might benefit led to a strong bias towards very old people prone to fall or suffer medical emergencies. In both case study schemes half of the users were over 80 and one in ten was over 90; 'falls' was given as a prime reason for referral, closely followed by medical conditions associated with falling. Most people referred to the schemes had previously suffered some fall or medical emergency where urgent treatment was needed. This bias perpetuated the stereotype of alarm services users, leading to more referrals of people with similar circumstances and comparative neglect of others who might benefit.

The emphasis on the vulnerability of alarm service users perpetuates the assumption that 'falls' are necessarily harmful and obscures the needs of people with limited mobility who from time to time need physical assistance to carry on with the activities of daily living. As it turned out, an analysis of calls made in the two case studies demonstrated that people used the service for the latter reasons more than for treatment of injuries or for medical attention. Indeed, incidents seen from outside as 'falls' actually were often the result of people being unable to cope alone with activities of daily living—getting out of bed, using the lavatory or transferring to or from a wheelchair. This fact is not reflected in promotional material and appears not to inform the practices of those whose job it is to propose service options to potential users.

Interestingly, however, social and health care workers interviewed showed a greater awareness of *younger* disabled people with mobility needs and were more inclined to view the service as an aid to independent living for them than for older people. There was little evidence from the research of older people being encouraged to use the service for rehabilitative purposes, in order to regain lost abilities or freedoms, although again this purpose was seen as central to the situation of younger disabled people. For older people the service was about reducing risk in their lives; for younger people it was seen as facilitating risk-taking.

The research found that users not only had to contend with the imposition of rules about what the service was for but also had to comply in accommodating and getting to grips with the technology. This had notable consequences for their self-esteem. Instruction on the techniques needed was for some difficult to assimilate and the consequent feelings of inadequacy in understanding and using the equipment caused some distress: people tended to see themselves rather than the instruction as inadequate. Some were nervous about using it in case they made an error. They also had to adapt their style of living to accommodate the equipment and to wear the portable trigger. Users tended to set off the alarm accidentally in the course of ordinary everyday actions and were obliged to modify their activities as a result. The modifications were relatively minor—not carrying objects close to the chest or not levering jars or bottles against the body when trying to open them—but the effect was to impose limitations on their activities.

New users were keen to conform to what the service expected of them because they were anxious about a repetition of a recent frightening event. Long-term users, on the other hand, were found to be less compliant, particularly with regard to wearing the pendant. The SPRU study, in line with all other national and international research, found the majority declined to wear the pendant constantly. Arguably, they rejected the premise that they needed constant protection (Thornton with Mountain, 1992). They set the pendant aside despite considerable pressure to wear it from social workers, district nurses, neighbours and family, as well as from scheme staff.

Scope for Change?

In England and Wales new communication services are now being set up, not as an extension of provision designed for residents of sheltered housing, but with the expressed aim of providing a service to people living in ordinary housing. Nevertheless, the dominant model of provision still obtains, in that the interpretation of 'needs' remains narrow and does not reflect the day-to-day difficulties experienced by disabled people who need help at non-routine or unpredictable times.

There is some small evidence that the dominant model of communication alarm service provision is being eroded by new approaches to community care. A notable example is the innovative use of communication alarms for intensive home support within the West Glamorgan Staying at Home Initiative. Here, older people are able to contact their care assistant, either to alter planned care arrangements or to ask for extra or unanticipated help, as well as for urgent help in a crisis. A prominent aim of the initiative was to move away from institutionalising, routine organisation of services towards an interactive pattern of care. Evidence from other countries is patchy but Danish municipalities, in some places at least, are using communication alarms to allow older people to summon personal assistance round the clock (Friediger, 1991). According to Friediger, this kind of development reflects official changes in policy away from standardised institutional 'total care' towards 'self-care', meaning self-determination and use of individual's own resources.

The emergence of these new models of communication alarm services is encouraging and suggests that cultures which make explicit service users' rights to control and self-determination are better able to employ communication alarms as a means to empowerment. There are, however, many difficulties in the way. Not least among them is the influence of traditional ways of providing services on users' expectations. It is clear that reluctance to take control is not just a product of the restrictive way in which alarm services are provided. Users of the West Glamorgan Staying at Home Initiative also were reported to be hesitant about using the communication alarm to alter planned care assistance; a report commented that this was understandable, given the striking contrast to normal service arrangements (West Glamorgan Staying at Home Initiative, 1989). Similarly, an interim report of the Haringey On-call Support and Creative Management Project (which employs conventional telephones and a paging company to enable people to call up help when they want it) commented on the influence of a historical legacy of low expectations on users asserting their own choices (Zarb, 1991).

A further difficulty is the probability that communication alarm service provision will continue to be dominated by housing providers working within traditions of standard services and paternalistic care. Accountability for the welfare of those who use their services remains a strong influence. Housing providers' approaches to provision have developed within a frame set by the manufacturers of the equipment: many have been reliant on them for publicity material and computer software; and developments in the technology itself have been led more by manufacturers than by their local authority customers. In order to maximise sales of the equipment, manufacturers promote the view that the technology can stand alone and play down the resource implications for providers of incorporating the equipment within a service framework. Encouraging users to define for themselves their own needs means building in to the service people who are able to respond to a wide range of needs. The narrowness of existing response systems is a major obstacle to broadening the use of communications technology to sustain independent living.

Cultural differences between housing and social services departments are a further obstacle to change. Although the two can work well together on the ground, housing departments so far have had a marginal role within the formal community care planning and development processes (Arnold & Page, 1992) and consequently have difficulty recognising the new 'values' of user definition of need which are supposed to inform community care. The 'social market' appears to have had more impact and housing providers are looking now to social services as a major customer for their services. There is little evidence, however, of providers being willing to adapt their services to meet the needs of new customers. Often, social services departments are not the only customers of housing departments' alarm services and their purchasing 'muscle' may well prove to be weak.

Change is premised on social services departments, in their role as enablers of community services for disabled people, acting to facilitate self-determination and user control over services. This premise is in itself questionable, particularly in regard to community care for older disabled people. Arguably, the imperative to prevent older people from entering institutional care, and increasing attention to the views of informal carers concerned about the safety of their elderly relatives, will lead to more protection against risk and less opportunity for self-determination. I have already remarked on the markedly different attitudes of social and health care workers to the potential of communication alarm technology for younger physically disabled people needing care assistance. The increasing 'client group' specialisation within social services departments in the UK may mean that attitudes to the care and protection of older people remain unaffected by changes in attitudes to the needs of younger disabled people.

But is a service so centrally dedicated to the 'frail and vulnerable elderly' likely to be acceptable to younger disabled people who increasingly have different expectations? Many communication alarm services pay lip-service to the inclusion of younger people but it is clear that take up is low. It has been argued that opening up such services to a wider range of groups—parents caring for chronically ill children and people at risk of racial harassment have been offered as examples—will, incrementally, erode the influence of the special needs view of the world (Fisk, 1990). But this proposition merely compounds the problems of inappropriate assumptions about 'need' (Thornton, 1992) and reinforces the association of communication alarms with crisis response.

Implications for the Mixed Economy of Care

Communication alarm services are a good illustration of the contradiction within the new arrangements for community care now facing social services departments charged with implementation. The 'new community care' supposes a revolution in the way in which needs are identified and met and in the part that services play in supporting people at home. It supposes not only that the mix of services can be adjusted to meet individual circumstances and preferences but also that existing services somehow can be adapted and made more 'flexible', 'responsive' and amenable to user control. It imagines that alternative and additional personal social services provided by the 'independent' sector will be similarly sensitive to individual need. Social services departments have a new enabling role in encouraging such services to come about and a new purchasing function in buying in services from external providers.

The example of communication alarms points up the conflict between, on the one hand, the aim of creating user-centred, flexible, non-institutional and interactive services and, on the other hand, being required to buy in services developed in the market-place. In the market, providers of services have their own reasons for being providers. They operate within a set of organisational values which differ from those of the organisations purchasing the services. Although conflict of values and ideologies in working across health and social services sectors is now recognised (Dalley, 1991), and some attention has been given to the impact on the voluntary sector of the 'contract culture' (Thornton, 1991), to date the difficulties of working across the private and public sectors have been ignored.

This article has taken a close look at one service already being bought in from the independent sector by social services departments. It has drawn on empirical research to demonstrate the conflict between providers' values which permeate the design, process and impact of services and the ideals of self-determination said to underpin the new community care. As the mixed economy of care takes effect the gap between users' and service providers' needs will become ever wider. The diversification of providers of services will merely reinforce assumptions about technological solutions to the support of disabled people in the community and fail to challenge the power of providers to determine the uses to which the technology is put. Control, and not technological innovation alone, will determine the potential benefits of communication technology for disabled people.

REFERENCES

ARNOLD, P. & PAGE, D. (1992) *Housing and Community Care: bricks and mortar or foundation for action?* (Hull, School of Social and Professional Studies, University of Humberside).
BALDOCK, J. (1991) Local innovations: England and Wales, in: R. J. KRAAN, J. BALDOCK, B. DAVIES, A. EVERS, L. JOHANSSON, M. KNAPEN, M. THORSLUND & C. TUNISSEN (Eds) *Care for the Elderly: significant innovations in three European countries* (Frankfurt am Main/ Boulder, CO, Campus/Westview).
BUTLER, A. (1985) Dispersed alarms: an evaluative framework, in: M. MCGARRY (Ed.) *Community Alarm Systems for Older People*, 2nd edn (Edinburgh, Age Concern Scotland).
Butler, A. (1989) The growth and development of alarm systems in sheltered housing, in: M. J. FISK (Ed.) *Alarm Systems and Elderly People* (Glasgow, Planning Exchange).
CLAPHAM, D. & SMITH, S. (1990) Housing policy and special needs, *Policy and Politics*, 18, pp. 193–205.
CORNES, P. (1991) Impairment, disability, handicap and new technology, in: M. OLIVER (Ed.) *Social Work: disabled people and disabling environments* (London, Jessica Kingsley).
DALLEY, G. (1991) Beliefs and behavior: professionals and the policy process, *Journal of Aging Studies*, 5, pp. 163–180.
DIBNER, A. S. (1991) Personal response services today, *International Journal of Technology & Aging*, 4, pp. 5–7.
FISK, M. J. (1990) *Dispersed Alarm Systems in the United Kingdom* (Glasgow, Planning Exchange).
FRIEDIGER, H. (1991) Services for the Danish elderly: the role of technical aids, *International Journal of Technology & Aging*, 4, pp. 69–72.
GRIFFITHS, R. (1989) *Community Care: agenda for action* (London, HMSO).
HARBERT, W. (1992) The challenge of ageing. Paper presented at *Marginalisation of Elderly People International Conference*, Liverpool.
OLDMAN, C. (1989) The role of dispersed alarms in community care, in: M. J. FISK (Ed.) *Alarm Systems and Elderly People* (Glasgow, Planning Exchange).
PELLOW, J. (1987) *Keeping Watch: a study of caring for the elderly at home with the aid of electronics* (London, John Clare Books).
SHALINSKY, W. (1989) Interdisciplinary and interorganisational concerns in the development of technology for physically disabled persons, *Disability, Handicap & Society*, 4, pp. 65–79.
THORNTON, P. (1991) Subject to contract? Volunteers as providers of community care for elderly people and their supporters, *Journal of Aging Studies*, 5, pp. 181–194.
THORNTON, P. (1992) Community alarm services: who needs them? in: A. CORDEN, E. ROBERTSON & K. TOLLEY (Eds) *Meeting Needs in an Affluent Society: a multidisciplinary perspective* (Aldershot, Avebury).
THORNTON, P. with MOUNTAIN, G. (1992) *A Positive Response: developing community alarm services for older people* (York, Joseph Rowntree Foundation).
TINKER, A. (1991) Alarms and telephones in personal response: research from the United Kingdom, *International Journal of Technology & Aging*, 4, pp. 21–25.
WEST GLAMORGAN STAYING AT HOME INITIATIVE (1989) *Supporting the Spirit of Independence. Report of the First Year of the Project 1988–89* (Swansea, West Glamorgan Social Services Department).
ZARB, G. (1991) Haringey on-call support and creative case management project. *Unpublished progress report* for Kings Fund Community Care Grant Workshop.

In Whose Service? Technology, Care and Disabled People: the case for a disability politics perspective

LIZ JOHNSON & EILEEN MOXON[1]

Community Care Division, Nuffield Institute for Health, University of Leeds, and
[1]*Department of Applied Social Studies, University of Bradford, Bradford, UK*

ABSTRACT *This paper discusses the introduction of telematics technologies, which are advancing rapidly in Britain and throughout the world, and which impact increasingly on the lives of disabled people. The authors argue that, to date, technology-based services have been largely, if not exclusively, determined by the interests of care service professionals, technologists and the commercial sector. Missing from the debate has been the perspective of the disability movement, which challenges professional hegemony, and introduces important issues such as choice, control and access to the wider environment. Such a perspective is needed if technological advances are to empower disabled people and not simply provide administrative solutions to the problems of increasingly hard-pressed service providers.*

Introduction

With the twenty-first century just round the corner, radically new forms of care services for disabled people [1,2] are emerging . What distinguishes these services is their reliance on sophisticated technologies. Some are already commonplace, such as the prevalence of community alarm systems in the homes of many older people, especially those who live alone (Thornton, 1993). Other, more complex systems are just beginning to emerge, with pilot projects often receiving funding from a variety of specialist programmes within the European Union and elsewhere (Daunt, 1991; Roe, 1995).

This paper is inspired by the authors' involvement in one such project which aims to pilot telematics technology [3] in the homes of a number of disabled people living in and around a city in the north of England. The project receives funding from the European Union, and is one of six Telecities projects to be developed in different cities within the EU. The ground rules for the project as a whole are clearly defined at European level, with each city developing its own technology. In the city with which the authors have been concerned the key participants in the design of the project are the City Council, a local University and British Telecom. The four main types of service which the project will provide are:

- teleshopping;
- telecare (providing two-way video access to a social care worker);
- an information package designed specifically for disabled people living in or around the city;
- a videophone facility which will connect all participants in the project.

The system will be accessed via computer terminals located in participants' homes. A variety of technologies will be available so that people with a wide range of impairments can take part in the project. These will include touch-activated screens, voice-activated screens, one-handed keyboards, key guards and a wide range of adaptive technologies.

Both authors have been actively involved in the initial stages of this project. One of the authors played a key part in the first phase of the project—informing disabled people about it, seeking their views on the potential usefulness to them of new technologies in general and the telematics technologies of the project in particular, and assisting in the selection of a core group of 18 people to pilot the system over a 12-month period. At the time she was also employed in the Department of Applied Social Studies at the University of Bradford, working alongside the second author. By chance, the second author, who is a member of the City Council in which the project is located, had been actively involved in designing the application which led to the successful funding of the project. So it happened that both authors were involved in the same project and were keen to explore some of the issues arising from it.

This Telecities project requires the City Council to liaise closely with funders and partners in different countries, and across a range of linguistic and cultural divides. At the same time, the Council must also work in partnership at local level with a number of disparate sectors, spanning the academic, the commercial and the care-providing worlds. Given the diversity of agendas which such a complex picture inevitably entails, the role of the disability movement in projects such as this presents an important area of study. In this paper the authors offer an exploration and analysis of the relationship between the new technology-based services, and the priorities and perspectives of the disability movement.

So far the disability movement has targeted its efforts on other issues, often to great effect. A number of these relate to technological developments such as the design and production of wheelchairs, and the conversion of cars and vans. As yet, though, little attention has been paid to the development and emergence of telematics technologies as resources for social care. This is almost certainly because the disability movement as been pursuing more active political agendas, and lacks human and financial resources to fight on all fronts.

Disability politics [4], which stem from personal rather than professional experience of disability, have exerted an increasingly influential pressure on social and health services in recent years, offering a powerful challenge to both professional and popular perspectives on disability, insisting on the rights of disabled people to be given choice and control over the support they receive, and pressing for change in the wider environment. Much attention has focused on the idea of independent living, and on the specific interpretation of 'independence' which the movement advocates:

> We do not use the term 'independence' to mean someone who can do everything for themselves, but to indicate someone who has taken control of their life and is choosing how that life is led.... The most important factor is not the amount of physical tasks a person can perform, but the amount of control they have over their everyday routine. (Brisenden, 1986, p. 178).

Given this interpretation of independence and the emergence of new technologies which are capable of radically altering both the types of services provided, and the relationships between disabled people and the wider society, it seems reasonable to expect that these would attract attention from within the disability movement. Indeed, the claim is made by one of the leading spokespersons of the movement that 'the disability movement is central to ensuring that technology is used to liberate rather than further oppress disabled people' (Oliver, 1990, p. 126).

Nonetheless, a review of the literature of the disability movement provides little evidence of a serious analysis of the implications of telematics and other new technologies. Whilst it is possible to identify a number of statements such as the one above, for the most part the concerns of the movement continue to focus on more traditional, personnel-dominated services. At the same time, what emerges from a review of the literature on technology-based services is the dominance of perspectives from outside the disability movement—designers and retailers of new technologies, funders of pilot projects, and the providers of social and health care services. This means that important issues about choice, control and access to the wider environment are at serious risk of being overlooked as the technological bandwagon picks up pace.

The Disability Movement and the Social Model of Disability

There are fundamental and far-reaching differences between the perspectives on disability which the disability movement advances and the dominant, 'medical' [5] model of disability. First and foremost, disability politics advocate a *social model* of disability. Whereas other perspectives focus on the individual's impairment and how that can be minimised or normalised, the disability movement is concerned primarily with the disabling effects of the environment—both physical and social. In other words, 'the social model focuses on the steps, not the wheelchair' (d'Aboville, 1991, p. 70). According to this model, then, what matters is not so much a person's inability to walk as the fact that most buildings and transport systems are inaccessible to people with mobility impairments. Consequently, where the dominant medical perspective focuses on the individual and his or her treatment, disability politics are concerned principally with disabled people's *collective* experience of discrimination and oppression, and hence with the need for social change.

This social model of disability, which first emerged some 20 years ago, presents a major challenge to the authority of professional 'experts', and of doctors and social workers in particular:

> Disabled people and their organisations are increasingly insisting that we are the experts on disability and that if we had control over the response to our needs we would develop very different policies from the ones which currently dominate our lives. (Morris, 1991, p. 173)

Thus, the social model of disability maintains that, far from taking charge of the lives of disabled people, and thus perpetuating a highly dependent relationship, health and social care professionals should 'see themselves as a resource to be tapped by disabled clients, rather than as professionals trained to make highly specialised assessments of what is appropriate for individual disabled people' (Finkelstein, 1991, p. 36).

As a consequence, the disability movement has become associated with a number of campaigns—calling for direct payments so that disabled people can design and take control of their own support arrangements; insisting that the more traditional disability organisations incorporate the voices of disabled people and revise the images of disability which they present; and campaigning for a comprehensive and meaningful Civil Rights Bill, which finally looks likely to be given government backing.

New Technologies: responses from within the disability movement

New technologies appear to be playing an increasingly important part in the way society functions—how people communicate with one another, how they work and organise their daily lives. Teleworking is on the increase, with significant numbers of people working from home at least part of the week; telebanking, teleshopping, even teledating are increasingly commonplace. A variety of devices, such as faxes, the World Wide Web, along with television and the telephone, make instant global communication possible for increasing numbers, and mean that events occurring in even the remotest parts of the world can be communicated almost instantaneously via newspapers and TV screens. Some people are excited by the emergence of the new global village; others are alarmed by the prospect of being reduced to an existence of virtual relationships, or fear that those who are older or less affluent will be excluded from this brave new world. Yet it is abundantly clear that technological developments cannot be ignored and are already playing a significant part in the changing shape of the society in which we live (Rowe, 1990; Moran, 1993).

Given the attention which the disability movement pays to the environment one might expect that telematics and their usage would be high on its agenda. Surprisingly, although the 1990s have seen the publication in Britain of a large number of books and articles bearing the clear imprint of the disability movement, few of these make anything other than the most cursory reference to new technologies. Many ignore these developments altogether. Some analyses from within the disability movement do exist, and these are reviewed below, but these represent only a fraction of the total output of the literature of the disability movement, and a minute proportion of the overall literature on disability and new technologies.

One of the most comprehensive books to emerge from the disability movement in recent years (Swain *et al.*, 1993) devotes only one chapter specifically to computer-based technologies (Roulstone, 1993). This chapter adopts a fairly narrow focus and is concerned with the impact of new technologies on disabled people's access to employment. Another collection of essays (Oliver, 1991) includes a chapter on new technologies. This opens with the following statement:

> The products of modern science-based industries and the new technologies which underpin their operation are now too much in evidence for their potential to improve the independence and quality of life of people with disabilities to be overlooked. (Cornes, 1991, p. 98)

Cornes (1991) touches on some crucial issues and suggests that technology in its own right is of little use if discriminatory attitudes and practices continue to prevail. Both he and Roulstone (1993) note that the fact that new technologies exist does not mean they will necessarily benefit more than a handful of disabled people. First, a number of issues need to be addressed, concerning costs, training, and the need for many disabled people to be enabled to overcome the effects of years of being rendered passive and dependent.

Despite the issues which Cornes raises his essay is disappointing because it locates the debate about new technologies within the narrow framework of employment opportunities for disabled people. Even within this limited framework it fails to discuss the fact that, whilst teleworking may increasingly provide disabled people with access to employment, by its nature it will perpetuate their exclusion from the wider social world of the workplace.

French (1993) takes a more sceptical view of the perceived benefits of new technologies, commenting that the question for her is not how to access them, but how to avoid having them thrust upon her. A cornerstone of disability politics, it will be remembered, is the rejection of the medical model of disability and French suggests that it is this medical model of disability which still most frequently determines the use to which technology is put. This model, with its focus on treatment and rehabilitation, sees the purpose of intervention as being to make the disabled person as 'normal' as possible—to adapt the individual to the conditions of society in which she or he lives. French challenges the idea that technical aids are necessarily helpful. She cites her own experience of being offered a special machine so that she and other partially-sighted students could find their own references:

> The thought of this machine filled me with foreboding. If it were to be installed, chances are it would not suit me, as people's problems, even within the same disability pigeon-hole, differ so much. Worse still, if I were able to use the computer, I would almost certainly take longer than the

librarian, and having located the references on the screen I would still need her assistance to pick them from the shelves! ... The introduction of this aid would, at best, enable me to cope inefficiently with half a task, while at the same time disallowing me from asking for help. (French, 1993, p. 45.)

As she points out, 'if librarians continue to help me find my references I will have more time to read them' (French, 1993, p. 46). So, according to French, technologies can subvert the goals of disabled people at least as much as they can enhance them, since the assumption which so frequently underpins their design and application is that disabled people should be 'normalised'.

Hasler is less sceptical about new technologies, but she points out that central to the issue of the use and usefulness of technologies is the question of how need is defined and by whom:

The [disability] movement does not reject the idea of gadgets. One of the basic requirements for independent living is appropriate technological equipment. But even here, appropriate can be defined differently by a non-disabled person and a disabled one. (Hasler, 1993, p. 15.)

Oliver (1990) looks briefly at the relationship between new technologies and disability politics. Unlike Cornes (1991) and Roulstone (1993), he does not restrict his comments to the sphere of employment, but instead acknowledges the significance of new technologies across a range of domains. Yet his exploration amounts to just three tantalisingly-short pages, which take the form of a literature review and which draw heavily on ideas first articulated as long ago as the early 1980s (Finkelstein, 1980; Zola, 1982).

Oliver cites Finkelstein's version of disability politics, which adapts Marxist analyses of society to describe a three-stage evolutionary process. In this process disabled people move from being part of a large underclass (pre-Industrial Revolution) through an intermediate stage where they are separated from their class origins and thus from capitalist society as a whole, and finally, to a stage where they are fully integrated within a new, socialist society. Within this analysis technology is seen as a tool which can facilitate integration. Oliver, whilst coming from a similar ideological background, is critical of Finkelstein's faith in the benevolent effects of technology, stressing, like Hasler, 'the ambiguities of the role of technology in modern society' (Oliver, 1990, p. 29). He, like Zola (1982) before him, suggests that often the effects of new technologies are to disempower rather than empower, and to isolate rather than integrate. Given this double-edged nature of technology, it is imperative, according to Oliver, that new technologies are placed high on the agenda of the disability movement. 'The disability movement', he insists, 'must work out an appropriate political strategy' (Oliver, 1990, p. 127).

Several years on from this statement, a strategy has yet to emerge. Meanwhile, providers of health and social care services are increasingly looking to new technologies to help them resolve the dilemmas which they face as they struggle to contend with the dual pressures of increasing demand and diminishing resources.

Commercial, Technical and Service Provider Interest in New Technologies

A number of interest groups come together to create projects such as the one to which this paper refers. These include commercial organisations, care providing agencies and, of course, the technical experts. No matter how well-intentioned or enlightened the representatives of any of these interest groups may be, it is important to recognise that ultimately each has its own concerns and agendas: for instance, British Telecom has to make profits, the Council has to balance the books, the University has to innovate. All have to work together collaboratively, according to the specific requirements of the major funder of the project. These stakeholders are considered below, with particular emphasis on the motivation of each and on the different agendas which they bring to these collaborative enterprises.

Commercial Stakeholders

In the past disabled people have been largely ignored by commercial organisations other than those in the specialist disability field:

> Many companies, particularly those whose products are marketed across the full spectrum of the population, considered disabled customers as a niche market at best, and an unwanted intrusion at worst. (Perrett, 1995, p. 41.)

Today demographic changes are causing commercial companies to focus their attention for the first time on disabled customers. Life expectancy in Britain has risen by over 20 years in the course of this century (Office of Population Censuses and Surveys, 1993), and the numbers of older people seem set to continue to rise rapidly, with the group aged 85 and over currently representing the highest growth rate among any of the age groups (Jeffreys, 1988). As more people live into advanced old age, the incidence of impairment increases dramatically. At the same time, increasing numbers of older people are living alone (Bond, 1993), as a result of the development of community care policies and of other demographic changes, such as the increased numbers of women in the work force, higher divorce rates, smaller families and increasing geographical mobility (Jerrome, 1993).

The telephone was invented in 1876 by a former teacher of deaf people, Alexander Graham Bell. Ironically, though, this invention meant that 'a new gap was created between the possibilities of those who can hear and speak and those who are hearing and speech impaired' (von Tetzchner, 1991, p. 2). Perhaps as many as one in ten of the population today (Roe *et al.*, 1995, p. 15) have impairments which mean that they are unable to operate a standard telephone. As this group grows in size, so telephone companies increasingly view them as potential customers rather than an irrelevant minority.

Working on a rough figure of six million households where at least one person is over 65 years old or is disabled, Perrett (1995) concludes that this population represents a potential market which is worth £1.6 billion to British Telecom. It is small wonder that the company feels they can increasingly comfortably balance commercial and humanitarian interests; disability, in an ageing society, is rapidly becoming big business.

British Telecom now has its own Age and Disability programme, which publishes a guide specifically aimed at older and disabled people (British Telecommunications plc, 1996). One example of the specialist services which the company now provides is Typetalk. This service, which operates in conjunction with the Royal National Institute for the Deaf, makes telecommunications accessible to significant numbers of hearing impaired people.

Given that the correlation between disability and low income is high (Thompson *et al.*, Borsay, 1988; 1986), it is reasonable to assume that many disabled people will be unable to purchase the services which companies such as British Telecom produce, no matter how carefully these are designed with their needs in mind. However, when these companies combine with service-providing organisations, such as social services departments, the potential exists for a much larger number of customers to be brought on board.

Technical Stakeholders

As with the commercial world, the involvement of the technical sector in collaborative projects such as the Telecities project is largely inspired by the increased numbers of disabled people and by the needs of care service providers to identify new ways of responding to this expanding population. Additionally, the rapid pace of technological advances such as artificial intelligence makes the field of disability an obvious arena in which to develop new systems. It therefore becomes possible to contemplate a future which could involve 'robotic arms which ... carry out a range of household chores such as cooking and serving meals, feeding and bathing the user, and operating and controlling other appliances on command' (Sandhu and Freitas, 1995, p. 271).

However, not all disabled people will respond enthusiastically to this scenario. Some may share Zola's view that 'to be handled by a machine ... where once I was handled by a person can only be invalidating of me as a person' (Zola, 1982, p. 396).

Unlike Zola, most technical experts cannot be relied on to question the assumption that technologies are intrinsically useful. This is not to suggest that the designers and producers of new technologies are uninterested in the opinions of the people who may use the machines which they create. Many insist, like Taipale, that 'the user has to be the crucial person in this process of development' (Taipale, 1993, p. 33), noting that the chances of ending up with an efficient and effective product are greatly enhanced if disabled people are involved at an early stage. The point, rather, is that technical experts deal with technical problems, so their starting point is with the question, 'How can I enable this person to carry out a physical task which at present she can't do unaided?' Their background makes it unlikely that they will pause to consider the question of whether the goal of independence is always best served by enabling people to perform tasks for themselves.

One of the problems with technology stems precisely from its exalted position within society. In comparison with social policy and social care its goals and outcomes are clear and easily assessed. It can apparently 'solve' problems where other disciplines operate in muddier waters. All this elevates the status of technical expertise within these collaborative projects, which are essentially about human issues, and increases the risk that they will end up being driven by technology, rather than by needs (Taipale, 1993, p. 30). There are other aspects of technological advances which demand consideration:

> Western society has involved the construction of female identities around technological incompetence ... To the extent that technologies reflect male values in their design, production and marketing, they create barriers for women as consumers and users. (Moran, 1993, p. 42.)

This is likely to have important implications for disabled women, who make up the majority of disabled people (Morris, 1993b). It raises important equal opportunities issues and highlights the need for positive action, both in terms of the design of new technologies and the availability of training and support services available for users.

Service Providing Stakeholders

In considering care service providers it is important to look at the cultures of these organisations, at the assumptions which underpin them, and at the particular challenges which they currently face.

The culture which historically has dominated care services derives from a perception of disabled people as dependent and vulnerable, and thus in need of 'care'. Expertise, according to this perspective, is vested in professionals, whose task is to decide which services are needed and to organise their implementation. 'The construction of older and disabled people as dependent means that they are treated as incapable' (Morris, 1993a, p. 47); hence, all that is required from disabled people in respect of the services they receive is compliance.

In recent years a number of relatively new concepts have entered the discourse of social policy and related disciplines. These spring from a variety of sources, including central government directives, the demands of the disability movement, and a desire among some practitioners for a change in the power dynamics between client and professional (Hugman, 1991). These new concepts are concerned with independent living, user involvement, user expertise, and relationships between users and professionals which are based on partnership rather than patronage.

Although the image of the dependent disabled person continues to influence the design and delivery of services, some of the paternalism which has informed services to younger disabled people is now weakening. However, such progress shows little sign of extending to older people (Bond & Coleman, 1993, p. 348), and the stereotype of the dependent disabled *older* person is proving very resistant to change. The new technology-assisted services with which this paper is concerned are aimed primarily at responding to the growing numbers of older people. This fact has important implications for the types of technology-based services which are provided and means that, rather than extending choice, the majority of these services are designed to minimise risk. (Thornton, 1993; Roe *et al.*, 1995, p. 10).

The trend away from residential services and towards enabling 'people to live as normal a life as possible in their own homes' (Department of Health, 1989, p. 4) inevitably ensures that service providers have to respond to the logistical problems posed by an increasingly widely dispersed user group. Technology appears to offer an obvious solution to some of the dilemmas which service providers now face:

> [It represents] a major opportunity to facilitate independent living and to improve the quality of life for many individuals who might otherwise be in institutional care. In doing so it also presents an opportunity to limit or reduce the financial burden on care providers and on member states. This is especially important with the forthcoming care crisis and boom in the proportion of elderly people in the population (Richardson & Poulson, 1993, p. 88).

Technological developments can indeed benefit disabled people substantially, but it is important to question the assumptions which underpin statements such as the one above. We need to ask who defines 'quality of life', what is meant by 'independence', and whether the twin goals of improved quality of life and reduced expenditure can be accomplished with such apparent ease.

Difficulties of Collaboration

Any form of collaboration between commercial, technical and service-providing organisations is unlikely to be simple (Glastonbury, 1993, p. 3). The collaborative process is made more complex because large numbers of projects of this type are linked in to and sponsored by European-wide projects. For instance, the Telecities project is only one of many EU-financed projects within the TIDE (Technology for the Socio-Economic Integration of Disabled and Elderly People) programme, which in turn is one of several international programmes dedicated to issues relating to disability and technology (Daunt, 1991; von Tetzchner, 1991; Roe, 1995). Consequently, in addition to the different agendas which have been outlined so far, these projects must accommodate to the specific culture of an international bureaucracy. Since they must also collaborate with a number of schemes in different countries, this already complex picture is made even more problematic by the need to incorporate even more cultural and linguistic differences.

Examples of Teleservices, Present and Future: a critique based on the social model of disability

It is easy to see how the complexity of the relationships between these different groups could result in the needs and perspectives of service users receding into the background. Only with the introduction of an alternative view, one which stems from the perspectives of the disability movement, is the liberating potential of new technology-based services likely be realised.

Teleshopping

Opportunities for teleshopping seem set to expand dramatically over the next decade. Some people are already able to shop from lists on television or computer screens, and the day may not be far away when there will be widespread access to 'virtual shopping', so that from within one's home it will be possible to walk around the virtual supermarket, select virtual items, put them in a virtual trolley and pay for them at the virtual check-out.

Recent years have seen the development in Britain of several specialist home shopping services. One such project was introduced recently in Ealing. This relatively low-tech service is aimed at older people and enables users to do their shopping from home. It appears, however, to be experiencing some difficulties. Many users find it difficult to operate, since 'an eye-teasing seven-figure computer code has to be copied out for each item of a whole week's supplies'. In addition, 'it removes a vital element—the regular contact between clients and trained home helps' (Hebert, 1996).

The Ealing scheme frees home care assistants from shopping tasks so that they can concentrate on providing personal care to people with intensive support needs. As a result, those less frail older people are deprived of an important source of social contact and support. Presented to service users as a development which would improve their quality of life, the scheme appears in some cases to be having the opposite effect, since it further increases the isolation of its users.

Teleshopping facilities are a feature of the project to which this paper refers. Many participants in this project are enthusiastic about the prospect of no longer having to negotiate a succession of obstacles such as transport and parking difficulties, turnstiles and narrow check-outs, inaccessible shelves and the difficulties of carrying heavy bags (Disablement Income Group, 1983). Some currently rely on friends, family members or care workers to do their shopping, and find the need to do so quite burdensome. However, not everyone has been equally enthusiastic about the prospect of teleshopping. Some initial enquirers decided against applying to the project, precisely because they saw teleshopping as a constraint rather than a freedom. These people valued their trips to the shops, notwithstanding the difficulties and felt that teleshopping would diminish rather than enhance their quality of life.

In her analysis of the future electronic home, Hillman (1993) looks at the value of teleshopping. She concludes that it will be useful in so far as it exists as an additional option for people (Moran, 1993, p. 30). She suggests that few people will want to make exclusive use of this option but many may use it occasionally. For most people, shopping is likely to remain a social, visual, tactile, stimulating, if sometimes exhausting, acquisitive experience (Hillman, 1993, p. 2).

Central and local governments have to make difficult decisions in the face of growing demand and ever diminishing resources. When the medical model of disability is applied it appears that teleshopping services can conveniently meet the two goals of cutting care costs and increasing user independence. However, the social model of disability equates independence with choice and control rather than with the ability to perform physical tasks. Looked at from this perspective, teleshopping may not so easily satisfy the twin goals of maximising scarce resources and enhancing independence. In the short term, teleshopping may reduce people's social contacts by dispensing with the need for the involvement of friends, family or care assistants. In the longer term it may also act as a disincentive to the development of more accessible public buildings and transport systems.

Telecare

Similar concerns arise with telecare services. A project in Germany illustrates some of the key issues. This project (Erkert & Robinson, 1993) provides a videolink between care providers based in a residential centre and older people who live alone. It enables care workers to monitor the well-being of older people, and to provide advice and information, and it guarantees users of the service instant access to help in the case of emergency. By comparison with the audio contact which the telephone affords, this audio-visual communication has been found to encourage more natural and more effective contact between older people and care workers. It significantly enhances the quality and scope of information communication because care workers can see the person they are speaking to and more accurately gauge their needs. They can also show the older person on the other end of the videoline how to perform certain tasks such as completing forms, using medication or performing rehabilitative exercises. Even when this system is compared with face to face contact it is evident that there are benefits to both parties; for instance, the care workers avoid the time and expense which they might otherwise incur in travelling to the older person's home, and the older person gets instant access to advice, information and counselling. However, as with teleshopping, it is important to look beyond this very superficial analysis.

From the perspective of the medical, rehabilitative model of disability there appears to be little conflict between the goals of independent living and reducing the load on services. However, when the social model of disability is employed what emerges is a rather less comfortable fit between the two. For instance, the following question arises: 'Is it preferable to take into use a new aiding device which will greatly facilitate daily life but may also reduce personal contacts with nurses/home helpers?' (Taipale & Pereira, 1995, p. 60).

With older people this question may be especially pertinent, as research has consistently shown the important role that home care assistants play in the lives of many isolated older people. For example, these carers not only provide much-valued social contact, but offer an ongoing relationship within which key concerns may be safely aired and changing needs addressed (Hillman, 1993, p. 25; Johnson, 1995, p. 39).

Most telecare services provide a means by which isolated people can be monitored by care workers and can access help in the event of a crisis. One example of telecare services which are already widely used is the community alarm system. Targeted primarily at single older people, these services aim to minimise risk and to reduce the anxieties which may stem from the combination of frailty and living alone.

Thornton (1993) suggests, however, that although community alarm services enable substantial numbers of older people to live alone they may also maintain people in a dependent relationship *vis-à-vis* service providers. These systems have a double-edged nature, providing reassurance that help will be at hand in an emergency, but also acting as a constant reminder to the user of his or her vulnerability. Perhaps this is why many younger disabled people have shown little enthusiasm for community alarm systems (Thornton, 1993) and why large numbers of older people with community alarms in their homes choose not to wear the pendants which can trigger instant access to help (Thornton & Mountain, 1992).

Social Networks, Self-help and Solidarity: the potential for empowerment through telematics

Many of the technology-based services which have been developed so far are founded on a perception of the disabled person as vulnerable and, therefore, in need of professional help. Their aim is to facilitate communication between helper and helped, and so they tend to perpetuate dependency rather than foster independence. What is frequently overlooked in the introduction of these systems is the fact that disabled people, like everyone else, need access to ordinary social contact which involve reciprocal rather than dependent relationships.

Social networks, as defined by Berkman (1984) are central to the fulfilment of a number of basic needs such as intimacy, self-worth, a sense of belonging, and the satisfaction of both giving and receiving help. These networks may be especially important for many disabled people, whose relationship to society in general, and to family members and service providers in particular, is most commonly constructed as one of dependence. Indeed, in the literature on carers (Twigg & Atkin, 1991) the emphasis is firmly on the multiple problems of the caring role, to the extent that the disabled person is frequently defined simply as a burden. As if to reinforce the importance of social networks, many of the participants in the Telecities project cited among their reasons for being involved in the project the hope that it would enable them to share experiences with other disabled people and to feel that they were in a position to help others.

> Professionals in health and social services have yet to appreciate sufficiently
> the role of self-help groups in helping to deal with isolation and in enabling
> people to develop their potential. (Wilson, 1996.)

Wilson's research into self-help groups concluded that these groups are highly valued by their members and contribute significantly to users' empowerment. It is clear from her analysis of these groups that they perform most if not all of the functions of social networks—boosting members' self-confidence, helping people overcome isolation and anxiety, enabling them to help one another, and to share information and experiences. In addition, some of these groups have developed a campaigning role and have become actively involved in lobbying for improved services.

Some self-help groups are linked to overtly political disability groups, such as those which come under the broad umbrella of the British Council for Disabled People (BCDP). Morris describes the development of these organisations as a milestone in the history of disability politics:

> The significance of disabled people coming together to form an international movement cannot be underestimated. Disabled people are imprisoned within institutions, constrained within inaccessible housing and obstacle-ridden physical environments, dependent on unpaid care by family members, discriminated against in the labour market. Such people lack power by virtue of their socio-economic circumstances. The foundation of Disabled People's International was about disabled people taking control over their lives. (Morris, 1991, p. 174).

As far back as 1977 Umpleby recognised the potential for computer-based technologies to enable groups with widely dispersed membership to organise and campaign around quite specific issues (1977, p. 229). That a global movement of disabled people has now developed into a significant political force is thanks in no small measure to the wonders of communication and information technologies. Yet, in spite of this, the disability movement in Britain continues to distance itself from the debate about the development and application of new technologies. By contrast, disability activists in the United States appear to be far less reticent. Indeed, they have ensured that the right to appropriate assistive technologies is enshrined in federal legislation, through the Amendments to the Rehabilitation Act of 1986, the Technology-Related Assistance for People with Disabilities Act, 1988, and more recently, the United States of America Disability Act of 1990 (Cobut *et al.*, 1991, p. 9).

> Perhaps the most effective way of empowering people with disabilities ... is to provide them with the means to come together to benefit from the liberating effect of sharing common experiences. (Ellis, 1993, p. 43.)

New technologies can facilitate such access: for example, by enabling people with no speech to communicate via lightwriters or e-mail; by making it possible for people who are ill or otherwise isolated within their homes to have audio-visual contact with other people, and by facilitating simultaneous contact with a number of people in different locations. Perhaps the most valuable feature of the Telecities project with which the authors have been involved will be its ability to facilitate contact between disabled people—locally, nationally and globally.

Conclusions

> The question is to know whether all this new technology will lead to greater integration or further exclusion. (Roe, 1991, p. 61)

Technology-based services are likely to play a significant part in future health and social care provision for disabled people. Some services are already in place. So far, the disability movement has distanced itself from these developments, due in part to a determination to avoid compromising their integrity (Daunt, 1991, p. 53) and, in part, to a suspicion that new technologies will be used to the ultimate disadvantage of disabled people.

Scepticism about the alleged benefits of technology has deep historical roots, which are not restricted to the disability movement. Sivanandan suggests that:

> Those who control the means of communication control also the economic, the cultural and the political. It is no longer the ownership of the means of production that is important, but the ownership of the means of communication. (Sivanandan, 1996, p. 2.)

Yet he also acknowledges that new technologies can now be accessed by disadvantaged groups and so can become powerful weapons of resistance. For instance, he notes that the growth and effectiveness of the Zapatista rebellion in rural Mexico owes a great deal to technological advances such as e-mail, the fax machine and mobile phones. The rapid growth of a world-wide disability movement is itself evidence of the part which new technologies can play in facilitating the empowerment of disabled people.

Of themselves, technologies are neutral; how they are used determines the extent to which they will meet the needs of disabled people. Technology-based services could lead to the greater exclusion or disabled people; alternatively, they could enable people to take increased control of their lives.

Far from withdrawing from the debate, the disability movement needs to act to ensure that certain key questions are explored, not least of which is the question raised by the American anthropologist, Hakken:

> What should be done to insure that ... technology is not substituted for access? ... Supplying people with machines can come to be a way to avoid supplying them with access and an excuse for not making public places accessible. (Hakken, 1995, 518)

It is a matter of some concern that the disability movement has not been at the forefront of the debate about telematics technologies and disabled people. It seems highly probable that the next decade will see a burgeoning of collaborative ventures between care providers, and commercial and technical organisations, with telematics technologies being seized on increasingly as a means by which service providers can respond to the needs of a rapidly-growing population of disabled and elderly people. There is an urgent need for the disability movement to engage with this process, as it has done with other issues relating to community care and independent living (Kestenbaum, 1992; Oliver & Zarb, 1992; Morris, 1993a).

New technologies can be used to empower or to confine; now is the time for the disability movement to play its part in ensuring that the former of these outcomes is achieved.

NOTES

[1]   The expression 'disabled people' is the preferred terminology of the disability movement. Whereas other expressions locate disability exclusively within the individual, the use of the term 'disabled people' incorporates the notion of disability as a social construct, with people being disabled as much by the prevailing structures and attitudes within society as by their physical or mental impairments.

[2]   Unless otherwise stated, the term 'disabled people' is used generically, and includes older people as well as those under 65.

[3]   Telematics combine information and communication technologies. In the project to which this paper refers, participants are able to access information and make contact with other people via a computer link—using e-mail facilities to communicate with people across the globe, establishing audio-visual contact with other participants, accessing and inputting into specialist databases.

[4]   Disability politics are identified with the disability movement. Hence, in this paper the two terms are used interchangeably.

[5]   Oliver, in defining the medical model, describes 'the failure of the medical profession, and indeed of all other professions, to involve disabled people in a meaningful way except as passive objects of intervention, treatment and rehabilitation' (Oliver, 1990, p. 5).

REFERENCES

BERKMAN, L. (1984) Social networks, social support, and physical health, *Annual Review of Public Health* 5, pp. 413–432.

BOND, J. (1993) Living arrangements of elderly people, in: J. BOND, P. COLEMAN & S. PEACE (Eds) *Ageing in Society: an introduction to social gerontology* (London, Sage)

BOND, J. & COLEMAN, P. (1993) Ageing into the twenty-first century, in: J. BOND, P. COLEMAN & S. PEACE (Eds) *Ageing in Society: an introduction to social gerontology* (London, Sage).

BORSAY, A. (1986) *Disabled People in the Community* (London, Bedford Square Press).

BRISENDEN, S. (1986) Independent living and the medical model of disability, *Disability, Handicap & Society*, 1, pp. 173–178.

BRITISH TELECOMMUNICATIONS PLC (1996) *The BT Guide for People who are Disabled or Elderly* (London, BT)

COBUT, G., EKBERG, J., FREDERIKSEN, J., LEPPO, A., NORDBY, K. & ROLLANDI, G. (1991) Policy and legislation, in: S. VON TETZCHNER (Ed.) *Issues in Telecommunication and Disability (COST 2'9)*, (Commission of the European Communities, France).

CORNES, P. (1991) Impairment, disability, handicap and new technology, in: OLIVER, M. (Ed.) *Social Work: disabled people and disabling environments* (London, Jessica Kingsley)

D'ABOVILLE, E. (1991) Social work in an organisation of disabled people, in: OLIVER, M. (Ed.) *Social Work: disabled people and disabling environments* (London, Jessica Kingsley).

DAUNT, P. (1991) *Meeting Disability: a European response*, (London, Cassell).

DEPARTMENT OF HEALTH (1989) *Caring for People: community care in the next decade and beyond* (London, HMSO).

DIG (1983) *Tell Me What You Want and I'll Get it for You: a study of shopping when disabled* (London, Disablement Income Group)

ELLIS, K. (1993) *Squaring the Circle: user and carer participation in needs assessment* (London, Joseph Rowntree Foundation).

ERKERT, T. & ROBINSON, S. (1993) An application of video telephony to maintain the quality of life of elderly people with special needs, in: B. GLASTONBURY (Ed.) *Human Welfare and Technology: papers from the Husita 3 conference on IT and the Quality of Life and Services* (Netherlands, Van Gorum).

FINKELSTEIN, V. (1980) *Attitudes and Disabled People: issues for discussion* (New York, World Rehabilitation Fund).

FINKELSTEIN, V. (1991) Disability: an administrative challenge?, in: M. OLIVER (Ed.) *Social Work: disabled people and disabling environments* (London, Jessica Kingsley).

FRENCH, S. (1993) What's so great about independence? in: J. SWAIN, V. FINKELSTEIN, S. FRENCH & M. OLIVER (Eds) *Disabling Barriers—enabling environments* (London, Sage).

GLASTONBURY, B. (1993) *Human Welfare and Technology: papers from the Husita 3 conference on I.T. and the Quality of Life and Services* (Netherlands, Van Gorum)

HAKKEN, D. (1995) Electronic curb cuts: computing and the cultural (re)construction of disability in the United States, *Science as Culture*, Vol. 4, part 4, no. 21., pp. 502–534.

HASLER, F. (1993) The place of information provision in the disability movement, in: *Information Enables: improving access to information services for disabled people*. Papers presented at the National Disability Information Projects' 1993 conference, Nottingham (London, Policy Studies Institute).

HEBERT, H. (1996) Shop till you drop, *The Guardian*, January 31, Supplement *Community Care*, p. 26.

HILLMAN, J. (1993) *Telelifestyles and the Flexicity: a European study. The impact of the electronic home* (Dublin, European Foundation or the Improvement of Living & Working Conditions).

HUGMAN, R. (1991) *Power in Caring Professions* (Basingstoke, Macmillan).

JEFFREYS, M. (1988) An ageing Britain—what is its future?, in B. GEARING, M. JOHNSON & T. HELLER (Eds) *Mental Health Problems in Old Age* (London, Wiley)

JERROME, D. (1993) Intimate relationships, in: J. BOND, P. COLEMAN & S. PEACE (Eds) *Ageing in Society: an introduction to social gerontology* (London, Sage).

JOHNSON, L. (1995) *Getting the Message: users' and carers' experiences of community care in Leeds* (Leeds, Leeds Community Health Council).

KESTENBAUM, A. (1992) *Cash for Care: a report on the experience of Independent Living Fund clients* (Nottingham, Independent Living Fund).

MORAN, R. (1993) *The Electronic Home: social and spatial aspects. A Scoping report*, (Dublin, European Foundation for the Improvement of Living and Working Conditions).

MORRIS, J. (1991) *Pride against Prejudice: transforming attitudes to disability* (London, The Women's Press).

MORRIS, J. (1993a) *Independent Lives: community care and disabled people* (Basingstoke, Macmillan)

MORRIS, J. (1993b) Gender and disability, in: J. SWAIN, V. FINKELSTEIN, S. FRENCH & M. OLIVER (Eds) *Disabling Barriers—enabling environments* (London, Sage).

OFFICE OF POPULATION CENSUSES AND SURVEYS (1993) *The 1991 Census: persons aged 60 and over, Great Britain* (London, HMSO).

OLIVER, M. (1990) *The Politics of Disablement* (Basingstoke, Macmillan Education).

OLIVER, M. (1991) *Social Work: disabled people and disabling environments* (London, Jessica Kingsley).

OLIVER, M. & ZARB, G. (1992) *Greenwich Personal Assistance Schemes: an evaluation* (London Greenwich Association of Disabled People).

PERRETT, B. (1995) Marketing Considerations, in P. ROE (Ed.) *Telecommunications for All* (Lausanne, Commission of the European Communities)

RICHARDSON, S.J. & POULSON, D.F. (1993) Supporting independent living through adaptable Smart Home (ASH) technologies, in: B. GLASTONBURY (ed.) *Human Welfare and Technology; Paper from the Husita 3 conference on IT and the Quality of Life and Services* (Netherlands, Van Gorum).

ROE, P. (1991) in: S. VON TETZCHNER (Ed.) *Issues in Telecommunications and Disability* (COST 219), p. 16 (France, Commission of European Communities).

ROE, P. (1995) *Telecommunications for All* (Lausanne, Commission of the European Communities).

ROE, P., SANDHU, J.S. & DELANEY, L. (1995) Consumer overview, in ROE, P. (Ed.) *Telecommunications for All: COST 219* (Luxembourg, Office of Official Publications of the European Communities).

ROULSTONE, A. (1993) Access to new technology in the employment of disabled people in J. SWAIN, V. FINKELSTEIN, S. FRENCH & M. OLIVER (Eds) *Disabling Barriers—enabling environments* (London, Sage).

ROWE, C. (1990) *People and Chips: the human implications of information technology* (London, Blackwell Scientific Publications).

SANDHU, J.S. & FREITAS, D. (1995) The role of artificial intelligence in telematics, in P. ROE (Ed.) *Telecommunications for All* (Lausanne, Commission of the European Communities).

SIVANANDAN, A. (1996) Heresies and prophesies—the social and political fall-out of the technological revolution: an interview, *Race & Class*, 37 (4), pp. 1–11.

SWAIN, J., FINKELSTEIN, V., FRENCH, S. & OLIVER, M. (1993) *Disabling Barriers—Enabling Environments* (London, Sage)

TAIPALE, V. (1993) Development of Information Technology and Social Welfare and Health Services—a dialectic process, in B. GLASTONBURY (Ed.) *Human Welfare and Technology*: papers from the Husita 3 conference on IT and the Quality of Life and Services. (Netherlands, Van Gorum).

TAIPALE, V. & PEREIRA, L.M. (1995) The social aspects of telematics, disabled and elderly people, and future challenges, in: P. ROE (Ed.) *Telecommunications for All* (Lausanne, Commission of the European Communities).

THOMPSON, P., BUCKLE, J. & LAVERY, M. (1988) *Not the OPCS Survey: being disabled costs more than they said*, (London, Disablement Income Group).

THORNTON, P. (1993) Communications technology—empowerment or disempowerment? *Disability, Handicap and Society*, 8, pp. 339–349.

THORNTON, P. & MOUNTAIN, G. (1992) *A positive Response: developing community alarm systems for older people* (York, Joseph Rowntree Foundation).

TWIGG, J. & ATKIN, K. (1991) *Carers Perceived: policy and practice in informal care* (Buckingham, Open University Press).

UMPLEBY, S.A. (1977) Is greater citizen participation in planning possible and desirable? in: G. BOYLE, D. ELLIOTT & R. ROY (Eds) *The Politics of Technology* (London, Longman/Open University Press).

VON TETZCHNER, S. (1991) *Issues in Telecommunication and Disability (COST 219)* (France, Commission of the European Communities).

WILSON, J. (1996) Self service, *Community Care*, 15th February, pp. 24–25.

ZOLA, I. (1982) Social and cultural disincentives to independent living, *Archives of Physical Medicine and Rehabilitation*, 63, pp. 394–397.

Information and Communication Technologies and the Opportunities of Disabled Persons in the Swedish Labour Market

DIMITRIS MICHAILAKIS

Department of Sociology, University of Uppsala, Sweden

ABSTRACT *This article attempts to outline the prospects of disabled persons to gain and retain employment within the Information Society by presenting and discussing the results of a labour market policy programme in Sweden based on information technology. The effects of Information and Communication Technologies (ICTs) for unemployed and employed persons with disabilities can be assessed on the micro, as well as on the macro levels. Technological optimism has given rise to expectations about the great potential of ICTs in creating employment opportunities for disabled persons. Technological optimism, however, derives from a deterministic point of view, i.e. ICTs are regarded as an independent variable. This article suggests that ICTs must be regarded as a variable dependent by the economic, social and cultural order. Its effects on disabled persons employment opportunities are not independent by the power relations at a given time.*

Introduction

We are living in a society that for the last few decades has been marked by increasing computerisation and the possibilities that have been brought to us by the ease with which information of different kinds can be transmitted around the world. Information technology has changed the stock market, as well as the communication patterns at workplaces. Enthusiastic proponents of this development have claimed that this society will open up new prospects for persons with disabilities—as well as for other disadvantaged groups—of entering the labour market. [1] The basic component—the microprocessor—is not limited to computer applications only, it can also make up an important component in various aids. Computers can thus facilitate education and training, give access to jobs that were unattainable before and make the activities of daily living easier to carry out.

A growing body of theoretical and empirical research within the social sciences indicate that a fundamental shift in society has taken place. It has often been described as a move to a new, third era in human society, i.e. the first being agricultural and the second being industrial, which has transformed itself into the information society. According to Jordan, the unifying claim in the various theories on this change is that a move began in the 1970s that took global economies away from the industrial forms that emerged in the nineteenth century and transformed them towards economies in which information plays a central role. This move from the industrial to the information age implies the replacement of capital and labour as chief resources of economic growth by information and knowledge as primary means of development.

Despite the fact that grand theories describing coherent development in step like phases leave us a bit uncomfortable nowadays, there is striking change in the daily life and on the labour market. Computers have entered the workplaces, as well as the homes. However, as Jordan points out, one must be aware that 'information societies' are not so called because previous societies did not utilise information, but because information has become the central principle by which production, consumption and—more generally—power is distributed across a global economy (Jordan, 1999). The emerging information society is evident in the shift that has taken place within industry, as Loader notes (1998). Traditional manufacturing industries no longer dominate the generation of national wealth in advanced societies. In contrast, the information industry is expanding at the expense of manufacturing industry in terms of employment, investment and market share. One consequence of this development is that the work is not predominantly confined to a particular location, as was the case in the industrial society (the factory and the office), nor restricted by the traditional nine-to-five working day. Instead, the 'information worker' adopt to different patterns of employment more suited to the flexible organisation of working life (Loader, 1998). The development in technology, and especially in Information and Communication Technologies (ICTs), implies the replacement of physical strength or simple intellectual tasks that are very formalised with computer technique; thus, a lot of manual work can be—and has been—automated. [2]

These changes bring a totally new situation to the worker in the labour process. The workplace is no longer necessarily the enterprise; the working hours of the individual is not necessarily the same as the normal working hours at that enterprise. A decentralisation of the workplace takes place as implied by homework and telework. In turn, it results in new modes of communicating with fellow workers or colleagues. Furthermore, ICTs are transforming the working methods and the organisation of companies by stressing training, education and communication skill. What employers now are required is ability to work in team, to be efficient and flexible, and to communicate clearly.

Looking on this new situation from the perspective of disabled persons' and their job opportunities there are certain aspects to take into consideration, namely:

(1) whether persons with disabilities will be able to keep up with the speedy development of technology; [3]

(2) whether there are real possibilities of adapting workplaces;
(3) whether job opportunities really are created directly through ICTs or through the re-organisation of the labour process;
(4) whether the new requirements on labour power in the information society includes everybody or if it can be claimed that disabled persons can be excluded.

Some answers could be given by looking at a programme that has going on in Sweden with the objective of exploring the dynamics of information technology for finding jobs for persons with disabilities.

As a part of the labour market policy for persons with disabilities in Sweden a special programme on creating ICT-based adaptations of workplaces has proceeded since mid-80s with the intention of improving the labour market prospects for persons with disabilities by applying the new technologies in order to remove or reduce the functional impairment. Since empirical research has been rather sparse in the subject and since disabled persons suffer from high-level unemployment compared with non-disabled, it has been considered very important to evaluate the programme. [4] Persons with disabilities form a large group (10–15% of the population in Sweden) with a lower employment rate, [5] lower level of education and lower average earnings compared with non-disabled persons. It must also be born in mind that the financial resources that have been spent on labour market programmes, such as ICT-based adaptation of workplaces are substantial. The need of evaluating programmes of this kind is also necessary from the point of view of the rather dramatic transformation that labour markets undergo today due to information technology. Who can compete and on what merits?

Key Terms in the Evaluation of ICT-based Accommodation of Workplace

For the purpose of this study, three terms should be clarified, i.e. the terms *'evaluation'*, *'information and communication technology'*, and *'workplace accommodation/ adaptation'*.

The term 'evaluation' is understood to mean a process by which programme inputs, activities and results are analysed and judged against explicitly stated norms. The norms may be the stated programme objectives, work schedule, budget, etc. Evaluation of effectiveness involves questions such as: 'What impact does the programme have on the employment conditions of its intended beneficiaries?' and 'How were its results achieved?' Since the purpose of the ICT-based workplace adaptations for the disabled programme is to increase disabled persons' possibilities to gain or retain employment, the evaluation has to measure the degree to which these possibilities have increased.

The term 'information technology' is wide and could mean a lot of different things, and it is even more difficult when it comes to determining 'information and communication technology' products for workplace access. It is not sufficient that some components of the products are electronic. A more thorough definition is needed that takes into consideration the purpose, the position and the payer of the product. Generally speaking, the term 'information and communication technology' (ICT) signifies the handling of information with the aid of technical instruments. Handling of information includes computerisation and telematics. *Computerisation* signifies the use of computers, including hardware (computers and accessories) and software (program and systems design). *Telematics* signifies the transmission of information, be it speech, text, data or pictures. From the user's point of view, telematics is also synonymous with a solution to an information transfer problem, i.e. a technical solution to the user's demand regarding his possibilities to send, obtain information in an appropriate mode and retrieve information actively (Lindström, 1984). The ICT-based workplace adaptations that are studied here, are in some cases examples of computerisation, but in many cases they can be viewed as examples of both computerisation and telematics.

'*Workplace accommodation/adaptation*' means the introduction of 'a product, instrument, technical system or equipment used by a person with a disability, specially produced or freely available, to prevent, compensate, reduce or neutralise the impairment or disability' (WHO definition). This definition has been criticised for being too narrow and a material definition. It covers adaptations of the workplace, but not changes of the job or the way the tasks are allocated (including, for instance, change in work activities, variation in tasks, a move to another job with the same or another employer, work from home, etc.; ILO, 1998a,b).

Advantages and Disadvantages of ICTs for Disabled Individuals

There are—as in every important change—adverse effects, and in assessing these effects one may choose to look at them on a micro- and macro-level. As regards individuals with disabilities there are several advantages with ICTs and the information society that can be discerned on the *micro-level*. Most of the communication barriers that have long confronted blind and visually impaired persons can, with these, be removed. Since ICTs bring work to persons, rather than transporting persons to work—by telework at home or other location, thus avoiding problems of access to buildings, transportation, etc.—they create new possibilities to work for persons with physical impairments. ICT-based accommodations also open up new possibilities for persons with mobility impairments by diverting manual skills from data processing. For persons with visual and hearing impairments, ICTs implies a move from physical tasks towards perceptual ones (Hunt & Berkowitz, 1992). Through ICTs individuals with visual impairment, those who are deaf or hard-of-hearing, the speech-impaired and mobility impaired can gain great benefits. [6]

However, for disabled persons—as for other groups in society—ICTs may also have negative and/or unexpected effects. One disadvantage for persons with disabilities is connected to the very speed of development that takes place within information society, leading to a great amount of information to follow and an increase in the demands on efficiency. Therefore, persons with disabilities complain that they—despite devices—can never be as fast as non-disabled. Output—and increasingly input—from and to computers rely upon CRT's and other visual displays, which prevent visually disabled persons from using the devices without extended modification. Specifically concerning ICT-based adaptations and devices, it is an unavoidable fact that they are quite expensive, since they cannot be mass-produced.

Looking on the *macro-level*, there are structural changes going on brought about by the development of information technology, and these structural changes are not always advantageous to persons with disabilities or to any other group. The increasing incorporation of information technology into work processes and production leads to profound changes at the workplace. Together with the introduction of ICT devices follows an increasing automation, robotisation and more complex information systems. The production process speeds up, the organisation of the work focus around this new equipment, and consequently the skill to administrate, operate and handle the technology, gain utmost importance in the work process.

People with disabilities are—of course—not a homogenous group. As Albeda (1985) points out, ICTs might have the reverse effect on different disabilities; what includes one group, excludes the other. In some cases, automation or robotisation replaces menial tasks, in some places it means that jobs are lost. For unskilled disabled workers, automation may mean the loss of a job, but for the physically impaired person it may mean that old barriers disappear, since it no longer becomes necessary to possess physical strength or be able to move along in order to perform a specific job. However, alongside this move away from strength and physical endurance, new capacities are demanded. In precision work, design, engineering, programing, etc., skills are demanded that presuppose a higher education. Furthermore, as jobs become physically easier, there is a trend that the demands on efficiency increase. These altered requirements on labour may adversely affect individuals with disabilities, at least in some groups of disabled. Persons with intellectual disabilities have, for instance, a particular disadvantage when it comes to planning, teamwork skills, rotation of tasks, etc.

ICT Programme for Disabled Persons in Sweden

One of the main goals of the Swedish labour market policy is that the labour market should be accessible for all. Persons with disabilities should, as everyone else, be in a position to find a job on the open labour market. Within the framework of labour market policy, several programmes for increasing the opportunities for disabled persons to become employed have thus been realised. The Government and the Ministry of Labour launched a programme to strengthen the position of disabled persons in the labour market through promoting the usage of information technology in the mid-80s. The Swedish Labour Market Board was given the task to work out the programme. [7] In 1987, a programme on ICT-based adaptations of the workplace started. Agreements with enterprises on development of ICT-based workplace adaptations were made. Within a decade about 4000 adapted work places had been delivered (Keijer, 1997).

An ICT adaptation can be requested either to the Swedish Labour Market Board's authorities, i.e. vocational assessment and rehabilitation-institutes, or the National Social Insurance Board, i.e. its regional social insurance offices. Individuals who, due to illness, accident or some other cause, need assistive devices in order to *retain* their job apply at the regional social insurance offices, while individuals who yet have not entered the labour market apply at the vocational assessment and rehabilitation-institutes, for help with finding a job and to get the appropriate accommodation of the workplace adaptations. A wage subsidy is provided to the employer who employs an individual with disability, who thereby enters the labour market. This subsidy is provided as a complement to the ICT accommodation of the workplace, during the first 12 months.

Irrespective of the financing authority, the rules for receiving subsidies for the different parts of this programme are similar. An employer can apply for subsidy concerning accommodation of the workplace, whereas an employee can apply for subsidy concerning assistive technology. Subsidy may be given for the cost of buying or renting of assistive technology or other adaptations of the workplace that are necessary for the employee to perform his/her job. Subsidy can also be given for an expert investigation to specifically adapt a workplace. The maximum subsidy an employer can receive for this is 50,000 SEK (c. 6000 Euro). Employees and self-employed persons can receive much more than 50 000 SEK for ICT-based devices. Equipment and education usually costs several-hundred thousand SEK per individual.

The Sample and the Design of the Study

The true test of a programme is its impact on the persons for whose benefit it has been designed. Nevertheless, despite a general agreement that programmes should be measured in terms of their effects, few programmes systematically collect comprehensive information on the impact made on intended beneficiaries. As a consequence, few programmes are able to demonstrate what they have achieved and fewer still are able to indicate precisely why they succeeded or failed in the effort.

In the case of this programme, extensive collections of data were gathered from each responsible authority—regional social insurance office, or vocational assessment and rehabilitation institute—in a non-systematic way. (Attempts to create a database at one of the authorities failed, but the need was felt since every renewed application must be evaluated against the background of the earlier one.) A sample was created on the basis of the collection of data on all persons who have received subsidy for ICT adaptations of the workplace under the period 1991–1998 at all regional social insurance offices in the municipality of Uppsala, six regional social insurance offices in the municipality of Stockholm, and one vocational assessment and rehabilitation institute in Uppsala and three in Stockholm. [8]

The evaluation was carried out in three phases. In the first phase, a thoroughfare and statistical analysis of 611 cases was performed. It became clear that the 611 registered cases corresponded only to 422 individuals. During the 7-year period that was investigated, some individuals had sought renewal of ICT-based adaptations, or a supplement to one already received; thus cases and numbers of persons are not equivalent. In the second phase, the 422 individuals were contacted by telephone in order to arrange an interview. The questions were aimed at discovering whether the individual still worked in the same workplace that s/he had originally received ICT adaptations for and if those met their needs, together with some questions concerning job satisfaction and discrimination. In cases where the individual was no longer employed, the telephone interview was made with a colleague or a superior at the workplace. In the third phase, the objective was to obtain further data about both successful and unsuccessful cases in order to gain more thorough knowledge. Thus, 23 cases were collected among those already interviewed by telephone, and contacted in order to arrange a visit at the workplace and an in-depth interview.

Individuals Receiving ICT Adaptations

The first question was who received ICTs? Looking at the group in terms of gender, it was clear that there were more men than women who received ICT adaptations to their workplace (56% men and 44% women).

When comparing different disability groups, it is clear that the largest group were those with a visual impairment. More than half of the receiplants were visually impaired (56%), while only 26% have hearing impairment and 19% mobility impairment. It is a well-known fact that information technologies open up great possibilities for those with visual and mobility impairments. The surprising result in this study is that the visually disabled persons are in such an overwhelming majority among those in receipt of ICT-based adaptations, even more if one takes into consideration that the development towards an increased use of graphical display during the 1990s has been unfavourable for the visually impaired. Furthermore, many of those who had applied for and received ICT-based adaptations several times during the investigated period (some of them up to 10 times) were visually impaired. Other groups of disabled persons are not included in this study because there were so few—according to the authorities—within each group. Persons with intellectual disabilities, for instance, have benefited very little from ICT's so far. [9]

The cost of ICT-based adaptations of workplaces also differs both between men and women, and between the different disability groups. The average costs for men's ICT-based adaptations are 1.5 times higher than for women's (an attempt to interpret this is undertaken below when other gender-related facts are at hand). The cost for ICT-based adaptations for the visually impaired are four times higher than it is for those with hearing impairments and twice as high as those with mobility impairment. Furthermore, it is very unevenly distributed when comparing them as individuals. Some individuals have, during the investigated period, had their ICT-based adaptation renewed or supplemented twice or more. The average cost for an ITC-based adaptation is 103 000 SEK (about 12 000 Euro), while the maximum received sum is about 1 200 000 SEK (about 141 000 Euro). The total sum of subsidy for accommodation of workplaces during this period is ca 41 million SEK (c, 5000 000 Euro).

Because there are two different types of financers, one for the employed and one for the unemployed, it is interesting to study which authority paid for the ICT-based accommodations. There are 141 individuals that have received ICT-based accommodation of workplaces through regional social insurance offices, while twice as many, 281 individuals, have received it through vocational assessment and rehabilitation institutes. This means that, the greatest part of the population who have received ICT-based adaptations of the workplace are disabled persons who previously were outside the labour market, not employees who, through illness or accident, become disabled during their working life.

To Enter and to Remain in the Labour Market

Another interesting factor to study is where the workplaces that have been ICT-adapted for disabled employees are located. Between the two sectors there is only a slight difference. The main part of the individuals in this study (35%) are employed in the private sector, followed by 32% in the public sector. As much as 19% of the individuals in this study are employed in non-profit-making-associations, while only 7% of are business owners. Comparing the figures on the basis of gender, it is clear that there is no great difference in the public sector (only a few more women work in the public sector than men—(53 versus 47%, respectively). There is although a considerable difference as regards employment within the private sector, as much as 64% of the men in the study are working in the private sector, while only 36% women.

Comparing the variable authority that finances the accommodation of workplace [10] with the variable private/public sector, there is a significant difference: only 26% among the private employees have received subsidy from regional social insurance office, while 74% of the private employees have received subsidy from vocational assessment and rehabilitation institutes. Among those employed within the public sector, there is a very even distribution; half of the ICT-based accommodations are financed by regional social insurance offices (51%) and half by vocational assessment and rehabilitation institutes (49%).

Among men who work within the public sector, 41% have received ICT-based accommodation from regional social insurance offices, i.e. they already had an employment. The figure is the same for women. Forty-four per cent of men and 32% of women work within private enterprises that have received ICT-based adaptations from vocational assessment and rehabilitation institutes, i.e. they were outside the labour market.

As stated above, one of the main objectives of the study was to find out how many of those who received ICT-based adaptations of the workplace have been helped in entering the labour market more permanently. The study reveals that 52% could still be found at the same workplace, while 45% had left. According to information given by a fellow worker or a superior, there are not one, but several causes behind the fact that the disabled person no longer works at the enterprise. It was claimed that the person in question had left because the enterprise did not need him, s/he became redundant, because the employment was nothing more than a temporary job, a project, the person now works at another enterprise, s/he had gone back to study, she had became pregnant or they had received early pension. The most frequent answer was that there was no need for the employee or that the employee himself had left. In a very few cases, it was claimed that there had been communication or cooperation difficulties.

Another important factor for evaluating the programme was the size of the workplace. Of those who are still in the same workplace 1–7 years after they had received an ICT-based adaptation of it, 28% are employed in workplaces with a maximum of nine employees, 43% in workplaces with 10–99 employees and 12% in workplaces with more than 100 employees. It is evident that small enterprises provide the best opportunities for employment.

Those who have received ICT-based adaptations from a regional social insurance office are, to a much great extent, still in the workplace, as many as 75%. A significantly smaller number could still be found in the same workplace, among those who have received ICT-based adaptations from a vocational assessment and rehabilitation institute this was about 40%. These figures verify a well-known trend in the labour market for persons with disabilities, namely that those who already have a job who become disabled are better off than those who are trying to enter the labour market in the position of already being disabled. Bearing in mind that the employer not only receives subsidy for workplace adaptations, but also a wage subsidy for the first year when employing someone who was outside the labour market, it could be expected that the figures between these two groups would not differ greatly. Evidently there are other, invisible obstacles that are stronger than the subsidies provided (in all likelihood negative attitudes about their working capacity and communication skills).

If one relates the high figures reported above of disabled persons within the private sector who receive ICT-based adaptations, with the figure of how many of them are still at the workplace, one become even less optimistic.

A great amount of those who had been employed in the private sector have received their ICT-based adaptations through the vocational assessment and rehabilitation institute—i.e. disabled that are unemployed or just finished an education (about 70%). Among those employed in the private sector that received ICT adaptations from the vocational assessment and rehabilitation institutes, 56% were still at the same workplace. The difference between the two figures indicates that those who enter the labour market, leaving behind them unemployment and/or education, tend to do so only temporarily. Another interpretation could also be that employers within the private sector 'consume' a lot of persons paid with wage subsidy. Persons with disabilities are entering the labour market, going to a workplace that the vocational assessment and rehabilitation institute has found for them, working there, and then becoming redundant in one way or another. It emerged in the telephone interviews that, for many, there is a circle of unemployment: work with wage subsidy, than back to unemployment or receive pension. The disability pension system is the most common exit pathway for those who have so called insufficient ability to work. [11]

Looking at the gender variable, we find that there are 61% of the men who are still in the same workplace, but only 48% of women. The differences among men and women are even greater when compared between the disability groups, especially within hearing and visually impaired groups. Looking at the variable disability group we find that hearing and visually impaired to a greater extent than persons with mobility impairment are still in the same workplace. [12] The chances of still working in the same workplace are connected to impairment, gender and whether the individual had already a job before s/he became disabled (Table I).

To sum up, the evaluation shows that the distribution of subsidy is uneven both with regard to the kind of impairment and gender. Persons with visual impairments are in a majority among those who have received ICT-based assistive technology. The accommodation for men costs 1.5 times more than for women. Few of the workplaces studied were unsubsidised, in a competitive position.

Cooperation—Dependency—Special Treatment

In order to single out if there are other, non-technology-related factors that render difficult the permanent entrance in the labour market, questions were asked about social relationships, cooperation and treatment at the workplace. Research concerning attitudes against persons with disabilities have been inconclusive whether the negative attitudes many persons with disabilities experience, really are negative attitudes, or solely the result of uncertainty of how to behave, fear and other factors (SOU, 1998, p. 16).

On the question of the employees still being in the same workplace if they had experienced that they are treated differently from non-disabled workers due to their impairment, 17% replied in the affirmative. Among them, 4% experienced a positive kind of treatment, while about 13% experienced a negative kind of treatment. Related to the variable kind of impairment, experience of different treatment were more frequent among visually disabled than among hearing and mobility impaired.

As regards cooperation with non-disabled the experiences were positive for the overwhelming majority. As many as 72% of those responding to the question responded that cooperation is good, 7% responded that cooperation is quite good and only 2% responded that cooperation is directly bad. Some reasons stated for bad cooperation experiences were lack of understanding from hearing individuals, not being allotted sufficient tasks, or being treated with suspiciousness from non-disabled fellow-workers or superiors.

Regarding the ability to perform their tasks without assistance from their non-disabled workmates, the study shows that there are 42% of the disabled employees who said they need help from others in order to fulfil their tasks (Table II). Related to the authority that financed the accommodation of the workplace, a greater share of those who need help have received subsidy from vocational assessment and rehabilitation institutes. Related to kind of impairment, the need of help is greatest among visually impaired and smallest among mobility impaired. Related to gender we find that among visually impaired and hearing impaired, the men need in greater extent than women help to perform their tasks. A subsequent question concerns whether they receive the help they needed. Of those responding to the question, only 3% reported that they do not receive the help they need.

On the question if disabled and non-disabled employees have tasks to be accomplished in cooperation, 63% answered in the affirmative, while 10% responded that they do not have any such tasks (Table III). These results are quite positive in the sense that they indicate that disabled and non-disabled can work

TABLE I. Distribution of sample according to whether or not they are still employed by the same company, allowing for different disabilities, authority providing subsidy and sex

| Disability/authority providing subsidy/sex | | Whether or not they are still employed by the same company | | | | |
		Yes	No	Information missing	Sum %	N
Hearing impairment						
S.I.O.*	Men	77%	18%	5%	100%	22
	Women	59%	41%		100%	17
	Both sexes	69%	28%	3%	100%	39
V.A.R.I.**	Men	55%	36%	9%	100%	33
	Women	42%	58%		100%	36
	Both sexes	48%	48%	4%	100%	69
S.I.O. and V.A.R.I.	Men	64%	29%	7%	100%	55
	Women	47%	53%		100%	53
	Both sexes	56%	41%	4%	100%	108
Visual impairment						
S.I.O.	Men	86%	10%	5%	100%	42
	Women	86%	9%	5%	100%	22
	Both sexes	86%	9%	5%	100%	64
V.A.R.I.	Men	48%	50%	2%	100%	92
	Women	39%	59%	3%	100%	78
	Both sexes	44%	54%	2%	100%	170
S.I.O. and V.A.R.I.	Men	60%	37%	3%	100%	134
	Women	49%	48%	3%	100%	100
	Both sexes	55%	42%	3%	100%	234
Mobility impairment						
S.I.O.	Men	67%	33%		100%	15
	Women	50%	42%	8%	100%	12
	Both sexes	59%	37%	4%	100%	27
V.A.R.I.	Men	35%	55%	10%	100%	29
	Women	38%	63%		100%	24
	Both sexes	36%	59%	6%	100%	53
S.I.O. and V.A.R.I.	Men	46%	48%	7%	100%	44
	Women	42%	56%	3%	100%	36
	Both sexes	44%	51%	5%	100%	80
All						
S.I.O.	Men	79%	19%	2%	100%	85
	Women	70%	29%	2%	100%	56
	Both sexes	75%	23%	2%	100%	141
V.A.R.I.	Men	45%	50%	5%	100%	149
	Women	36%	62%	2%	100%	132
	Both sexes	41%	56%	4%	100%	281
S.I.O. and V.A.R.I.	Men	57%	39%	4%	100%	234
	Women	46%	52%	2%	100%	188
	Both sexes	52%	45%	3%	100%	422

*S.I.O.—Social Insurance Office,
**V.A.R.I.—Vocational Assessment and Rehabilitation Institute.

TABLE II. Distribution of sample according to whether or not they need help from others to carry out their tasks

Do you need help to carry out your work tasks?	Number	%	Valid %
Yes	93	22	42
No	104	25	47
Information missing	24	6	11
Total	221	52	100
Do not have their employment	201	48	
Total	422	100	

TABLE III. Distribution of sample according to whether or not disabled persons and non-disabled have common working tasks

Common tasks with non-disabled persons	Number	%	Valid %
Yes	140	33	63
No	22	5	10
Information missing	59	14	27
Total	221	52	100
Do not have their employment	201	48	
Total	422	100	

together and that teamwork is a fairly common practice. Among the 10 percent who responded that they did not have tasks to be accomplished in cooperation with non-disabled employees, individuals with mobility impairment are in a majority.

Since the early 1990s, teamwork has become a very important feature of labour organisation. Teamwork is the principle for structuring and restructuring the organisation of work. Our research cannot answer whether teamwork implies risks or possibilities for workers with disabilities. According to Feldes (1999), the implementation of teams has been accompanied by a reduction of traditional employment areas in which persons with disabilities have often been employed in stand-alone workplaces. The study indicates that disabled employees work within a team do not face discrimination and isolation due to performance restrictions or negative attitudes.

Regarding regular contact with non-disabled workmates during lunch and coffee breaks, only 4% responded that they did not have regular contacts. This indicates that the persons with disabilities in this study, who have been at the same workplace for a period between 1–7 years, are well integrated at their workplaces. One must also bear in mind that the disability itself in some cases imposes hindrance to communication at informal breaks (for instance, deafness). The visits at the workplaces gave several examples of slight distance between the disabled and the non-disabled due to the very impairment.

In summary, the results on the topic of cooperation, dependency and social relationships at the workplaces are very encouraging. The great majority of the disabled persons in the study are not facing discriminatory attitudes at their workplaces, they work together with non-disabled, they receive the help they need and they are not socially isolated. We cannot, however, exclude that among the 45% who have left the workplace there were those who had endured acts of discrimination and bad treatment, or cooperation problems. The answers given by fellow workers or superiors who were interviewed in these cases do not support such assumption. Only a few of them mentioned anything negative that could be connected to the person (cooperation difficulties for instance) and no one mentioned the disability as a reason why the individual no longer worked at the work place. However, on the other hand, on the issue of attitudes we are entering a grey area were the truth is hard to reveal, as research has concluded for the last decades.

We also added an open question in order to learn about their experience of ICT-based accommodations of workplaces. Had it been positive or negative? The great majority had very positive experience of their ICT-based accommodations. ICT-based accommodations reduce the impairment; they increase/improve possibilities for two-way communication, they make it possible to retain the job; they reduce dependence from others; they open up a new world. Among negative experiences of ICT-based accommodations, which were comparatively very few, it was claimed that the adaptation rather quickly became out-dated; that ICTs do not always function as promised and that visual displays create problems for visually impaired. In the in-depth interviews among negative experiences was the growing importance of graphic interface for those with visual impairment. Another negative experience was that the adaptations of the latest information technology lag behind, so when the new program or the new version finally reached the disabled employee, the non-disabled workmates were already working with something else.

Even so, many of those interviewed in this last part of the study, have benefited a lot from the ICTs. Thanks to the ICT adaptation they had been able to maintain the employment or gain an employment. However, the results from the in depth interviews in this study indicates that if ICT-based adaptations of workplaces have been highly successful in assisting disabled employees to retain their jobs or in finding new jobs, technology alone has not been the only factor. Other key factors for success were receiving support from the superiors, having an understanding employer with whom one can make agreements about appropriate tasks, of flexible hours of work or reduced working-hours, and in some cases the individual's own fighting spirit (not subsuming under the circumstances of the disability, but trying to make the best of it).

Unequal Distribution of Accommodations

The study reveals that the administrative routines are time-consuming both from the point of view of the authority and from the point of view of the person who applies for the ICT-based devices/adaptations. As part of this problem there seem to persist a certain vagueness concerning what counts as an ICT-based device/adaptation and what is the criterion in order to receive them. [13] There seems also to be a persistent lack of adequate information. Many of those interviewed, by telephone and in-depth, stressed that you have to follow on your own the latest technical development in order to know what is going on and thus to apply for relevant adaptation/devices. Maybe the less and the cheaper ICT-based adaptations to women could be explained by this informal sifting process (they do not follow the development within information technology, thus they do not seek to gain the best devises for themselves).

At the visits to the workplaces, a rather traditional picture emerged. Many men had great opportunities to develop themselves within their disability, going on courses, working with computers (even if, with their specific disability, it meant a very costly adaptation), while many women had not received the same opportunities or had actually gone backwards in their careers, becoming clerks and assistants, or at least being paid as assistants.

Holding in mind the difference reported above between how many women receive ICTs compared with men and at what costs, it seems that disabled women also are subjected to the traditional discrimination of women or, more precisely, that officials do not give the same priority for the needs of women (more or less consciously). Other research give evidence for this trend. [14] To some degree, the uneven distribution can be an effect of different vocations between men and women, men being more technical orientated in their vocation. For only 21% of those who are still in the same workplace, the ICT-based adaptation has lead towards more qualified tasks.

Both these trends of unequal distribution, due to gender and the kind of disability, raise questions about the guiding principles at the responsible authorities and the power relations among groups of disabled persons.

Addendum: Subsidised Work Force

Although, it was not a specific topic to be focused on in this evaluation, the wage subsidy system emerged as a problematic feature in the course of the study. Below some findings and some conclusions will be reported.

The Swedish labour market policy defines disability as a reduction of working capacity. The concept 'occupational handicap' is most explicitly defined in the 'Regulation of wage subsidy'. The Regulation states that 'occupational handicap' embraces those persons in search of work who, on account of physical, mental, intellectual or medical disabilities, have reduced working capacity and because of this can be expected to have difficulties on the regular labour market (SFS, 1992, p. 338). The system of disability-benefit—e.g. for work subsidy—uses some quantitative standards to measure disability in terms of loss of earning capacity. Sometimes a disabled worker's productivity is assumed. Alternatively, productivity may be assessed and an incentive given on a case-by-case basis, depending on the assessed loss.

The purpose at the wage subsidy programme—which is older than the ICT programme—is to encourage employers to employ a person with disability by reimbursing him for part of the wage costs. The employer pays a market adjusted, contractual wage for the part of the work—counted in per cent—that is considered satisfactory and not affected by the disability. The employer receives a wage subsidy for the rest. It is stipulated that it is the working capacity of the employee that decides the amount of the subsidy. In the case of the newly employed, the subsidy can reach as much as 80% of the wage. Wage subsidy is usually provided for a maximum of 4 years and shall, according to the rules, be reconsidered regularly. In the long run, the wage subsidy is reduced and normally ceases after a couple of years. Subsidies vary in that some may be time-limited and others may taper off with time, while others may involve a reassessment after a certain period of time has passed. There are, however, no conditions attached to employers receiving a subsidy; for instance, they are not expected to maintain the disabled employee when the subsidy period has ended. There has been some criticism against financial measures that do not have such conditions attached (Eriksson, 1995, 1996).

Looking at the results from the telephone interviews and the in-depth interviews, the wage subsidy system does not seem to function as a first step into the labour market. Many of those interviewed on the telephone and in the in-depth interviews were employed with a wage subsidy. In several of the in-depth interviews, the employees expressed an open criticism against the wage subsidy system. The argument was that it transforms the persons with disabilities into second rate, cheap manpower. The enterprise or the authority does not try to employ the person after an introduction with wage subsidy (although it had been part of deal), but they rely on the wage subsidy continuously or will let him/her go if no renewed, favourable agreement with vocational assessment and rehabilitation institute can be reached. According to our study, the employer can be either a private enterprise or a public authority (even an authority responsible for labour market issues).

Several of those who were visited at their work places worked for non-governmental organisations. They were pleased with their employers and reported that they were given opportunities to develop their skills; they did not express negative opinions about the wage subsidy system. In these cases, although the disabled individual works for a church, a disability organisation or other non-governmental organisations, the reliance upon the wage subsidy is permanent. In these cases, it is hard to claim that the wage subsidy system functions as a way of removing obstacles to employment for the disabled, because there are no prejudices to remove in these organisations, neither that it is functioning as compensation to the employer for lower efficiency of the disabled employee, because these organisations do not work according to a profit principle. The wage subsidy functions rather as an extra resource for employing personnel that otherwise could not be financed. From the perspective of persons with disabilities these organisations are key employers (cf. the above-mentioned figures on location of work place—almost a fifth work at non-Governmental organisations (NGO's)); NGO's create a labour market, offering jobs and an affirmative working milieu.

There was one astonishing, almost sad, discovery in the in-depth interviews at the workplaces. Several of those interviewed had been working for many years for the same employer, in ordinary employment and with a normal wage, doing a good work. They could easily have been picked out as good examples of successful disabled employees. Nevertheless, they had found themselves in the course of a reorganisation becoming employed with a wage subsidy. Besides the lower status at the work place for the persons involved, wage subsidy also leads to an economic loss since the part of the wage becoming subsidised—the greatest part—cannot be part of the annual wage negotiations at the enterprise/public authority. Thereby, they will have lower and lower wages in comparison with their non-disabled colleagues. The question arises how established employees can be transformed into a subsidised workforce. A tentative interpretation could be that behind these acts lies an increasing pursuit of reduced costs, both in private enterprises (due to competition) and in the public sector (due to lesser resources).

There is, indeed, a clause in the regulation that permits, if there is a risk that the employee may be excluded from the labour market, wage subsidy to be provided to someone who is already employed. In some cases this could maybe be a way to avoid employees with disability to become redundant, but the clause could easily be misused as a means to pay less for an existing workforce. It was disappointing to learn about this practice of inverted disability policy—altering the status of competent employees into subsidised work force on no personal grounds—which occurred both in private enterprises and public authorities. What prospects does this give to those who are fighting to gain employment on the open labour market?

If one wants to avoid becoming over optimistic—which is a very common trait in the disability field—one must confront this fact. The labour market is striving towards an increasing demand on efficiency from everybody within the system. The non-disabled workers are under an increasing amount of pressure from the tempo and the requirements of their jobs. There are many studies, both on national levels and internationally that made manifest this trend (in Sweden it has been highlighted by a rapidly growing number of long-term illnesses due to stress-related sickness). Being unable to work full time, not to mention being unable to work overtime, is a serious obstacle for anyone in the labour market today (not only for the disabled, but for parents with small children or seniors as well). There is a trend in Sweden that the labour market that functions outside a sheer economist perspective is shrinking. Since the 1990s there is an ongoing reduction of personnel working in the public sector, which goes hand-in-hand with an increased demand on existing personnel on higher efficiency (the declared aspiration of making authorities function as were they private enterprises, thus making the efficiency a prime objective in order to reduce state expenditures). How can disabled employees or disabled unemployed cope with this?

No doubt, some disabled employees may need shorter working hours in order to work well. Some have a reduced capacity for work and they know it. A great majority in the telephone interviews answered the question about their own efficiency in comparison with their non-disabled work fellows/colleagues, by estimating that they were less efficient. Leaving aside that this high figure could reflect a lack of self-confidence, it is a fact that a great many of them do not work full time and many of them chose to remove some tasks in order to concentrate upon a fewer.

One may question if the underlying hypothesis with wage subsidy is wrong. Maybe it is wrong to suppose that an employer will or can deviate from the underlying rule in all business of keeping costs as low as possible. Will not the employer in all likelihood try to bend the rules to his advantage? Will not the head of an authority try to reduce all 'unnecessary' costs, thus increasing resources that can be used more on promoting activities than being just towards disabled employees? Since the trade unions in the reported cases did not seem to bother when the disabled employees were unjustly treated, who else will?

The Improbability of Full Employment

Being employed is a necessary condition for social recognition, for personal and economic autonomy. However, in the current circumstances of high unemployment rates, the employment opportunities is an especially complicated issue regarding disabled persons. The ICTs themselves are part of a transformation of the labour market towards increasing rationalisation, with fewer job opportunities. The favourable results of ICTs at the micro-level are counteracted by the unfavourable results at the macro-level. If the rate of unemployment for the population as a whole is already high, amongst disabled persons the rate is four or five times higher. In order to gain or retain employment, disabled persons not only have to confront the barriers produced by a competitive and unstable labour market, they have also to overcome the additional barriers that are the result of their personal circumstances. [15]

While everybody seems to agree on the importance of promoting employment for disabled persons, there is much evidence that the various approaches—such as quota systems, reserved jobs, financial support to employers for workplace adaptations, or subsidies for wages and salaries—have not solved this problem. Despite the programmes and measures adopted for many years in Sweden, persons with disabilities experience growing difficulties in finding and keeping employment. The increased competition and greater constraints on the allocation of public resources for social and economic support programmes are factors contributing to these difficulties (SOU, 2000, p. 3).

In my view, a better understanding of the pros and cons of ICTs must distinguish between effects on the micro-macro-level, on the organisation of the labour process and the labour market system. Looking at effects of ICTs on these two levels is very contradictory. ICTs have positive effects for the individual with disabilities in terms of compensating his/her functional impairment but at the same time ICTs leads to exclusion from the working life, i.e. long-term unemployment with no prospect of new work, as a result of the increasing rationalisation of the working process they generate. The macro-effects of ICTs diminish jobs on all levels (a late example can be found in the banking sector due to the increasing use of the Internet) or change the work inherently. The expectations which technological optimism has given rise to are all related to the micro-level with an almost total disregard of the effects on the macro-level.

According to some theorists (Bauman, 1998; Vobruba, 1999), we are now living in a transition period toward societies after full employment. Since work has been central to capitalist societies both in the sense of structuring individual life and social institutions, the change affected by the end of full employment are rather dramatic. Full employment is a precondition for welfare benefits, social security systems, the tax system and generally social inclusion. The basic tenet of these theories is that, in the long run, labour-saving technological progress drastically reduces the workforce. Thus, a major disadvantage that ICTs bring upon the disabled person is the increasing unemployment rate as a result of the reduced need for labour due to the advance of technology. We are living in a society where a growing part of the population is not needed (Bauman estimates the figure as one-fifth of the working population) at the same time as economic growth is achieved by rationalising labour intensive enterprises, thus these excluded persons do not have any prospect of becoming employed (Bauman, 1998). Keeping in mind the weak position of the disabled persons in the labour market already before this development took place, the prospects looks increasingly worse. Presumably as a result of this decreasing amount of jobs on the labour market—with the exception of the fast growing ICT-consultancy sector that helps enterprises to find technological solutions that enable them to reduce their costs and rationalise the work process even more—the level of qualifications that is needed in order to find a job is constantly rising (every job presuppose a kind of formal education). Since persons with disabilities at times have lower educational level, this tendency makes it all the more difficult for them.

It was originally thought that the growing automation and robotisation of the workplace would, by reducing dependence on mobility and dexterity, open additional jobs to disabled persons. This has happened to some extent, but the total impact is varied. As these trends have reduced the number of workers needed, they have curtailed the number of job openings available and have thus added to the difficulties experienced by disabled persons in finding employment. Jobs given to disabled persons are often simple ones. Unskilled jobs, however, whether in factories, offices or the service sector, are the first to lost when labour costs rise. As technological change increases the possibilities of adapting workplaces to disabled persons, it will also increase the possibilities of cutting back on costly human labour. Employers may then prefer workers who can be used more flexibly and do not require as much support as disabled persons (Köning & Schalock 1991). Moreover, as technology has created more jobs requiring a combination of high intelligence, and more than basic education and training, the proportion of jobs available for persons whose disability is intellectual, or who have not been able to obtain the necessary education and training has declined (Acton, 1981).

According to Bauman, economic progress in today's world of big corporations means, first and foremost, 'down-sizing', while technological progress means replacement of living labour with electronic software. For the present day streamlined, down-sized, capital and knowledge-intensive industry, labour is a constraint on the rise of productivity. In contrast to the classical labour theories of value (Smith, Ricardo, Marx), a labour intensive enterprise is problematic and has difficulty surviving in a competitive market; therefore, any search for higher efficiency (i.e.

more profit on capital invested) focuses first on further possibilities of cutting down the number of employees. 'Economic growth and the rise of employment are, for all practical intends, at cross-purposes; technological progress is measured by the replacement and elimination of labour' (Bauman, 1998). Under such circumstances the promises of the fervent proponents of technological optimism sound, rather hollow and has given rise to false expectations about what ICTs can contribute towards disabled persons' possibilities to gain and retain employment. Confidence in technology's potentialities for disabled persons prospects to gain and retain employment does not reflect the changes taking place at the macro-level, i.e. a decreased demands for labour force generally and when labour power is needed it must be educated, flexible and independent.

Disabled persons are vulnerable to two negative trends. The first is the increase in unemployment, which has a specially damaging effect on all those who are, for one reason or another, less favoured in a competitive employment labour market. The second is the current trend to reduce public expenditure, a trend that generally has consequences for persons outside the labour market and for disabled employees, especially in the public sector, to retain employment. A more restrictive policy on the rules for wage subsidy may also lead to a considerable increase in the unemployment rate of disabled persons. Both these trends can be seen as effects of the economic system, which creates conditions that force people to leave the labour market. The economic system forces continuously those involved in the production of commodities and services to improve their efficiency, due to competition. As a result, pressure for change is created which leads to a lower demand for labour and a higher pressure on those within the labour market to be more and more efficient. Under these conditions disabled persons, as well as those with a poor education and above 55 years, are at high risk of being excluded.

Exclusion from the labour market system and, consequently, with a low income can lead to exclusion from other systems in society as well, since the problems of poverty and associated social isolation are, in part, attributable to a denial of employment opportunities. 'In a society where active citizenship for those other than the very rich is associated with individualistic notions of "earning your keep", the perceived inability to do so poses a problem in terms of one's overall social membership' (Jenkins, 1991). Jenkins argues that disability is a factor contributing to the production and reproduction of social stratification in its own right, independently of class relations. Disability is strongly related to occupational class, economic disadvantage and downward social mobility. Thus, being disabled is strongly associated with economic handicaps. These handicaps affect not only the person with a disability, but also the non-disabled members in his family and their labour market careers. The disadvantages exist despite long-standing policy measures on the part of the state aimed at intervening in the labour market to the advantage of disabled persons. The question which must be asked, according to Jenkins, is whether the disadvantages experienced by disabled persons are a product of labour market processes—and therefore simply another dimension of the class system—or whether factors independent of the labour market are at work.

Social and moral considerations have always regarding the economic system been overshadowed by the economic viewpoint. A new tendency, however, is that this trend seems to be reinforced by the recession, and even extended in the public sector and non-profit organisations. Economic efficiency, then, seems to be in contradiction with social, cultural and moral principles. Arguments for equal opportunities in employment for persons with disabilities, advanced by moral principles, are often rejected on the basis of increased costs and loss of competitivity. From an over-arching point of view—if such a viewpoint is possible—the error of applying an economic point of view lies in the fact that we disregard the welfare benefits accruing to disabled persons, which by essence cannot be measured and retain only the financial costs of these actions. A proper evaluation ought to take into account both non-economic benefits and economic costs. However, here lies one of the major contradictions in any evaluation study of disability policy: the application of criteria of cost effectiveness in a field that is not ruled by market mechanisms only, but by moral considerations as well.

Conclusions

Many efforts to promote the integration and participation of disabled persons in the labour market have failed. An important reason for this is that disabled workers are associated with economic burdens due to the need for workplace adaptations, absenteeism due to illness and lack of flexibility (Hendriks, 1999). This state of affairs means that disabled persons as a group have always been dependent on social and welfare benefits.

An ICT-based accommodation of workplaces is a promising approach to opening up new opportunities for disabled persons. It offers new options to persons who have previously been excluded from the labour market. The present evaluation study has shown that the ICT-based accommodation of workplaces programme can bring many benefits for individuals with disabilities. In spite of this positive assessment, however, there are many serious problems, as have been noted above. In times when unemployment rates are high, it becomes even any harder for disabled persons. [16] There is a need of offering a particular motivation to employers to hire a disabled person. The incentives used in order to convince an employer to employ a person with a disability are wage subsidy and subsidy for adaptation of the workplace, where the former tends to be misused as the study indicates.

The effects of technological change in present society conditions are contradictory: the positive effects on the individual level are counteracted by the rationalisation of production at the societal level. This is an important reason why a simple summary judgement as to the implications of ICTs to the employment prospects of disabled persons is hard to judge. The employment prospects accompanying technological change have different implications on different levels and for persons with different skills. As the job content changes from production dominated by manufacturing to handling information and service centred production, the prospects for some groups of disabled persons can improve. Other things being equal, those highly educated with communication disabilities should be relatively more competitive in the labour market.

However, what our evaluation study has shown is that the ICTs, at best, can be only a partial solution to the problems faced by persons with disabilities in the labour market. Most of the individuals interviewed in this study stressed the importance of ICTs in its potential to remove barriers to participation in working life. However, ICTs can increase the possibilities of disabled persons in the labour market only to the extent that they are accompanied by the development of appropriate measures to compensate for the loss of effectiveness or that the working time is adapted to the abilities of different individuals. A precondition for this, however, is seeing persons with disabilities as different individuals with special needs, wants and capabilities. Luhmann (1995) provides a very interesting description of modern society as a complex system of communications that has differentiated itself horizontally into a network of interconnected social systems. Each social system, according to Luhmann, differentiate itself vertically in order to cope with complexity; so has, for example, the economic system differentiated vertically in many subsystems (banking system, market system, wage system, etc.). Each of these systems reproduces itself recursively on the basis of its own, system specific communication. Social systems are thus self-reproducing systems of communication. Each system observes itself and its environment, but their unique perspective marks whatever they observe, by the selectivity of the particular binary code they use for their observations. According to Luhmann, social systems owe their identity to this binary code. The market, for instance, functions according to the binary opposition cost/benefit. When the binary code is established, the system operates by interpreting the environment and choosing which relationships are to be counted as relevant for the system on the basis of the code. The binary determines what a system can and cannot see, and everything it observes is observed from that particular viewpoint.

In accordance with this theory, one could say that the binary opposition ability/disability is a construct—created by some economically determined and variable standards of what constitute a reduced working capacity, whose boundaries are dependent upon social and economic conditions. In real life, the binary ability/disability indicates a continuum where complete absences of ability/disability are imaginary states of the human condition. Therefore, when the boundaries between ability and disability are drawn, with the consequence that some persons are defined as disabled, while others as non-disabled, some persons defined as effective or ineffective, with reduced or not reduced working capacity, etc., we must take into consideration that those boundaries are drawn for economic and administrative purposes, and as such negotiable political and economic stances.

Acknowledgements

The author would like to thank Professor Mårten Söder for his criticism of earlier drafts of this paper and his valuable suggestions about its structure and argument. This article is based on an evaluation study conducted during 1999 'Accommodation and modification of workplaces for persons with disabilities by means of information technology'. The *Office of Labour Market Policy Evaluation* (IFAU) in Sweden financed the study.

NOTES

[1] For example, persons living in sparsely inhabited areas, where there are fewer job opportunities.

[2] ICTs replace not only workers at factories, but also more qualified personnel, for instance when applied in automatised library systems.

[3] Although ICTs already play a significant role, the uneven distribution of access to these technologies and the fact that certain skills are necessary in order to use them raise important questions about their consequences on social inequality, consumption, education, etc. (Loader, 1998).

[4] The only research on disabled persons needs of computer-based technology thus far conducted in Sweden is a study made by Stig Larsson in 1991. He has by means of a questionnaire and interviews mapped out what needs severe disabled persons have of computers in their work.

[5] 'Employment rate' includes persons of working age who are currently not considered to be economically active, but who would like to work.

[6] To mention just a few examples: reading machines can scan printed text and translate it into synthesised speech; personal computers can be linked up to Braille printers, a range of software can enable blind and visually impaired persons to make full use of computers; broadband communication opens up possibilities of remote document reading for the blind; Computer Aid Manufacture and Computer Aid Design facilitate the operation of machinery for mobility-disabled workers. Another example is the use of microcomputers with modems in text-telephones for the deaf and speech impaired.

[7] The Swedish Labour Market Board is the responsible authority for labour market policy. It issues guidelines and instructions to County Labour Boards, and supervises the activity. The County Labour Boards are responsible for the employment offices, and the vocational assessment and rehabilitation institutes, i.e. are agencies of great importance for persons with disabilities trying to enter the labour market. Some of the employment offices, and vocational and rehabilitation institutes are specialised in one or two disabilities in order to provide a suitable job and the right adaptations needed by the job seeker.

[8] The vocational assessment and rehabilitation institutes included in the study are specialised in providing services to persons with mobility, visual or hearing impairment.

[9] There are, however, on-going projects aimed at a better integration of the intellectually disabled into the workplace (Cacciabue, 1998).

[10] The variable 'authority financing the accommodation of workplace' signifies the difference between those employees who were already employed when they became disabled (receiving the ICT accommodation from the regional social insurance office) and those disabled employees trying to enter the labour market (they receive their ICT accommodation from vocational assessment and rehabilitation institutes).

[11] During the past two decades a large number of persons, varying from 40,000 to more than 60,000 per year, have left the labour market using this early exit pathway. The total number of disabled pensioners in the population is steadily increasing (Stattin, 1998).

[12] Persons with mobility impairments are, to a lesser extent, in the same workplace, despite the fact that ICT permits more flexibility in the place and the time schedule of work.

[13] With the growing possibilities of medical techniques it becomes crucial to define what is an assistive device. Everybody agrees that a hearing device, which is outside the ear, is an assistive device, but what about something that is put in place through surgery? Ought it to be deemed by the consequences, e.g. regaining the hearing capability to a high degree thus decrease the disability, or from it's placing (interior/exterior) or by looking at the organisation scheme of public authorities?

[14] In a study on regional social insurance offices regarding decisions about compensation due to disability Hetzler (1994) found that the rules were applied in such a manner that disabled women were discriminated against. Men are approved grants to a greater extent

and with a higher amount of money than women. This fact cannot be explained by their respective impairments. According to Hetzler, social policy reproduces and sometimes strengthens women's subordination, since it reflects the power of gender relationships already existing in society. Barron (1997) proposes that disability and gender can be studied as one powerful prism, since there is a common denominator in the social construction of these two subjects, namely dependency. This results in a congruity between the two roles where powerlessness is confirmed and reinforced by each other.

[15] It is not unemployment as such which excludes and marginalises disabled people. It is poverty, Bauman argues, which marginalises people and not the access to labour market (Bauman, 1998).

[16] Statistics indicate that, at times of high unemployment, employers, even in countries with a quota scheme, are less willing to hire disabled workers.

REFERENCES

ACTION, N. (1981) Employment of disabled persons: where are we going? *International Labour Review*, 120(1), pp. 5–19.

ALBEDA, W. (1985) *Disabled and their Employment*, Commission of the European Communities in Cooperation with the European Centre for Work and Society (Maastricht, Luxembourg).

BARRON, K. (1997) *Disability and Gender. Autonomy as an Indication of Adulthood* (Uppsala, Acta Universitatis Upsaliensis).

BAUMAN, Z. (1998) *Work, Consumerism and the New Poor* (London, Open University Press).

CACCIABUE, P.C. (1998) *Better Integration of Mentally Disabled in Industry*, Institute for Systems, Informatics and Safety, Annual Report (Luxembourg, Joint Research Centre, European Commission).

ERIKSSON, T. (1995) *Anställd på lika villkor?! Studie av översynsarbetet rörande anställningar med lönebidrag vid Uppsala universitet* (Forskningsrapport, Centrum för handikappforskning vid Uppsala universitet).

ERIKSSON, T. (1996) *Att vara anställd med lönebidrag. En studie av anställningar med lönebidrag vid Uppsala universitet* (Forskningsrapport, Centrum för handikappforskning vid Uppsala universitet).

FELDES, W. (1999) Modern team work and employment of persons with disabilities, *Rehabilitation*, 38(4), pp. 17–36.

HENDRIKS, A. (1999) From Social (In)Security to Equal Employment Opportunities—a Report from the Netherlands, in: M. JONES & L.A. BASSER MARKS, 1999, *Disability, Divers-Ability and Legal Change* (International Studies in Human Rights, Martnus Nijhoff Publishers).

HETZLER, A. (1994) *Socialpolitik i verkligheten. De handikappade och försäkringskassan* (Lund, Bokbox förlag).

HUNT H.A. & BERKOWITZ, M. (Eds) (1992) *New Technologies and the Employment of Disabled Persons* (Geneva, ILO).

ILO (1998a) *Proceedings of the International Symposium on Job Retention and Return to Work Strategies for Disabled Workers*, Washington D.C., 20–21 May.

ILO (1998b) *International Research Project on Job Retention and Return to Work Strategies for Disabled Workers* (Geneva, ILO).

JENKINS, R. (1991) Disability and social stratification, *British Journal of Sociology* 42(1), pp. 557–580.

JORDAN, T. (1999) *Cyberpower. The Culture and Politics of Cyberspace and the Internet* (London, Routledge).

KEIJER, U. (1997) Inventering inför en utvärdering av insatser för anpassning av arbetsplatser för funktionshindrade, Rådet för Arbetslivsforskning, Stockholm.

KÖNIG, A. & SCHALOCK, R.L. (1981) Suported employment: equal opportunities for severely disabled men and women, *International Labour Review*, 130(1), pp. 21–46.

LINDSTROM, J-L. (1984) *Information Technology and Disability—State of the Art and Trends in Sweden and Other Nordic Countries*, Study made for the Swedish National Board for Technical Development (Stockholm, SNBTD).

LOADER, B.D. (Ed.) (1998) *Cyberspace Divide. Equality, Agency and Policy in the Information Society* (London, Routledge).

LUHMANN, N. (1995) *Social Systems* (Stanford, Stanford University Press).

SFS (1987) Förordning om bidrag till arbetshjälpmedel m.m. SFS 1987:409.

SFS (1992) Förordning om ändring i förordningen (1991:333) om lönebidrag; SFS 1992:338.

SOU (1998) 16. *När åsikter blir handling—en kunskapöversikt om bemötande av personer med funktionshinder*, Delbetänkande av Utredningen om bemötande av personer med funktionshinder (Stockholm, Socialdepartementet).

SOU (2000) 3. *Välfärd vid vägskäl. Utvecklingen under 1990-talet*, Delbetänkande/Kommittén Välfärdsbokslut (Stockholm, Socialdepartementet).

STATTIN, M. (1998) *Yrke, yrkesförändring och utslagning från arbetsmarknaden—en studie av relationen mellan förtidspension och arbetsmarknadsförändring*, Doctoral Theses, Department of Sociology, Umeå University.

VOBRUBA, G. (1999) The end of the full employment society. Changing the basis of inclusion and exclusion, in: P. LITTLEWOOD, I. GLORIEUX, S. HERKOMMER, I. JÖNSSON (Eds), *Social Exclusion in Europe. Problems and Paradigms* (Aldershot, Ashgate).

Enacting disability: how can science and technology studies inform disability studies?

Vasilis Galis

The Department of Thematic Studies – Technology and Social Change, University of Linköping, Linköping, Sweden

This paper aims to discuss how science and technology studies (STS) can inform disability studies and challenge dominant approaches, such as the medical and the social models, in the ordering and representation of disability. Disability studies and STS have followed somewhat parallel paths in the history of ideas. From a positivist approach to their research objects to a strong social constructivism, both disciplines have moved to postmodern conceptualisations of science, technology and disability. In the same manner, this paper brings the conceptual vocabulary of actor-network theory (ANT) to the field of disability studies. ANT enables the ordering of disability as a simultaneous biological, material and semiotic phenomenon. The focus of the analysis shifts from merely defining disability as an impairment, handicap, or social construction (epistemology) to how disability is experienced and enacted in everyday practices, in policy-making, in the body, and in the built environment (ontology). This adoption of an ontological approach to disability allows the analysis to not only discuss how disability is done, but also to follow how disability groups and carriers of disability expertise and experience intervene in policy-making by developing 'research in the wild' and confronting scientific experts in different fora (ontological politics).

Points of interest

- Instead of solely examining the physical aspect of disability or removing entirely the focus from the body, this article introduces a theoretical vocabulary that allows disability theorists to deconstruct ableist science and technology and integrate the politics of reality (including the bodily experience) in the social analysis of disability.
- The theoretical discussion on actor-network theory reported here challenges dominant conceptual models such as the medical and the social models.
- The article removes the focus from interpretative approaches of what disability is and shifts the sociological analysis to how disability is created through different interacting practices between the impaired body, the built environment and policy-making.

- The article proposes a theoretical vocabulary that follows the work of disability organisations in policy-making spheres where disabled people have the opportunity to participate in the configuration of social policies, the design of infrastructure, and democratic institutions.

Introduction

After prolonged neglect, disability has become the subject of increasing attention among science and technology studies (STS) scholars (Moser 2000, 2003, 2005, 2006, 2009; Galis 2006; Winance 2006; Diedrich 2005). Drawing on Corker and Shakespeare's assertion that the global experience of disability is too complex to be rendered within one unitary model or set of ideas (2002, 15), the topic of this paper is how STS can inform disability studies in the ordering of disability and the representation of disability issues in different techno-scientific forums. I will review works that straddle the border of these distinct fields and their critics, and propose an alternative conceptual reasoning for the ordering of disability. This alternative is marked by a shift from medical or social constructions of disability to how disability is done within various practices and through different experiences. Special focus will be given to simultaneous relationships between material, semiotic and biological entities. This kind of material semiotic approach is poorly represented in the ordering of disability (cf. Moser 2006, 375), while most accessibility studies, despite their important role as policy evaluation/critique, have limited theoretical significance (Gleeson 2001, 252). As I will show, the dominant conceptual models of disability have produced distinct dichotomies between the body, and semiotic and material entities.

The introduction of the social model of disability in the early 1970s set the ground for a materialist account of disability. This initial materialist view of disability acknowledged the significant role of politics in reproducing disabling socio-material environments (Gleeson 1997, 197). At the same time, the commitment of disabled activists to their political struggle is so obvious that it cannot be dismissed (Siebers 2006, 179). Thus, disability studies have always been marked by strong politicisation. However – and it is a theoretical contribution that this paper aims to make – politics does not constitute a monopoly of governmental action or of the policy domain. Politics in this context is distributed among a hybrid arrangement of humans and non-humans as well as experts and lay people (Latour 2004, 223; 2007, 817). Politics may refer to very different meanings of the word. In this paper and inspired by Latour (2007), politics refer to: all new associations between humans and non-humans that modify the collective; and deliberative problem-solving by lay people in areas previously dominated by scientific experts (2007, 816–817).[1]

As a direct legacy from Enlightenment to modernity, technology and scientific knowledge has appeared as something that exists outside the irrationality of politics, and has been portrayed as a neutral and objective product of scientific expertise. During modernity, the unquestionable position of natural scientists and engineers allowed them to speak in the name of supremacy, precision and academic validity regarding matters that involved science and technology (cf. Collins and Evans 2002, 239). Urban planners and architects, for example, have treated the built environment as a process of 'geometrisation of lived space in which things became numbers to be understood as objective and intelligible forms' (Imrie 2003, 50). These forms, however, anticipated a human body as described by Euclidian geometry, the proportions of the Vitruvian man and romantic Renaissance conceptions of antique perfection. In other words, the design of the built environment failed to integrate bodily and physiological diversity by materialising architectural obsessions sourcing from an able-bodied, taut, upright, male, healthy body measure (Imrie 2003, 49). The authoritative character and 'ableist' politics of architecture and architectural theory also contributed to 'medicalising' disability and the impaired body, underrating the role of inaccessible urban environments in the creation of disability. Nevertheless, these were certainly not the only factors behind the entrenchment of disability behind scientific and biological citadels (clinical diagnosis and the 'abnormal' body).

In the following text, I will provide a short account of the evolution of disability studies from the so-called medical model of disability to postmodern approaches. The latter constitutes an entry point, or rather a bridge, to the broad field of STS. My ambition is to deduce concepts or even theoretical reasoning from specific STS strands and to apply them to the ordering of disability. Central focus will be given to the implication of the experience of disability with the material, semiotic, political and biological entities that constitute it; namely, the lived experience of impaired, gendered, ethnic bodies interacting with the configuration of the built environment and its materiality. The configuration of the built environment also touches on questions of representation and involvement: how are disabled people involved in the policy-making sphere and in techno-scientific debates? Who speaks in the name of whom? Who represents whom and what? (cf. Callon 1986a, 214).

From medical to social to postmodern approaches of disability

The rise of industrialisation and medical science – 'the techniques of power that were essentially centred on the body, on the individual body' (Foucault 2003, 242) – during the nineteenth century legitimised radical shifts in the approach to disabled people: the medicalisation of illness and impairment, the dominance of medical experts, and the broad institutionalisation of disabled people in asylums, followed by residential and educational facilities for the 'blind', 'deaf' and those classified as intellectually impaired (Barnes, Mercer, and Shakespeare 1999, 18–20). By the start of the twentieth century, the medical approach dominated the ordering of disability. Disability, as defined by medical experts, was exclusively situated in impaired, 'invalid' bodies that needed to be cured by medical science with possible solutions that aimed to overcome or minimise the negative effects of the individual's impairment (Siebers 2006, 173; see also Llewellyn and Hogan 2000, 158; Barnes, Mercer, and Shakespeare 1999, 21). Within this framework, disability is associated with the physiological status of the individual on the one hand, and the individual's socio-cultural beliefs and features on the other. The medical model was rejected by disability organisations and disability activists because it concentrated on impairment and the handicapped body as the determining factors behind disability (Oliver 1996; Barnes 1998, 67)

The social model of disability emerged as a reaction to the medical model. Although the politicisation of the disability movement can be traced back to the nineteenth century for most countries in the western world, the effects of the various social movements of the 1960s and early 1970s created the conditions for disability studies scholars and disabled activists to seek to replace the medical approach to disability with a social model of disability (Diedrich 2005, 654; Oliver 1990, 2; Shakespeare 2006). This approach, which refused the role of medical experts in the ordering of disability and related disability to social oppression, was first articulated in 1975 by the Union of the Physically Impaired Against Segregation (UPIAS 1976, 4) in Britain. The UPIAS, building on lessons learned during the agonistic 1960s and with the help of South African disability activist Vic Finkelstein, succeeded in establishing a theoretical grounding for the social model of disability (Barnes 1998, 73). These first political and theoretical steps in the social ordering of disability, however, have been accused of bearing a naïve and deterministic technological optimism (Barnes 1998, 74; Barnes et al. 1999, 84; Shakespeare 2006, 200). This initial social approach of disability lacked a critical link between bodily experiences of disability, the development of social policies and the configuration of technology (and the built environment). As a result, a number of disability scholars have called for more critical theoretical approaches that would address both material and ideological aspects of disability (see, for example, Abberley 1987). Such an approach was introduced in the book *The Politics of Disablement* (Oliver 1990), where disabled activist and academic Mike Oliver critically related disability to economic and social structures as well as to central values of particular modes of production (Barnes, Mercer, and Shakespeare 1999, 84).

The work of Oliver was to develop a social theory of disability that was situated in the experiences of disabled people as well as in their effort to organise a social movement for redefining disability (1990, 11). To Oliver, disability cannot be understood in terms of purely internal social or psychological relationships – a whole range of material factors (such as housing, finance, employment, the built environment and family) must be taken into account (1990, 69). Such a re-definition of disability implied a shift in the epistemological focus from the body to the socio-material environment, from the individual to society, and from illness to culture. The new approach bypassed the notion of self and classified disability in terms of urban and social environments that disabled people live in. In this framework, physical/structural and intellectual barriers in labour, urban design and institutions, together with biased cultural perceptions of difference and dissimilarity, are the sources of disability. One of the strongest arguments in support of the social model of disability is that it has been politically effective in approaching disability as social constructions and physical barriers imposed by able-bodied people. Disability is an ambiguous concept and it should not only be focused on the individual handicap or impairment, since it has some collective existence in the social and the material world beyond the existence or experience of individual disabled people (Priestley 1998, 83).

Although the contribution of the social model of disability to the disability rights movement and the liberation of disabled people is unquestionable, critical voices from a postmodern framework have raised serious scepticism about the inattention of the social model towards everyday experiences of disabled people with regard to gender, ethnicity, sexuality and the body. Corker and Shakespeare (2002) argue that the social model defines disability as something unrelated to the impaired body. In this way, it disregards personal experiences, the range of impairments and their impact on individuals over their lifetime, and interactions of the body with its surroundings; in other words, how disability is experienced in everyday life and through different subject positions. This is where STS can contribute, by bridging modernist divides (body versus society, materiality versus culture), linking the disability experience with socio-material configurations, and providing some conceptual tools for life beyond the social model of disability.

Beyond the social model: the ontological politics of disability

A number of scholars have attempted to address disability experiences as they are articulated and come into being within specific practices, cultures and institutions (see, for example, *Cultural Studies* 2005, special issue on Genealogies of Disability, vol. 19, no. 6). Diedrich (2005, 650) argues that the social model has not adequately problematised disability experience as a category of representation that emerges and evolves within a particular socio-material and political/historical reality. What is needed, then, is a theoretical vocabulary that answers the question of how people become and are made disabled (cf. Moser 2006, 668), but also who has the authority to determine what disability is and how it is represented. This is not merely a claim about external material or semiotic constructions of disability, but about a political account of the enactment of disability in material and semiotic practices. What is interesting here is how disability is produced and reproduced in material and semiotic performances of realities (cf. Landström 2000, 477). Such a vocabulary/claim creates the possibility for two radical shifts in the ordering of disability.

The first shift is an epistemological rectification of the object against the hegemony of the individual subject as sole generator (or autonomous agent) of socio-material realities, in sociological analysis. Corker and Shakespeare (2002, 3) argue that disability experience is embedded in complex networks of not just social but socio-material relationships. Abandoning the subject as the unit of analysis marks a shift from modernist divisions (body/socio-material environment, individual/society, illness/culture) towards an ordering of disability as a simultaneous biological, socio-material and semiotic effect produced by heterogeneous objects. The second shift is extending politics to the formation of reality/ontology (experience of disability). Inspired by the work of Mol (1999), this vocabulary creates a link between the experience of disability (the real, the conditions of possibility and disability that disabled people live with) and the political (who has the power to determine what is real and in which locations) (cf. Mol 1999, 86; Landström 2000). As Siebers (2006, 180) puts it, one of the most important issues for disability studies is that the struggle of disabled people is linked to a realistic concept of the disabled body. This struggle refers to how disabled people influence the disability ontology by participating in the configuration of policy-making, urban environment design, and other such activities.

Against the rational independent modern subject: towards an analytical symmetry between humans and non-humans

Disability studies resisted an earlier interaction with STS, since disability activists attempted to order disability outside the positivist medical model (Diedrich 2005, 658). Indeed, the first generation of STS scholars appeared to attempt to understand, explain and effectively reinforce the hegemony of science and scientists, rather than to question their basis (Collins and Evans 2002, 239). As already discussed, the reaction of the disability movement against the positivist approach of disability was expressed by the emergence of the social model of disability. The social model treats disability as socially constructed, beyond the impairment (Corker and Shakespeare 2002, 3). During the same period, a new wave of scholarship occurred within STS that focused on the social construction of knowledge. However, social constructionism failed to approach the complex and difficult physical realities faced by disabled people (Siebers 2006, 175).

A theoretical strand emerging from the field of STS in the early 1980s, introduced as actor-network theory (ANT),[2] has strongly resisted the notion of social construction concerning science and technology. ANT scholars argue that both nature and the built environment are produced by society *and* culture instead of being 'given' outside society or socially constructed (Latour 1997; Moser 2003, 26). This is where STS can be valuable to disability studies. Following ANT, the study of disability should depart from the assumption that the impaired body is imminent in reality, and *vice versa*.

Hess (1997, 108) notes that ANT succeeds in avoiding the limitations of social constructionism by providing a way for non-humans to influence the processes and results of socio-technical processes. To emphasise material semiotics (in contrast to social constructions), ANT researchers introduced the specific concept of actor-networks. Actor-networks are interconnected complexes through which human and non-human entities evolve, interact and produce effects, such as the loss of function or a diminished ability to function, or disability (Moser 2000, 205). The metaphor of actor-network was introduced to monitor the dynamic activities that link together different entities such as bodies, places, ideas, artefacts and realities (Moser 2005, 670). ANT describes how actors (objects) within a network take their form and acquire their attributes (subject positions[3]) as a result of their interactions with other objects in the network (cf. Law 1999, 3). For example, a fully accessible metro system equipped with ramps, guiding lines, sign-posted facilities in Braille, visual and audio beacons, and other aids produces disability/ability as an effect of associations between the human body and these material semiotic entities (Galis 2006). When the speech machine of a person with a reduced ability to speak does not work, she/he is incapable of making herself/himself understood (Moser 2000, 223). In other words, ANT illustrates how actors and networks are enabled/disabled in relationships and applies this to all materials, both human and non-human (Law 1999, 5).

In an ANT framework, the study of disability involves identifying and addressing interactions between human bodies (including the disability experience) and non-humans, not on top of impairment but as an intermixing phenomenon. ANT attempts to cancel the divide between subject and object, by ascribing a 'generalised symmetry' between human and non-human actors. Latour (1988, 301) accuses sociologists of discriminating against non-human actors in the sense that they ignore the fact that non-human entities can delegate behaviour to humans. Thus, using ANT does not involve the privileged study of either impaired bodies or social–material constructions but the analysis of situations where the interactions of bodies and materiality/culture produce action or inaction, ability or disability (agency). As with all controversial approaches in the social sciences, ANT attracted followers but also faced hard criticism. Two main critiques that are relevant to this paper focused on the issue of generalised symmetry, and ANT's disinterest in power asymmetries of network formation.

The claim of ANT scholars that sociological analysis should treat both humans and non-humans symmetrically has confused many social scientists and remains controversial. Does the symmetrical approach imply that non-humans have intentions and feelings? Can non-humans be actors? Do non-humans have agency? Collins and Yearley (1992, 320), proponents of the social constructivist strand within STS, accused ANT of mixing the notions of behaviour and action, which constitute the great distinction between machines and human responsibility. In other words, this kind of criticism stemmed from the modernist sociological concepts of actorship and agency, where actors are generally assumed to be humans (cf. Kjell-berg 2001, 555).

ANT scholars, responding to Collins and Yearley's criticism, argued against the modernist separation of things and humans and instead proposed that the sociologi-cal analysis should follow the attribution of roles; that is, to follow the exchanges of agency within a network (Callon and Latour 1992, 355–356). This means that agency depends on the object's role or position within the network – that agency can be continuously transformed from one object to another (Pickering 1995, 15). While humans are endowed with logic, choice, experiences and intentions, this per-formative agency would not be possible if not for the existence of material semiotic surroundings. By themselves, things and humans do not act, but there are relations, negotiations, interactions and effects between human and non-human entities (Callon and Law 1995, 485). The way ANT scholars approach subjects is the same as they previously approached objects (Moser 2000, 223). In other words, the gen-eralised symmetry principle implies that disability is an *effect* of a process of associ-ations in a network. To empirically illustrate this, different bodily forms, abilities and disabilities are not independent of architecture, but are mutually constitutive (Imrie 2003, 51). For example, pavements, ramps, stairs, elevators, washrooms, benches, signs, public buildings, wheelchairs, and other infrastructure enact action/agency: disability/ability.

This does not, however, imply that non-humans consciously choose to facilitate disabled people or that ANT extends intentionality to non-human entities. These objects perform actions rather than construct or possess them. Disability/ability (action) is analysed here in functional terms (Winance 2006, 66). Thus, in a human-centred vocabulary, these actions are often called 'intentions' or 'goals', while in a non-human terminology these are called 'functions' (Latour 1994, 8). Thus, the attribution of agency cannot be detached from the surrounding material semiotic entities; disability cannot be detached from the existence or not of accessibility pro-visions. To be disabled is not only determined by the physical impairments of an individual's body but also by the interaction of the body with material and semiotic entities. As Gleeson puts it, in the post-positivist era it is not only social processes that produce material space; 'produced space' also forms social norms (2001, 252) and bodily experiences. In the postmodern era, it is not only socio-material pro-cesses that perform disability, but also impaired bodies that enact ontological poli-tics. Imagine what would happen if we were to design and construct urban environments only for wheelchair users, write books mostly in Braille, or communi-cate in sign language. Who would be disabled in those cases? Thus, as Moser (2000, 224–225) notes, disability/ability is also a matter of attribution of agency and actorship, depending on the actor-networks a person is part of. The associations between actors determine their experiences.

Put another way, ANT proposes an alternative vocabulary that goes beyond social constructions or medical understandings of disability. On the contrary, a material semiotic approach is interested in how disability is 'done and enacted' (Mol 1999, 77). How one becomes disabled plays a central role for this theoretical story. As Mol notes, objects that are performed do not come alone: they carry modes and modulations of other objects (1999, 81). Thus, in order to understand disability as a form of enactment, to track down how we do disability, the researcher must study multiple objects (both human and non-human) and multiple domains (Diedrich 2005, 659). Accordingly, the sociological analysis ought to study the ordering of disability and the experience of impairment in locations that are not merely socially constructed or medicalised by social policies, the media, special education, economics and rehabilitation (Moser 2005, 671). We have to also look at locations where the ordering of disability meets and enacts everyday life, governmental action to configure the built environment, scientific debates to confront impaired bodies, and so on. These locations often imply exclusions and trials of strength between disabled people, professional politicians and experts.

The second main source of criticism that is relevant to this paper concerns ANT's lack of interest in the power asymmetries of network formation and its epistemological obsession with powerful actors that overlooks the contributions and participation of other social groups (see, for example, Law 1991, 13; Star 1991, 33; Lee and Brown 1994). Traditional ANT refers to human competence through a cunning perspective: empire-building abilities as manifested by Machiavelli's prince are essential for establishing and spreading a technology (Latour 1987, 124). This aspect of ANT is problematic since it does not allow for recording discriminations and exclusions. ANT does not say anything about which actors are excluded from the network and why, despite the fact that the formation of networks often entails the efforts, practices, and functions of less visible actors. Moser (2005, 668) wonders how the study and ordering of disability can avoid reproducing asymmetries (between subjects and objects, between strong and weak actors) in the distribution of power and agency. Latour (1988, 302) himself has acknowledged this deficiency by stating that ANT does not solve all problems, since it excludes segments of human populations such as old people and disabled people.

The question emerging from this preoccupation with power is what happens to less privileged actors in the network? How does ANT record the exclusion or the influence of less powerful actors? Disability – this could be a second contribution of STS and this paper to disability studies – is also enacted by different exclusions of disabled people and their organisations from the ordering of disability ontological politics. Historically, organisations for disabled people have been relatively weak in representing the interests of their disabled members in different governmental or techno-scientific spheres. Instead, social service managers, medical or other scientific experts have had the interpretative prerogative to define and enact the bodies and interests of disabled people (Drake 1994, 1996; Barnes, Mercer, and Shakespeare 1999; Galis 2006). The limited influence of disability organisations did not initially allow for considerable interventions in policy-making processes, and this fact made them immediately invisible to traditional ANT analysis. Thus, one issue for disability ontological politics is central here: how disability studies can (with the help of ANT) support and conceptualise the struggle of disabled people to take control of disability ontological politics and participate in the enactment of the disability experience in the policy-making sphere, setting aside asymmetries in the distribution of power and agency in the network.

From the tyranny of experts to the insurrection of anti-science: disability concerned groups

To address the issue above, one has to delve into postmodern thought and re-establish its links to the various social movements of the 1960s and early 1970s. During this period, general attacks on science, the juridical system, morality, the traditional approach of sexuality and other areas contributed to what Foucault (2003, 7) termed 'the insurrection of subjugated knowledges'. 'The insurrection of subjugated knowledges' constitutes an autonomous and decentralised production of knowledge that ignores the established scientific tyranny in seeking validity: anti-science. This sort of knowledge, which has been previously disqualified as non-conceptual, insufficient, and hierarchically inferior by the gatekeepers of 'scientificity', appeared from below, based on what people know/experience at a local level and contribute to open up for a critique of the modernist 'hierarchy of erudition and sciences' (Foucault 2003, 5–10; see also Diedrich 2005, 653).

It is these 'anti-sciences' that this paper also aims to conceptualise and support as well as draw attention to how anti-science is represented in the material politics of disability. In this case, the analysis should not treat disability groups merely as political associations but as carriers of anti-scientific knowledge and experience of indisputable significance for disability ontological politics. How do ANT scholars address anti-science? For example, we need concepts and methods to follow how urban disability movements have unsettled the forms of positivism crystallised in the built world and social shaping of the modern industrial city (cf. Gleeson 2001, 255). Callon and Rabeharisoa (2003, 193–194) note that while theoretical tools within ANT have been valuable for analysing technology and the controversies that it creates, they have not paid attention to questions regarding relationships between experts and non-experts, and scientists and lay people. In line with Callon and Rabeharisoa's suggestion, the contribution and involvement of social groups (they call them *concerned groups*) should be incorporated into the scope of the analysis of disability studies. It might be fruitful to consider concerned groups as (potentially) genuine researchers who are capable of working cooperatively with professional scientists (2003, 195). Concerned groups (such as patient organisations, environmental groups, consumers' associations, involved individuals, and disability associations) are those social groups that are influenced by the development of techno-sciences and seek to intervene in research processes and the development of technology. This kind of involvement lacks, however, the endorsement of the conventional scientific regime. The involvement of these groups in the production of techno-scientific phenomena affects their socio-material role and deranges their social, political and economic status for better or for worse.

Employing this concept brings the sociological analysis of disability one step forward by abandoning conceptualisations of disability groups as merely pressure groups, charity organisations, traditional voluntary and self-help groups, civil rights and anti-discrimination lobbyists, labour unions, and other organisations. The concept of concerned groups describes a dynamic process, an anti-science, by which different types of disability groups influence the collection of associations between humans and non-humans that modify the enactment of disability. These are groups that have entered the arena of disability ontological politics, appeared before experts and made themselves credible co-speakers by becoming competent, by participating in conferences, by dissecting research protocols and architectural blueprints in order to obtain mastery of the technical vocabulary, and by tracing rehabilitation methods back to medical education (cf. Callon, Lascoumes, and Barthe 2009, 84). How can the analysis capture this participation and what are the spaces that mark the involvement of concerned groups?

To sociologically consider anti-science in the ordering of disability delivers a blow to the modernist division between experts and lay people. Analytically, this implies following what Callon (2003) refers to as *research in the wild*; namely, knowledge produced by non-expert groups through their participation, practices, exploitation of existing experiences, negotiations with other groups, and new organisational configurations. Rabeharisoa and Callon (2002, 62) define research in the wild as the process through which concerned groups accumulate and compare the experience of their members and build up a collective expertise that is just as authentic as that of 'experts or scientists', even if it is different. In contrast to confined research (i.e. research that is conducted by experts in milieus that are not part of the public sphere, such as laboratories, architects' offices, scientific committees, and private offices), research in the wild does not claim or possess 'scientific' purity. Instead, it is confronted with compound, impure, polluted realities (Callon 2003, 46). The concept of research in the wild highlights the perspective that the configuration of techno-sciences does not have to follow the traditional route via confined scientific environments (e.g. the architectural office), which often implies a relatively passive role for the public sphere and a domination of scientists and engineers. New settings for novel modifications of associations between humans and non-humans involve moments of interaction and negotiation with different concerned groups such as disabled people, who were otherwise invisible in the ANT context. After all, concerned groups possess expertise and experience concerning their own needs and bodies, which is important knowledge for the design and implementation of urban environments, and which emerges from research in the wild.

Negotiations between research in the wild and confined research cannot take place in what Gleeson (2001, 254) calls 'institutions of industrial modernity', which exercise power through the 'truth' codified in science, technology and parliamentary democracy. These negotiations demand public spaces such as those that Callon (2003) calls *hybrid forums*: forums because they are open spaces where diverse groups can discuss technical choices concerning the collective, and hybrid because these heterogeneous groups and the spokespersons who claim to represent them constitute different concerned groups consisting of patients, citizens, politicians, architects, doctors, engineers and others (2003, 59). Hybrid forums constitute assemblies of ontological politics where concerned groups, which carry out research in the wild, negotiate with scientists, engineers and other experts, who conduct confined research on techno-scientific issues, and collectively modify the enactment of disability. In the case of the new metro system in Athens, for example, several hybrid forums, such as working groups on accessibility organised by disabled civil servants, meetings between various disability organisations and the company that supervised the construction of the metro, and two cross-ministerial accessibility committees consisting of engineers, public servants and disability representatives, addressed disability issues and developed specific proposals and recommendations regarding the realisation of accessibility in the system (Galis 2006, 265). These hybrid forums enabled collective (expert and non-expert) modification (ontological politics) of an assembly of humans and non-humans (disabled bodies, accessibility provisions, metro system). In other words, hybrid forums constitute cooperative research efforts that not only encompass discussions on technical or scientific choices, but also the exploration and exploitation of anti-science – that is, expertise and experience that lies outside the frame of confined research. This is not a claim in support of the research collective, but rather a claim for collective research crystallised in subjugated knowledge and confined research. The sociological analysis of the ordering of disability ought to look for existing hybrid forums or normatively suggest the inauguration of such arenas.

Conclusion

This paper offers disabled activists (both within academia and elsewhere) a theoretical alternative to the ordering of disability that escapes the epistemological extremes of modernity (external interpretations of disability by either proponents of the medical/ industrial complex or radical social constructivists). Instead of solely examining the physical aspect of disability (medical model) or removing entirely the focus from the body (social model), this article proposes a conceptual vocabulary that monitors the multiplicity of the experience of being disabled by *simultaneously* addressing interactions between the impaired body, disabling social and institutional barriers, and inaccessible urban environments. In so doing, I turned to ANT and applied the discussion on performative agency to the enactment of disability. The important point here is that disability does not reside solely in the body or in society. Disability is an effect that emerges when impaired bodies interact with disabling infrastructures/culture.

For instance, does non-driving (agency/action) constitute disability? It depends on the accessibility of the public transport system, how mobile a body is, how driving culturally is defined, and so on. What we learn from applying ANT in the field of disability studies is that we cannot reduce disability to impairments or social constructions. Instead, the analysis concentrates on ontological peculiarities, or how disability is simultaneously experienced through bodily functions, constructed in social and cultural norms, anticipated and manufactured in policy-making and technology development, and created by architecture. ANT is interested in the symbolic, material, physical and cultural practices within which disability ensues.

The second contribution of ANT to disability studies that this paper addresses is a theoretical vocabulary that monitors the exclusion of disabled people from disability (ontological) politics and an empirical methodology to accentuate and promote the involvement of non-experts in the configuration of policies and techno-sciences related to disability issues. The inability of early ANT to follow politically weak actors generated a number of concepts on the involvement of concerned disability groups in the configuration of the built environment, conceptualisations of accessibility (rules, regulations, norms, definitions) and the impaired body. Inspired by these discussions and abandoning the dominant approaches of disability that have constituted external researchers, social service managers or physicians as the only legitimate experts, this paper suggests an analytical focus on the contribution of disability organisations in the configuration of disability politics and policy-making. This approach does not have to be limited only to issues of deliberative representation, but to how disability associations, as carriers of disability knowledge and experience, can actively address disability issues and develop proposals and recommendations regarding the realisation of an inclusive society. These proposals could be a product of disabled people's own anti-science or research in the wild. In turn, research in the wild and the interests of disabled people may be represented in hybrid forums, challenging the hegemonic authority of experts.

I would thus like to encourage research that addresses the experience of disability with the help of the conceptual vocabulary that I have discussed here, to follow disability as it is enacted in everyday life, in policy spaces, in infrastructure, and among disabled people, academics, experts and politicians. For the social researcher, the ontological politics of disability imply that she/he must follow the action/agency concerning disability, and normatively propose forms of participatory research on disability issues.

Notes

1. Accordingly, I do not address politics performed within parliaments, political parties and professional politicians.
2. Central references for the ANT include: Callon (1986a, 1986b, 1991), Callon and Latour (1992), Callon and Law (1995), Latour (1983, 1987, 1988, 1993, 1996), Law (1992, 1997, 1999).
3. Moser explains that a subject position is not something one possess, occupies or is structured into, but rather a set of differently ordered positions one moves between fluidly (2006, 377).

References

Abberley, P. 1987. The concept of oppression and the development of a social theory of disability. *Disability, Handicap and Society* 2, no. 1: 5–19.

Barnes, C. 1998. The social model of disability: A sociological phenomenon ignored by sociologists. In *The disability reader*, ed. T. Shakespeare, 65–78. London: Cassell.

Barnes, C., G. Mercer, and T. Shakespeare. 1999. *Exploring disability: A sociological introduction*. Cambridge: Polity Press.

Callon, M. 1986a. The sociology of an actor-network: The case of the electric vehicle. In *Mapping the dynamics of science and technology, sociology of science in the real world*, ed. M. Callon, J. Law, and A. Rip, 19–34. London: The Macmillan Press.

Callon, N. 1986b. Some elements of a sociology of translation: Domestication of the scallops and the fishermen of Saint Brieuc Bay. In *Power, action and belief: A new sociology of knowledge?*, ed. J. Law, 196–223. London: Routledge.

Callon, M. 1991. Techno-economic networks and irreversibility. In *A sociology of monsters: Essays on power, technology and domination*, ed. J. Law, 132–64. London: Routledge.

Callon, M. 2003. The increasing involvement of concerned groups in R&D policies: What lessons for public powers? In *Science and innovation, rethinking the rationales for funding and governance*, ed. A. Geuna, A.J. Salter, and W.E. Steinmueller, 30–68. Cheltenham, UK: Edward Elgar.

Callon, M., P. Lascoumes, and Y. Barthe. 2009. *Acting in an uncertain world: An essay on technical democracy*. London: MIT Press.

Callon, M., and B. Latour. 1992. Don't throw the baby out with the bath school! A reply to Collins and Yearley. In *Science as practice and culture*, ed. A. Pickering, 343–68. Chicago: The University of Chicago Press.

Callon, M., and J. Law. 1995. Agency and the hybrid collectif. *The South Atlantic Quarterly* 94, no. 2: 481–507.

Callon, M., and V. Rabeharisoa. 2003. Research 'in the wild' and the shaping of new social identities. *Technology in Society* 25, no. 2: 193–204.

Collins, H., and R. Evans. 2002. The third wave of science studies: Studies of expertise and experience. *Social Studies of Science* 26, no. 2: 235–96.

Collins, H., and S. Yearley. 1992. Epistemological chicken. In *Science as practice and culture*, ed. A. Pickering, 301–26. Chicago: The University of Chicago Press.

Corker, M., and T. Shakespeare. 2002. Mapping the terrain. In *Disability/postmodernity*, ed. M. Corker and T. Shakespeare, 1–17. London: Continuum.

Diedrich, L. 2005. Introduction: Genealogies of disability. *Cultural Studies* 19, no. 6: 649–66.

Drake, R. 1994. The exclusion of disabled people from positions of power in British voluntary organizations. *Disability and Society* 9, no. 4: 461–80.

Drake, R. 1996. A critique of the role of the traditional charities. In *Disability and society: Emerging issues and insights*, ed. L. Barton, 147–66. London: Longman.

Foucault, M. 2003. *Society must be defended: Lectures at the Collége de France 1975–1976*, ed. M. Bertani and A. Fontana. New York: Picador.

Galis, V. 2006. From shrieks to technical reports: Technology, disability and political processes in building Athens Metro. Linköping Studies in Arts and Science No. 374. PhD diss., Department of Thematic Studies – Technology and Social Change.

Gleeson, B. 1997. Disability studies: A historical materialist view. *Disability and Society* 12, no. 2: 179–202.

Gleeson, B. 2001. Disability and the open city. *Urban Studies* 38, no. 2: 251–65.

Hess, D. 1997. *Science studies: An advanced introduction.* New York: New York University Press.

Imrie, R. 2003. Architect's conceptions of the human body. *Environment and Planning D: Society and Space* 21: 47–65.

Kjellberg, H. 2001. Organizing distribution: Hakonbolaget and the efforts to rationalize food distribution, 1940–1960. PhD diss., Stockholm School of Economics, EFI, Economic Research Institute.

Landström, C. 2000. The ontological politics of staying true to complexity. *Social Studies of Science* 30, no. 3: 475–80.

Latour, B. 1983. Give me a laboratory and I will raise the world. In *Science observed*, ed. K.D. Knorr-Cetina and M.J. Mulkay, 141–70. London: Sage.

Latour, B. 1987. *Science in action: How to follow scientists and engineers through society.* Milton Keynes, UK: Open University Press.

Latour, B. 1988. Mixing humans and nonhumans together: The sociology of a door-closer. *Social Problems* 35, no. 3: 298–310.

Latour, B. 1993. *We have never been modern.* Cambridge, MA: Harvard University Press.

Latour, B. 1994. *On technical mediation: The messenger lectures on the evolution of civilization.* Working Paper Series 1993: 9. Lund: Institutet för Ekonomisk Forskning.

Latour, B. 1996. *Aramis or the love of technology.* Cambridge, MA: Harvard University Press.

Latour, B. 1997. The trouble with ANT. *Soziale Welt* 47: 369–81.

Latour, B. 2004. *Politics of nature: How to bring the sciences into democracy.* Cambridge, MA: Harvard University Press.

Latour, B. 2007. Turning around politics: A note on Greard de Vries' paper. *Social Studies of Science* 37, no. 5: 811–20.

Law, J. 1991. Introduction: Monsters, machines and sociotechnical relations. In *A sociology of monsters: Essays on power, technology and domination*, ed. J. Law, 1–23. London: Routledge.

Law, J. 1992. Notes on the theory of the actor-network: Ordering, strategy and heterogeneity. Department of Sociology, Lancaster University. http://www.comp.lancs.ac.uk/sociology/soc054jl.html.

Law, J. 1997. Traduction/trahison: Notes on ANT. Department of Sociology, Lancaster University. http://www.comp.lancs.ac.uk/sociology/stslaw2.html.

Law, J. 1999. After ANT: Complexity, naming and topology. In *Actor network theory and after*, ed. J. Law and J. Hassard, 1–15. Oxford: Blackwell Publishers.

Lee, N., and S. Brown. 1994. Otherness and the actor network: The undiscovered continent. *American Behavioral Scientist* 37, no. 6: 772–90.

Llewellyn, A., and K. Hogan. 2000. The use and abuse of models of disability. *Disability and Society* 15, no. 1: 157–65.

Mol, A. 1999. Ontological politics. In *Actor network theory and after*, ed. J. Law and J. Hassard, 74–90. Oxford: Blackwell Publishers.

Moser, I. 2000. Against normalization: Subverting norms of ability and disability. *Science as Culture* 9, no. 2: 201–40.

Moser, I. 2003. Road traffic accidents: The ordering of subjects, bodies and disability. PhD diss., Faculty of Arts, University of Oslo, no. 173. Oslo: Unipub AS.

Moser, I. 2005. On becoming disabled and articulating alternatives: The multiple modes of ordering disability and their interferences. *Cultural Studies* 19, no. 6: 667–700.

Moser, I. 2006. Disability and the promises of technology: Technology, subjectivity and embodiment within an order of the normal. *Information, Communication and Society* 9, no. 3: 373–95.

Moser, I. 2009. A body that matters? The role of embodiment in the recomposition of life after a road traffic accident. *Scandinavian Journal of Disability Research* 11, no. 2: 83–99.

Oliver, M. 1990. *The politics of disablement.* Houndmills, Basingstoke: Macmillan.

Oliver, M. 1996. Defining impairment and disability: Issues at stake. In *Exploring the divide*, ed. C. Barnes and G. Mercer, 39–54. Leeds: The Disability Press.

Pickering, A. 1995. *The mangle of practice: Time, agency and science*. Chicago: The University of Chicago Press.

Priestley, M. 1998. Constructions and creations: Idealism, materialism and disability theory. *Disability and Society* 13, no. 1: 75–94.

Rabeharisoa, V., and M. Callon. 2002. The involvement of patients' associations in research. *International Social Science Journal* 54, no. 171: 57–65.

Shakespeare, T. 2006. The social model of disability. In *The disability studies reader*, ed. L. Davis, 197–204. New York: Routledge.

Siebers, T. 2006. Disability in theory: From social constructionism to the new realism of the body. In *The disability studies reader*, ed. L. Davis, 173–84. New York: Routledge.

Star, S.L. 1991. Distributions of power. Power, technology and the phenomenology of conventions: on being allergic to onions. In *A sociology of monsters: Essays on power, technology and domination*, ed. J. Law, 26–56. London: Routledge.

Union of Physically Impaired Against Segregation. 1976. *Fundamental principles of disability*. London: UPIAS.

Winance, M. 2006. Trying out the wheelchair: The mutual shaping of people and devices through adjustment. *Science, Technology, and Human Values* 31, no. 1: 52–72.

The use, role and application of advanced technology in the lives of disabled people in the UK

Jennifer Harris

The Interdisciplinary Disability Research Institute, School of Education, Social Work and Community Education, University of Dundee, Nethergate, UK

Disabled people are excited by the potential benefits of using advanced technologies at home. However, many devices are abandoned early and lie unused. This research project aimed to explore why this happens, what the users of such technologies require, how advanced technologies can rise to the challenges of flexibility and user choice, which applications enhance independence and improve quality of life and what the barriers are to take-up and future utilization. It was found that disabled people wish to use advanced technology to increase independence in and beyond home but the cost of both mainstream and 'specialist' devices are prohibitive. The role of advanced technology should be to enhance independence and provide mainstream solutions that disabled people request, rather than designing and engineering 'specialist' expensive products. Furthermore, the application of advanced technology for use in the home should be directed by disabled people, collectively and individually.

Terminology and orientation

For the purposes of this article, 'disabled people' are people between the ages of 18 and 65 who have impairments (physical/sensory/learning difficulties/mental health issues). 'Advanced technologies' are devices (often electronic) both mainstream and 'specialist' that assist disabled people at home. 'Independence' as used here does not necessarily mean the goal is for all tasks to be performed by the disabled person, but the person retains direction, choice and control, with appropriate personal assistance (Johnson and Moxon 1998).

The theoretical position adopted was the social model of disability (Oliver 1990), which holds that people are disabled by the mainstream society that takes little or no account of access requirements but expects people with impairments to 'fit in' with the non-disabled majority (Union of the Physically Impaired Against Segregation 1976). The research took a social model approach, using a social barriers perspective (Roulstone 1998) and utilising the tenets of the 'Outcomes for disabled service users' framework (Harris et al. 2005).

Background

The topic of this research project is one that is neglected within both the disability studies field (Johnson and Moxon 1998) and the design/engineering arena. However, for many years now researchers have been commenting that there are dangers in the silence of disabled people concerning the impact of technology on their lives and in allowing the processes of development and innovation to continue to be driven by designers and engineers (Johnson and Moxon 1998; Hammel et al. 2002). There is a widespread assumption that technology of all types can only improve disabled peoples' lives and, therefore, what is required is simply more sophistication. However, very few studies have previously examined exactly what requirements disabled people have for advanced technology to support independent living, what their aspirations are and what issues and problems arise from usage. Even fewer have taken a social model approach to this research topic.

For many years designers and engineers have been developing advanced and assistive technological devices and progressively these have been added to disabled peoples' homes (Dewsbury et al. 2002). Previous research in this area has shown that people with different impairments have differing requirements for service provision (Harris et al. 2005). Pioneering research in this field by Roulstone (1998) demonstrated the value of taking a social barriers approach to the identification of key issues in relation to advanced technology use. These studies laid a firm foundation and have, in many respects, paved the way for the 'universal design' paradigm, which emerged from the convergence of barrier-free environments, accessible design and assistive technology. Universal design aims to produce buildings, products and environments that are usable and effective for everyone, not just disabled people, and attention is paid to the aesthetics of the products.

Many technologies that are currently on the market hold the potential to enhance the lives and independence of disabled people (Dewsbury et al. 2002). Mainstream technologies that are already in people's homes could theoretically be used or customized to meet people's changing requirements over the course of their lifespan. IPods for example are widely used for leisure, but these devices can also remind users of medication times. Such use obviates the need for 'specialist' devices and avoids potential stigmatization of the users, as well as unnecessary financial outlay.

Prior studies on the use of 'assistive technologies' (specialist devices designed purposively to assist disabled people) at home have shown that one-third are abandoned early and lie unused (Sherer and Galvin 1996; Kittel et al. 2002; Sherer 2005). The pace of change in the area of assistive technology in recent years has been rapid. Whilst this is exhilarating, the current technological limitations of devices are all that constrain the designers and engineers. This has led to a situation where the excitement of possibilities drives the process of innovation. However, in all this there is a sense that the common sense notion of starting from the standpoint of disabled consumers has become lost.

Many disabled people voice a concern that engineers in particular work within an assumed medical model (Oliver 1990), i.e. that they are somehow 'broken' and that technology is a 'fix'(Dewsbury et al. 2004; Roulstone 1998). Thus, sometimes the motivation and orientation of designers and engineers are questioned by disabled people. For example, the area at the forefront of developments currently is automated prediction in smart homes (Dewsbury 2001, 2005a, 2005b). In practical terms this means the home can maintain a 'watching brief' and information on the use of everyday items (such as a washing machine or kettle) can alert remote personal assistants to take action.

To date there has been a dearth of debate by disabled people about the potential civil liberties issues that contact with such advanced technologies presents or how user rights can be maintained and protected. Whilst the social model has an impact across the full spectrum of disabled people's lives in public society, curiously, to date commentators are content to leave the domestic sphere in the clutches of those who perpetuate individual model approaches.

As advanced technology use in the home becomes a norm rather than an exception for disabled people in the UK issues of reliability and dependability have become major concerns to users (Demers et al. 2002). Increasingly, advanced technology is steadily pervading more areas of disabled people's lives. However, as the capacities of advanced technology increase ever apace it is important that the goal of empowering disabled people, recognized in this journal as far back as 1993 (Thornton 1993), is kept firmly at the forefront of developments.

In the UK 'community care' is a reality for the majority of disabled people, however, resources to provide comprehensive health and social care on demand are becoming increasingly stretched (Harris et al. 2003). Prevention of acute social care or health events is essential if quality of life is to be maintained and demands on health and social services are to be effectively managed. Advanced technology may have a significant present and future role in this process, but its use, role and application should be directed by disabled people, collectively and individually.

Objectives

The objectives of the research were to explore the challenges, barriers and facilitators to acceptance and acceptability of advanced technological devices designed to assist and support independent living. A systematic review of the existing literature was undertaken to critically appraise the extent to which advanced technologies usefully assist the lifestyles of disabled people and construct a typology of assistive technological solutions, devices and standard uses (Khan et al. 2005). This was followed by qualitative interviews which aimed to explore the possibilities, limitations and challenges experienced by disabled people in using advanced technology to support independent living, the learning challenges that contact with technology present, the capacity of technology to cater for individual choice requirements, the limitations to flexibility and instances of technology abandonment and the reasons for its failure.

A series of 'user clubs' explored with the national and local disability community their usage of, interest in, frustrations with and aspirations for advanced technology. Finally, at a 'user innovation day' disabled people from across the UK explored with user groups, charities, service providers and non-governmental organizations (NGOs), technology companies, designers, engineers, architects, manufacturers and vendors the technical limitations and potential of advanced technologies for independent living. The discussion centred on possible solutions to user issues, the exploration of the extent to which the advanced technologies can be designed to respond flexibly to individual requirements and the evaluation of cases of abandonment or under use of technologies.

Methods

Mixed methods were used in this research, using the principles of real world research (Robson 2002). The systematic review had two phases. Phase I was a non-systematic review of terminology use and definitions, while Phase II was a systematic exploration of the research literature focusing on review publications.

The in-depth interviews ($n = 45$) utilized qualitative semi-structured interview methods (Robson 2002) and focused upon examining disabled people's day-to-day use of advanced and assistive technologies in their own homes. A quota sampling strategy ensured that people with physical, sensory or multiple impairments, learning difficulties, mental health issues and/or chronic illness could participate.

The user clubs ($n = 7$) and focus groups ($n = 4$), in which 31 disabled people, personal assistants and family members collectively formed opinions concerning advanced technology usage, had an ethnographic methods base (Glaser and Strauss 1967), as did the user innovation day for users, designers, engineers and service providers. The resulting synthesized themes are presented below.

Possibilities, limitations and challenges

Users described hopes, dreams and frustrations with both existing and wish-list devices. 'Possibilities' were desired devices currently not possessed. Some participants had ideas for new products or services that are not currently available. In actuality, some ideas reported in the form of user dreams are actually now available, but the users did not know about them. Examples included a machine that videotapes several channels of TV at once and can overlap programmes, a portable computer that would download newspapers, a machine that meant a wheelchair user would not be rushing across the room to answer an unsolicited telephone call and a device that gets around 'monopolization' of a landline by a dial-up Internet connection. As these devices are readily available in the mainstream market it is clear that users lack up to date knowledge about potential devices and advanced technological solutions.

Some possibilities users desired that are not currently on the market include a facial expression controlled electric wheelchair, a small, light conference folder (portable loop system), an 'emotions clock' for autistic children who do not speak and a light and portable four-wheeled walker. There were many possibilities described by deaf and hearing impaired users, for example, a 'missed calls register' on a pager system similar to that on existing mobile phones, a cheap and useable videophone so that deaf people can sign to each other, a device that translates the spoken word into text instantly on a phone and for cinemas to caption (subtitle) all films. The dream of many deaf people is to find a machine that converts speech to text without going through the medium of a Palantypist or human operator (as in the Type Talk system). Even in 2008 not all television programmes are subtitled, and this dismayed deaf participants.

Other items described as future possibilities included a solar powered battery for a 'talker' (communication device), as the batteries are constantly wearing down, several devices for gardening, including one that would enable a person with the use of one hand to sweep up leaves and a wheelchair user to trim a hedge, as well as a robotic lawn mower. Also on the list was a multiple-use device that could enable a wheelchair user to turn small knobs, for example heating controls or light switches, via a long pole mounting. A voice activated fully automatic car was also desired, but the current models all require some degree of hand control.

Accessing leisure pursuits through computer technology was a goal for many users, but these are not always fully accessible. A user with dual sensory impairment used screen reader software on the computer but was using touch typing to input text. The user had learnt touch typing at college and navigated the key board by the raised key points. The user enjoyed playing 'who wants to be a millionaire', but the options read out by the computer (particularly B and D) were sometimes indistinguishable. A future possibility described would be to have coloured options, which would enable the player to choose (and differentiate between) 'red' and 'blue' options.

The possibilities of infrared switch technology, Bluetooth and wireless systems were found to be exciting to users and these systems have significant and desired advantages over wired systems. To many users these systems have revolutionized device control in the home. Originally, on return from hospital one user had every-thing 'hard wired' around the house. The development of infrared switching had enabled the user to effectively abandon wires all over the home. The same user was also excited by the possibilities of Bluetooth technology and had recently got a voice activated contacts book in a mobile phone.

Most participants who used voice recognition software were excited at the possibilities for communication purposes using computers, however, several reported that the software made copious errors and the process could be laborious, particularly in training the device (see below). In terms of alternative and augmentative communication (AAC) devices, several users described the rigidity of the programmed words and that only engineers or speech therapists knew how to enter new words, thus limiting the independence and creativity of the user.

There were a few examples that involved users making minor changes to existing mainstream or specialist products, some supplied through hospitals and social services, others bought privately. Three users had adapted technologies for different purposes, either to make it more efficient or comfortable to use. However, in the main users were very wary of 'tampering' with technological devices, especially if these had been supplied by public authorities.

Learning challenges that contact with technology presents

The participants had a wide range of impairments – consequently the list of learning challenges that came from contact with technology was extensive. These were divided into barriers and facilitators to learning (Table 1).

Notable in Table 1 is the number of participants that were not offered training or support (7). A feature of poor training is rushed or inadequate instruction. On the posi-tive side of training, it is of note that the participants accessed a huge range of formal and informal, human and virtual sources in order to procure training. Nineteen partic-ipants described accessing some training from a human being or virtual source. Instruction manuals that use complex language and are difficult to understand were disliked, whereas those that are easy to understand were preferred, and two participants preferred human instruction. Less obvious is that for some participants impairment effects caused issues with the assimilation of written instructions and concentration. An 'unusable instruction' given to one user for a telephone that was hands free was to plug it into a mains sockets to recharge at night, but the user could not do this independently. Five participants valued and benefited from assistance from their family members to learn technologies, although one was bothered by issues of dependence and taking advantage of the family.

Table 1. Barriers and facilitators in learning to use technologies.

	Barriers to learning	Facilitators of learning
Training	Poor/rushed training from: • provider (2) • family • technician • No training/support (7) Excessive cost of training	Good training from: • provider (3) • employer • social worker • electrician • technician (3) • on-line peers • friends (4) • helpline (3) • helpers at respite care centre • charity • speech therapist (3)

Instructions/manuals	Difficult to understand instructions/
	  manuals (5)
	Unusable instructions
	Specific problems with:
	• reading instructions (2)
	• concentration
	• commands
	Prefer human instruction(2)
		Easy to understand instructions/
		  manuals (6)
		On-line instructions
		Demonstration:
		• human
		• program talk through

Family	Depending upon/taking advantage
	  of family help to learn
		Family help with learning
		  valued (5)

The findings on learning to use technology were divided into pragmatic, manipulation and psychological issues. Pragmatic considerations include remembering functions on devices. This is a particular issue for participants with visual and/or cognitive/intellectual impairment, where lessons learned at one session may need to be repeated. In particular, participants with visual impairment described issues with needing to be shown where buttons are and their functions and having to remember their location on the next use. On the positive side, 11 participants described teaching themselves to use various devices.

Manipulation issues included physical manipulation of devices and the ensuing frustration. The issue of button size on remote controls and mobile phones was a repeated strong theme. On the positive side, the increased capacities for storage of very small devices (e.g. the iPod) and new service convergence facilities were welcomed (such as using a SIM card from a mobile phone to implant the phonebook into a new landline phone memory).

Psychological issues also divided broadly into negative and positive features. In terms of negative features, there were fears over breaking technological devices and an inability to use devices or to get the most from them. Seven participants described varying levels of frustration in trying to learn technologies of all kinds. In particular, learning to use new multi-function environmental control devices (one of which had 245 functions) was described as 'hard work'. However, on the positive side, participants reported enhanced self-esteem from mastering computer functions, feelings of confidence gained in mastering technologies and also 'transferable

Table 2. Pragmatic, manipulation and psychological issues in learning to use technologies.

	Barriers to learning	Facilitators to learning
Pragmatic issues	Time (2)	Symbols instead of words
	Patience (2)	Self teaching (11) through:
	Cost	• trial and error (3)
	Connecting older and new devices	• on-line/video learning
	Learning to use the functions on new items	• perseverance over years (2)
	Lack of on-going support	Aim for independence (2)
	Non-compatibility of software	Enjoyment (3)
	Knowledge/capacities assumptions by designers	
	Remembering functions (5), including:	
	• complexity of environmental control device	
	• phone memory	
	• commands for computer	
	• whereabouts of buttons	
	Terminology difficult to follow	
Manipulation issues	Electronic reader controls	Storage capacity of new technology in comparison with old
	Scooter controls	
	Size of buttons on remote controls (2)	Flexible and transferable functions between devices
	Navigation through menus on mobile phones	
Psychological issues	Fearing own inadequacy in capacity to understand how to use technology(2)	Enhanced self-esteem from mastering computer functions
	Fear of damaging device	Enhanced confidence from proficiency (3)
	Negative attitude to technology	Transferable confidence (3)
	Emotional dislike of technology	Learn only necessary techniques
	Embarrassment at 'computer ignorance'	
	Frustration (7), including:	
	• 'hard work' (environmental control unit)	
	• complexity of functions	

confidence' – skills gained in using computers assisting with learning other devices, such as mobile phones.

Individual choice requirements and flexibility limitations

When asking participants questions about choice an interesting dichotomy in the findings arose, depending on who financed the equipment. Where public funds supplied the equipment users were given no choice at all in the design or type.

These decisions were made by professionals. In cases where users had bought technological devices themselves there are descriptions of having a multiplicity of choice and in some instances being 'overwhelmed' by the choices available. Furthermore, there were also cases where disabled people requested advice on products from statutory service providers (e.g. wheelchair design) and these turned out to be unsatisfactory. An independent source of advice on advanced technological products was deemed by users to be necessary, but not a service that was available to them.[1]

Some users of advanced technology, such as AAC technologies, wanted the device to use abbreviations for words, but this was not possible with the current machines. The latter is a good example of how users are 'pushing the boundaries' of the technological devices through evolving choice requirements that are only bounded by the limitations of the machines. One user requested the inclusion of swear words in an AAC device memory and these were entered by the professional involved, however, it was not possible for the user to independently programme the device. Therefore, although the device had the capacity for flexibility, it did not allow full independent use. This is an important distinction.

In some cases users' frustrations with technology stimulated the search for the development of a flexible solution:

P1:   Well I have … a voice activated software in the office and at home and … the package comes with a headset which is plugged into the back of your computer, its got a wee microphone that comes with [it] … but somebody like me who can't use their hands, once that headset's on … – well especially at home, when I'm on my own, if its on, I can't do anything. If the doorbell rings or the phone rings I can knock it off and go and answer the phone but that's, of course that's it, can't go back on it again. … So … I thought if I could have something I could drive up to it rather than have it attached to my head … there was an organization called [name] is that right?

P2:   Yeah.

P1:   Anyway they had a local rep that came along and looked at my problem and he went away and he came back a week later and he'd … built a booth that sits on the top of my computer … and he'd taken the mike off the headset so, and it was made from a fishing, a bit of fishing rod that he'd painted black … .

P2:   Right.

P1:   So I just drive up to it … .

In this case, the charitable organization designed a pragmatic solution that made the technology more flexible and tailored to the user's individual requirements.

Other limitations to device flexibility noted were with communication devices, which limited the amount of personal phone contacts that could be stored and had no facility to ring back if the number was not in the user's address book. This meant that the independent functionality of the device was constrained. Flexibility was also linked to portability:

R: I'm very careful when I choose … a piece of equipment; I need it at home, but I might also, say, need it on holiday … .

An important consideration, then, is whether the device can be moved around locations with the user. Similarly, the issue of impairment changing over time and whether the device can cope in the new circumstances was raised in relation to digital hearing aids (which are individually tuned and programmed by computer):

R: So these are ... great and ... I'm not sure, but I think, it probably means that you can programme them for much worse hearing losses, than you could the old analogue aids ... So that means that people who before couldn't have a hearing aid probably can now – which is helpful isn't it?

I: And presumably you can re-programme them if your hearing ... changes ...

R: If your hearing changes, yes! Yes, you see, which is, which is fantastic.

Some users wanted and needed devices to be more flexible than they currently were. For example, if a deaf user of a pager system was in the shower the device had no 'missed call' or register of missed activity, so a caller at the door would still be outside and the deaf person would not know. However, such a feature is standard on modern mobile phones.

Computers and software caused general frustration, especially in learning to use new applications:

I: So you don't feel confident enough to link your MP3 player to start using it your-self, you'd feel better to have someone ... ?

R: Well I tried for a start I tried installing the disc, and then it came up with ... and I couldn't click on it and get it running after it had been installed. It kept coming up with 'cannot open, another programme is running' so I lost interest, 'Oh sod off then' and I thought I'd leave it til somebody else, because I'll probably have to 'uninstall' it and reinstall it and I can't be doing with it. That's sometimes I'll get like that. I'll try it but if it doesn't work I can't be. ... I have other things to do. I can't mess about, I want to get back on my message board and talk to people.

Flexibility of software was, however, valued:

I1:   How flexible do you think the software is? I mean can you change it ... .

R: Oh you can, yeh, if I show you this. I think the word's 'macro' – you can do macros. ... Now I don't do this very often, cos, I don't find I need it, but just as an example ... [to computer] wake up ... start Microsoft Word ... [Respondent's] address ... [computer prints entire address] ... select all ... right align that ... left click ... [computer replaces address with 'Backlight'] ... scratch that ... mouse left click ... [no response] ... mouse left click ... [no response] ... go to sleep ... [computer inserts the word 'consciously'] scratch that ... go to sleep.

This user was quite satisfied with the level of flexibility afforded by the software. However, close examination of the above quotation shows that the computer made several errors recognising the user's voice commands. This was a generalized prob-lematical area.

Some services, such as an automatic answerphone service on landline telephones, did not prove to be sufficiently flexible for users, who could not get to the telephone before the service started and were informed that the number of rings could not be extended.

Technology abandonment

The participants had used a huge range of mainstream and specialist items, most of which were supposed to support different aspects of everyday life, such as mobility and communication. Whilst many of the mainstream items that were reported to have been abandoned had merely been superseded by new technology (e.g. video recorders by DVD players), others proved impossible to use for impairment reasons. In one case a participant affected by thalidomide reported that the equipment given to them by a professional proved too time consuming and exhausting to use ('suck and blow' communication system) – this was abandoned in favour of the user's preferred method of communication, typing with their feet.

Several participants complained of the inadequacy of NHS wheelchairs and had bought their own lighter models that had more functions. The most difficult cases involved raising beds – participants were unable to use the equipment and described struggling to get out of bed manually.

Other cases involved giving up on landline telephones as increasing difficulties with manipulation effectively precluded using them. Some participants had a chronic illness/terminal condition and experienced multiple failures with items that could not usefully be used. A participant with visual impairment abandoned a universal remote control as the touch panel had no raised buttons and was impossible to use.

The general society level improvements in size and weight of materials available have filtered through into the specialist 'disability market', and many of the respondents described such improvements. In these respects, many of the devices abandoned had been superseded by improved models. Examples were an 'alphabet machine' that was superseded by an AAC unit, a fax machine with separate phone line used by a deaf person that was superseded by broadband working on one line, and large, bulky AAC communicator machines being superseded by small lighter devices that can be fitted directly to a wheelchair.

In terms of device 'failure' in strict terms, two participants described abandoning speech software because it was 'nasal' and difficult to understand and the other because it was not 'user friendly'.

Of the participants with hearing impairments, there were some interesting findings concerning updating of technology: one no longer used an inductive loop for TV owing to improved hearing aid technology; one no longer used a Minicom textphone owing to the availability of text on mobile phones and diminishing use by the deaf community; another had abandoned using mobile phone texting owing to availability of Internet chat rooms. One participant with a hearing impairment had abandoned three devices: a neck loop for telephone use, described as a 'hassle' (mobile phone texting had superseded this device); a 'very heavy and bulky communication folder' for meeting attendance, superseded by an improved loop; an amplified phone, which was superseded by the use of email and mobile phone text. There seems little doubt that such innovations in the communications technology market are having an impact on the deaf community and changing the ways they communicate within their social groups. From these general descriptions deaf people appear to be exploiting the opportunities of improvements in the mainstream communications market in a fortuitous fashion. The findings show that communication between members of the deaf community is evolving and they are starting to use new devices and services in response to the availability of new communication technologies.

Conclusion

The research has demonstrated that disabled people engage enthusiastically with advanced technologies and appreciate the increased independence that access to such devices can bring. Interestingly, this general finding applied to all impairment types. However, there are many challenges to continued productive engagement with advanced technologies for disabled people. Not least of these are the financial costs, which can prove a formidable barrier for many disabled people. The current policy position on financing advanced technologies in the UK revolves around whether the user is currently in education or employment. Thus, users find there may be support available, for example, to access computers if one is pursuing a college course or through Access to Work. However, users not in education or employment have no straightforward access to funding streams and for this group financing desired equipment is a major issue. Similarly, items such as computers that were financed through such streams require software upgrades, especially to run the newest programs, and these similarly prove unattainable.

There remain many obstacles at the policy level to the introduction of universal design standards for devices in the UK, and with these obstacles comes the issue of achieving a satisfactory interface with assistive technological devices:

> The Disability Discrimination Act does not require anything of product manufacturers. It deals with services and with the sale of goods, but not with the goods themselves. Legislation in other countries is also mostly silent about product design. ... One exception is the USA Telecommunications Act which requires service and equipment providers to make their products accessible where this is 'readily achievable'. ... Objections to legislation include the complexities of drafting a workable law which would take account of the diversity of impairments and the range of products it would need to cover. The analogy of safety legislation suggests the degree of complexity involved. There is a general requirement for products to be safe. How this is achieved is vastly different for ships and kettles, so general legislation in backed up by product-specific standards and laws. Legislation on inclusive design would need to be supported by specific requirements for each product group – a huge task.

> A further obstacle for the UK is that under EU law no country can impose local rules which would stop the free circulation of goods. So even if manufacturers in the UK adopted the principles of inclusive design, it would still be illegal to prevent the sale of less accessible products made in other EU countries. Current EU regulations about the free movement of goods mainly relate to safety and electrical interference.

> While it is theoretically possible to extend this legislation, it would mean renegotiating existing EU directives and backing them up with requirements for individual products. Given that current regulations took years to negotiate it would be difficult to persuade legislators to consider this as a priority. (http://www.ricability.org.uk/articles_and_surveys/inclusive_design/discussion_and_recommendations/legislation/)

In this study there was exciting evidence of user group appropriation of new technologies, for example mobile phone texting and Internet messenger use by the deaf community. Interestingly, these technologies are the first to truly hold the potential to overcome the barriers between deaf and hearing communication by providing a mainstream solution (Harris 1995, 1997; Harris and Bamford 2001).

As time moves on more devices become available that are more suitable for individual disabled people owing to increased choice in the market and general improvements, such as the development of lighter weight materials. In many respects this reflects the general trend of technological improvements in everyday life – consider, for example, that the first computer had to be housed in a large building and now much more powerful machines exist in the form of laptop computers. The participants in the study were making full use of these advantages and were keen to see more, particularly in the wheelchair market.

The evidence suggests that the advanced technologies currently available and being used in disabled peoples' homes hold significant potential for the exercise of user choice. An important distinction was found here, however, between those items provided through public services and those privately purchased. Those items given to users and funded wholly through the public system were 'prescribed' by professionals and the users did not get a choice of item. Thus, the medical model lives on in the world of public services. However, in the private purchase arena users are overwhelmed with choice and making choices between expensive items is often difficult. In terms of flexibility, the users in this study were keen to exploit the potential in all advanced technological devices for increasing independence. At the present time there are limitations to the flexibility that some devices can muster, but users are continuing to push the boundaries of device capabilities.

Mainstream markets still have a long way to go in making certain products fully accessible for disabled people. The *Disability Discrimination Act 2005* in the UK covers access to goods and services. Devices such as mainstream mobile phones, that this study showed are considered essential by disabled people, were found to be largely inaccessible. There is currently no law that means designers must incorporate the tenets of universal design into products or take steps to ensure disabled people can use them. However, the evidence of this study is that there is a great need for items such as accessible mainstream mobile phones. The mainstream market has a long way to go in 'user consultation' to avoid the pitfalls of blue skies design that results in inaccessible products.

Disabled people wish to use advanced technology to increase independence in and beyond home. The role of advanced technology is to enhance independence and to research and provide the mainstream solutions that disabled people request, rather than designing and engineering 'specialist' expensive products. The application of advanced technology for use in the home should, in future, be directed by disabled people, collectively and individually.

Acknowledgements

The author gratefully acknowledges financial support for this research from the Economic and Social Research Council, award no. RES-062-23-0177 and the support of colleagues at the University of Dundee, particularly, Dr Thilo Kroll, Prof. John Arnott and Dr Nick Hine.

Note

1. Although not found in this study, there is an implication from this finding that NGOs, their publications or mainstream media could all play important roles in increasing directed consumer information, which may assist disabled people in making informed choices concerning available products.

References

Demers, L., M. Monette, Y. Lapieree, D.L. Arnold, and C. Wolfson. 2002. Reliability, validity and applicability of the Quebec User Evaluation of Satisfaction with assistive technology (QUEST 2.0) for adults with multiple sclerosis. *Disability and Rehabilitation* 24, no. 1–3: 21–30.

Dewsbury, G. 2001. The social and psychological aspects of smart home technology within the care sector. *New Technology in the Human Services* 14, no. 1/2: 9–18.

Dewsbury, G. 2005a. Smart homes and assistive technology. http://www.smartthinking. ukideas.com/.

Dewsbury, G. 2005b. Smart thinking, person-centred design and specification. http://www. smartthinking.ukideas.com/.

Dewsbury, G., K. Clarke, M. Rouncefield, I. Somerville, B. Taylor, and M. Edge. 2002. Designing acceptable 'smart' home technology to support people in the home. *Technology & Disability* 14: 1–9.

Dewsbury, G., M. Rouncefield, K. Clarke, and I. Somerville. 2004. Depending on digital design: Extending inclusivity. *Housing Studies* 19, no. 5: 811–25.

Glaser, B., and A. Strauss. 1967. *The discovery of grounded theory.* New York: Aldine Publishing Co.

Hammel, J., J. Lai, and T. Hellers. 2002. The impact of assistive technology and environmental interventions on function and living situation status with people who are ageing with developmental disabilities. *Disability & Rehabilitation* 24, no. 1–3: 93–105.

Harris, J. 1995. *The cultural meaning of deafness: Language, identity and power relations.* Aldershot, UK: Avebury Publications.

Harris, J. 1997. *Deafness and the hearing.* Birmingham, UK: Venture Press.

Harris, J., and C. Bamford. 2001. The uphill struggle: Services for deaf and hard of hearing people: Issues of equality, participation and access. *Disability & Society* 16, no. 7: 969–80.

Harris, J., M. Foster, K. Jackson, and H. Morgan. 2005. Outcomes for disabled service users, University of York Social Policy Research Unit. http://www.york.ac.uk/inst/spru/pubs/ccatreps.htm#2005.

Harris, J., S. Piper, H. Morgan, C. Thomas, A. McClimmens, S. Shah, C. Barnes, G. Mercer, H. Arksey, and H. Qureshi. 2003. *Brief review study: National service framework for long term conditions, 'User's experiences of health and social care services'.* York, UK: University of York Social Policy Research Unit.

Johnson, L., and E. Moxon. 1998. In whose service? Technology, care and disabled people: The case for a disability politics perspective. *Disability & Society* 13, no. 2: 241–58.

Khan, K., R. Kunz, J. Klejnen, and G. Antes. 2005. *Systematic reviews to support evidence-based medicine: How to review and apply findings of healthcare research.* London: Royal Society of Medicine Press.

Kittel A., A. Di Marco, and H. Stewart. 2002. Factors influencing the decision to abandon manual wheelchairs for three individuals with a spinal cord injury. *Disability & Rehabilitation* 24, no. 1–3: 106–14.

Oliver, M. 1990. *The politics of disablement.* Basingstoke, UK: Macmillan Education.

Robson, C. 2002. *Real world research: A resource for social scientists and practitioner-researchers.* London: Blackwell.

Roulstone, A, 1998. *Enabling technology: Disabled people, work and new technology.* Milton Keynes, UK: Open University Press.

Sherer, M.J. 2005. Assessing the benefits of using assistive technologies and other supports for thinking, remembering and learning. *Disability & Rehabilitation* 27, no. 13: 731–9.

Sherer, M.J., and J.C. Galvin. 1996. An outcomes perspective of quality pathways to the most appropriate technology. In *Evaluating, selecting and using appropriate assistive technology,* ed. J.C. Galvin and M.J. Sherer, 1–26. Gaithersberg, MD: Aspen.

Thornton, P. 1993. Communications technology – empowerment or disempowerment? *Disability & Society* 8, no. 4: 339–49.

Union of the Physically Impaired Against Segregation (UPIAS). 1976. *Fundamental principles of disability.* London: UPIAS.

A common open space or a digital divide? A social model perspective on the online disability community in China

Baorong Guo, John C. Bricout and Jin Huang
Washington University in St. Louis, USA

This paper explores the use and impact of the Internet by disabled people in China, informed by the social model of disability. Based on survey data from 122 disabled individuals across 25 provinces in China, study findings suggest that there is an emerging digital divide in the use of Internet amongst the disability community in China. Internet users in our study do not appear to be representative of most disabled people in China. For the minority of disabled people who do have access to the Internet, however, its use can lead to significantly improved frequency and quality of social interaction. Study findings further suggest that the Internet significantly reduced existing social barriers in the physical and social environment for disabled people. Implications for future research, and strategies for increasing reducing the digital divide between the minority of Internet users and the majority of disabled people in China are discussed.

Introduction

Recently, scholars have noted that emerging information and communication technologies (ICT), led by the Internet, are having a profound impact on the knowledge, services, employment and social exchange opportunities available for people with disabilities (Ritchie & Blanck, 2003; Bricout, 2004). The Internet promotes social interaction by allowing people to communicate in a virtual space. Before 1998, the Internet was scarcely known or utilized by disabled people in China. Despite the fact that compared to the general population, people with disabilities still have far less access to the Internet, the increasing prevalence of the Internet in recent years has made it more feasible for individuals with disabilities to remain current on the latest news, obtain various information, make friends, form online self-support groups, and shop online (Zheng, 2002).

There are hundreds of web sites targeting the disabled population in China, most of which are designed and managed by disability organizations or individuals with a disability. Among these web sites, the most influential one claims that it has more than 20,000 registered users and numerous non-registered users. In an attempt to gain a rough idea of the size of popular Chinese disability web sites the current researchers observed several interactive boards (such as discussion boards and message boards) and discovered that each of these major web sites has more than 2,000 registered users. People with visual impairment, a group generally regarded as having substantial difficulties accessing the Internet, have built their own web sites as well. It appears that a vibrant online disability community is coming into being in China.

There are divergent opinions regarding the extent to which Internet use benefits the social and civic participation of disabled people, and thus it is important to discern the social reality of Internet users with disabilities themselves. Furthermore, given that public services (such as tele-education, job searching, disability organization and government agency information) provided for disabled people are multiplying on the Web, a better understanding of disabled persons' online interaction patterns will help promote more effective and relevant service delivery.

Based on self-reported data from a survey of 122 disabled individuals in China, this study examines the following questions: (1) What are the demographic characteristics of Chinese disabled persons who use the Internet, and how do they differ from those who are excluded? (2) Can Internet-based communications (exchanges) improve the perceived quality of disabled persons' social interactions?

Theories and proposition

The compensation model is often used to examine the Internet's impacts on disabled populations and other marginalized populations (Birnie & Horvath, 2002). This model suggests that people who are socially inactive or dissatisfied with their social interaction in the real world tend to use the Internet more frequently, and hence benefit more from the Internet. This model postulates that disabled persons are isolated and have low levels of social interaction, creating social interaction needs for which online communication can compensate (e.g., Bowker & Tuffin, 2002). In a study by Cummings et al. (2002), it was found that people with low or unsatisfactory interpersonal supports in the real world tend to seek compensatory benefits through online social interactions. However, when the Internet is viewed narrowly as a technological medium, the compensation model is not able to explain why or how the cyberspace can compensate for deficiencies in meaningful, supportive communication.

To understand the online disability community in China, the present study adopts the social model of disability (e.g., Goodley, 1997; Marks, 1997) whose explanatory power is superior to that of the compensation model in capturing the full significance of the Internet's social dimension. The social model of disability posits that the 'locus' of disability lies not in individual impairment, but rather in environmental barriers; hence the power of the Internet is to alleviate physical, geographical and attitudinal barriers to social interaction. Closely associated with the disability movement, the social model of disability has gained wide currency among disability researchers and the disability community (e.g., Coles, 2001; Tregaskis, 2002; Siminski, 2003), although not without criticism for its macro focus, potential for divisiveness, and disconnection from individual needs (e.g., Hughes & Patterson, 1997; Danforth, 2001).

The social model stands in stark contrast with the medical model, which posits that pathological conditions and functional deficits lie at the core of disability, and prescribes medical interventions that manage or alleviate disease, illness and impairment associated with disabilities (Marks, 1997). The social model eschews a vision of disability grounded in individual deficit and attributes disability in favour of a schema that locates disability in barriers existing in the social environment. Disability, in the context of the social model, means the limit or loss of opportunities to take part in community life because of physical and social barriers (Disabled People's International, 1982). It is not bodily impairment as such, but rather social discrimination and biases that in fact produce 'disability'.

From the social model perspective, traditional modes of interpersonal communication are not able to transcend normative expectations of appearance and/or behaviour that constitute barriers to disabled people seeking equal opportunities for social participation (Asch, 2001). To the extent that the Internet, as a new medium of communication, can successfully remove these barriers, it stands to significantly improve disabled persons' social interactions, with attendant benefits in terms of social support and social networks.

The social model in China

The medical model of disability has prevailed in China for a long time. In the *Law of China on the Protection of Disabled Persons* (1990), disability is defined as physical or mental 'deficit.' It is therefore based on the presence or absence of impairment, and there is a clear divide between those who are 'abnormal' (disabled) and those who are 'normal' (non-disabled). The tenor of the disability discourse can be illustrated by a widely-used Chinese term 'canji', corresponding to 'disability' in English. The literal meaning of 'canji,' however, is 'deficit' or 'disease,' implying a causal linkage between disability and the body deficit.

Although the social model is not widely known in China, and seldom explicitly applied, the disability community has embodied the spirit of the social model in its persistent battles against the predominant medical model. For instance, there was an online movement in 2000 calling for the elimination of the prevailing term 'disease' from the disability discourse in Chinese. Several other cases also reflect conflicts between worldviews implicitly embodying either the medical model or the social model. With an emphasis on returning deaf children to the world with sound and voice, China's rehabilitation policy suggests that they should be trained to use vocal language instead of sign language. This policy is seriously questioned by the deaf community, as well as by educators in special education programmes because of its normative stance on the production of aural language. Similarly, some deaf people tend to reject electronic cochlea, which however is strongly encouraged by China's rehabilitation policy. These normative conflicts pose serious questions about the medical model and its single-minded, technology-driven focus, contrasting strongly with core humanistic values of the disability community. The medical model implicitly assumes that there is a technological 'fix' for all impairments, and that fixing, or remediation, should be the chief aim of professionals working with disabled people. The disability community, by contrast, values integrity, wholeness and choice over a relentless drive towards reconstruction.

Despite these conflicts, the disability movement in China lacks a specific direction. Consequently, people with disabilities frequently face a perplexing question: where to go next? This question turns out to be of theoretical relevance to the social dimensions of Internet use. In this regard, to understand and utilize the social model will be critical from an analytical perspective. The Internet-disability relationship is proposed as a good starting point to examine how the social model can be applied to comprehend the Internet's social impact on the disabled community. The social model also makes possible a cogent critique of the single-minded technological bias implicit in the medical model.

The Internet and disabled people in the framework of the social model

Roulstone (1998) provides a good example of applying the social model to understand the impact of information and communication technology (ICT) on the lives of persons with disabilities. He examined whether new technologies can remove barriers existing in the environment, including attitudes amongst the general public and in the workplace. Significantly, Roulstone found that new technologies do not necessarily produce equal opportunities for persons with disabilities.

The Internet can have positive as well as negative impacts on the lives of disabled persons. It has been suggested by some researchers that the emergence of the Internet as a medium for information and communication generates opportunities as well as barriers for disabled persons (Blasiotti et al., 2001). From the perspective of the social model, which stresses the interaction between the social environment and disabled individuals, it is inevitable that the Internet functions within the boundary of extant social conditions and inequities. In this study, we propose the following propositions:

- Whether the Internet is accessible depends not only on the technical aspects of Internet accessibility, but also depends on a number of other factors, such as education, economic status, and geographical residence.

- The Internet can remove barriers inherent in the physical environment, and reduce discrimination towards disabled people.
- The Internet serves to promote social interaction by increasing the frequency and quality of exchanges.

Figure 1 depicts the relationships between these propositions. There is a so-called 'digital divide' between Internet users and non-users, depending upon a number of factors such as education, geographical residence, availability of Internet-related knowledge, and economic status (Charp, 2001). Once disabled persons become Internet users, they have access to a common open space, helping them break down barriers that exist in the real world physical and social environments. Internet use in turn brings about more social interaction opportunities and higher levels of satisfaction with friendships, social participation and social support. This is particularly the case for more knowledgeable users, who are ready to make optimal use of the medium and its resources.

Methodology

Instrument

To test the above propositions, a survey instrument with a total of 100 questions was developed by the researchers. All questions were written in Chinese. The consent form and the questionnaire were sent as an attachment to emails describing the purpose of this study and addressing confidentiality issues as well. Most of the questions are designed to query Internet-related experiences, asking the participant to respond using a 5-point Likert-type scale. This questionnaire also includes demographic questions and three open-ended questions. Although participation was encouraged, completion of the survey was strictly voluntary.

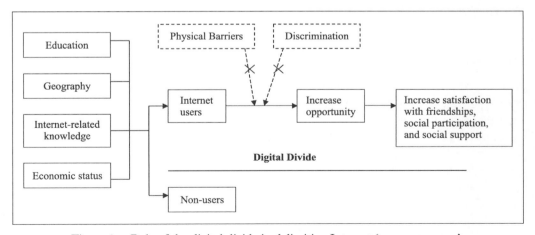

Figure 1.   Role of the digital divide in delimiting Internet 'common space'

Sampling

Several major Chinese web sites targeting disabled people were chosen in August 2003 to create an email address list for the purpose of sampling. It was observed that some users left their email information when posting a message on a discussion board, while others made their contact information available to the public on a friend-making board. Because these users have the option to make their contact information confidential, it can be assured that those whose email address were made available to the public are willing to exchange information through emails.

By collecting information from these boards 1471 email addresses became available to the researchers. Questionnaires were subsequently sent out to these email addresses. Three hundred and twelve (312) emails were immediately returned, either because the email addresses were flawed or they were no longer in use. One hundred and twenty-four (124) individuals with disabilities (11%) responded to the questionnaire. Of the completed questionnaires, 122 were valid; the remaining two were considered invalid due to substantial amounts of missing data. The modest response rate of 11% is at least partly accounted for by three facts: (1) The web sites utilized are open to both disabled and non-disabled people. Although we assumed that a large proportion of users would be persons with disabilities, it is likely that non-disabled people were also included in the sampling frame. Also, the questionnaire cover letter mentions that this survey is not meant for non-disabled people; (2) The web sites included in this study have an overlap in users, which means a person could receive the questionnaire more than once; and (3) Some users do not check emails on a regular basis, or the email address they left is not often checked. In fact, on the basis of the pattern and characteristics of certain response emails, we are convinced that this occurred in our study.

Despite the reasons discussed above, the sampling procedure may have resulted in an over sample of those persons who were easily accessible to the researchers. Given the small response rate and the vague population parameter in the Web-based survey, it is unknown whether the sample is representative. Therefore, the generalizability of the study findings is limited.

Measurement

In this study, the official definition of disability in China is employed to make it convenient for respondents to identify themselves. According to the *Law of China on the Protection of Disabled Persons*, disability refers to the deprivation of capacity due to physical or mental impairments, including hearing and speaking, visual, mobile, mental, and multiple impairments. Participants in this study reported the type of impairment according to their Disability ID issued by the government. *Use of the Internet* is measured along two dimensions: (1) When was the first time the participant used the Internet? (2) How long does the participant spend using the Internet each day? *Social interaction* is measured along three dimensions: friendships, social participation, and social support.

Descriptive statistics

Of 122 respondents, 45.8% are female and 54.2% are male. Their ages range from 17 to 49 with an average age of 28.4. They each have one of the following disabilities: mobility disability (60.7%), visual impairment (15.6%), hearing and speaking impairment (20.5%), mental disability (1.6%), or multiple disabilities (1.6%). Respondents are from 25 provinces of China. Most respondents have never been married (70.5%), while 22.1% are married and 7.4% are divorced or widowed (see Table 1).

On average, it has been 3.5 years since participants' initial exposure to the Internet. Respondents spend an average of 207 minutes on the Internet each day and an average of 73.7 Yuan (US$9) per month for Internet access. Of the respondents, 18.3% need ancillary equipment to use the Internet. This is roughly congruent with the percentage of respondents having visual impairments (15.6%). Most of respondents (77.7%) use the Internet at home. The Internet is used mainly for information, sending and receiving emails, chatting, shopping, and so on.

User characteristics: social barriers associated with Internet accessibility

The focus in this paper is not on the technical aspects of accessibility, which has been the subject of a broad array of studies (e.g., Aspinall & Hegerty, 2001; Davis, 2002; Noble, 2002; Yu, 2002); rather, the focus is social barriers associated with Internet accessibility. In the current study, education, economic status, geographic residence, and sources of Internet-related knowledge appear to be the most influential social factors associated with Internet accessibility, a list that is very similar to that compiled by Charp (2001) in her review of 'digital divide' factors in the U.S., Western and developing nations.

Educational barriers

As presented in Table 2, 17.3% of 122 respondents do not have a high school degree, and the majority of the respondents have a high school diploma (22.9%) or above (59.5%). Overall, disabled people who use the Internet have very high levels of educational attainment. This is illustrated by the following comparisons between Internet users with a disability and users in the general population:

1. The ratio of respondents having a diploma beyond high school (59.5%) is higher than that (55.2%) in the total user population according to the China Internet Network Information Center (CNNIC, 2003). The percentage of respondents with a graduate degree or above (9.9%) is substantially higher than that (2.2%) in the 2003 CNNIC report.
2. Disabled users' educational attainment is astonishingly high compared to the Chinese population as a whole. Only 3.8% of the Chinese population has a two-year college degree or more and only 15.8% of the total population has a high school degree or more (National Bureau of Statistics of China, 2000).

Table 1. Use of the Internet (N=122)

Variable	Mean or percentage
Months since the first exposure to the Internet (mean)	40.8
Time spent on the Internet each day (mean in minutes)	206.7
Monthly expense on the Internet access (Mean in Yuan)	73.7 (approximately US$9)
Use ancillary equipment to access the Internet (%)	
Yes	18.3
No	81.7
Location (%)[a]	
Home	77.7
Office	24.8
Net bar	24
School	6.6
Other	2.5
How to access the internet (%)	
Dialing	22.5
Cable	70.8
Both dialing and cable	1.7
Other	5
Purpose of using the Internet (mean)[b]	
Making friends	3.9
Entertainment	2.8
News	4.1
Seeking help	3.5
Sources of Internet knowledge (%)[a]	
Self-teaching	78.7
Friends	32.8
Colleagues	14.1
Family	13.2
School	8.3
Training	11.6
Other	1.7
Having personal homepage (%)	
Yes	26.7
No	73.3
Received distance education through the Internet (%)	
Yes	23.5
No	76.5

[a] More than one answer may apply.
[b] Responses range from 'strongly disagree (1)' to 'strongly agree (5).'

Table 2. Comparison of educational attainment of disabled users vs. non-disabled users

Educational attainment	Disabled users[a] (%)	Internet users as a whole[b] (%)
Less than high school	17.3	13.9
High school	22.9	30.9
Two-year college	28.1	27.1
Bachelor's degree	21.5	25.5
Graduate level and above	9.9	2.6

[a] Statistics based on our survey data.
[b] Data source: China Internet Network Information Center (CNNIC, 2003).

3. Disabled users' education levels are in sharp contrast to the overall low level of education of the disabled population. For instance, the elementary and middle school enrolment rate for disabled children is only 77.2%; only 2,547 disabled individuals were admitted to colleges or universities in 2001, which accounted for a mere 0.0002% of the total number of new college students that year (China Disabled Persons' Federation, 2002).

All these comparisons indicate that disabled users are better educated than the disabled population as a whole, and most strikingly, better educated even than the general Chinese population. In other words, disabled people with higher levels of education are more likely to have Internet access. Education, therefore, is an important factor associated with Internet use. Furthermore, in addition to these direct effects, education could also have indirect effects on Internet accessibility through the mediating influences of economic status and the availability of Internet-related knowledge, such as knowing how and where to access key information and/or services.

Economic barriers

Regarding major difficulties in accessing the Internet, our data show that monthly expense on Internet access is the leading factor, outweighing the other three factors, namely: lack of internet-related knowledge, lack of computers, and lack of ancillary equipment. The data, do not, however, support the view that the lower the personal income, the less likely that disabled people can afford a computer and Internet access. Although over two thirds of respondents are employed or self-employed (68.9%), most of them (61.5%) have monthly earnings below the national average in 2002.

Approximately 80% of respondents are in the three lowest income categories in our survey. An average cost of 73.7 Yuan (US$9) per month for Internet access accounts for almost 10% of the median income of all respondents. How then can persons with disabilities have access to the Internet despite their disadvantaged economic status? One possible explanation is that most disabled people in China live with and/or obtain financial support from their family. This premise is supported by the fact that among the 50 respondents who are in the lowest income category, 36 can still afford to use the Internet despite having no personal income whatsoever.

Geographic barriers

One of the most significant characteristics of disabled users is that most of them (89.3%) live in cities while only 10.7% live in rural areas, which is extremely disproportionate to the distribution of the total disabled population. Living in rural areas makes it much less likely for disabled people to use the Internet. The huge gap between urban and rural areas in terms of economic development accounts for this highly skewed geographical distribution. It is notable that of the 13.7 million disabled people below the poverty line in China, about 12 million live in underdeveloped rural areas where there are a number of socio-economic barriers (such as lack of a telecommunication system) not unique to people with disabilities (China Disabled Persons' Federation, 1998).

Barriers of Internet-related knowledge

Whether Internet-related knowledge is available is also related to the accessibility of the Internet, because such knowledge tends to be self-taught. Most respondents in this survey learnt Internet-related knowledge by themselves (78.7%). Other important sources are friends (32.8%), training programmes (11.6%) and schools (8.3%). Given that disabled individuals mostly depend on self-teaching to acquire Internet-related knowledge, it appears that other learning sources are either unavailable or insufficient. Given that 'friends' follow 'self-teaching' as the second most important source of Internet-related knowledge, there seems to be a demand for external learning support that is not adequately provided by public services. Solely relying on oneself for knowledge building requires that disabled people are capable of self-teaching and that the medium is sufficiently self-explanatory. This reinforces the fact that only highly educated disabled people can use the Internet, both to ensure well-developed learning aptitudes and the analytic tools for solving the more arcane aspects of Web-based information, knowledge pathways and utilities. To improve Internet accessibility, Internet learning resources and services need to be publicly provided to disabled people, especially those with low levels of educational attainment.

To sum up, disabled people who are well educated and financially supported, and who have obtained Internet-related knowledge, are more likely to use the Internet; living in urban areas also increases the likelihood of accessing the Internet. In contrast, disabled people who have less education and/or live in rural areas are less likely to access the Internet. What has been made clear here is that the Internet does not appear to be a miraculous technology that can universally compensate the 'deficit' facing people with disabilities. Embedded in the larger social reality, the positive effects of the Internet are limited to those who are well educated, live in urban areas, and have learning support. It is these constraints that cleave a divide between those who are Internet users and those who are not. It is also these constraints that make disabled people who cannot access the Internet even more socially marginalized and discriminated against. As one respondent noted pointedly:

> People with disabilities are poorly educated, and their economic condition is disadvantageous. Training services cannot be provided for free for disabled people. There is a digital divide and it can hardly be changed over a short period of time.

The respondent's comment poignantly touches upon entrenched social disadvantages facing persons with disabilities in China, including limited access to education and employment that defy any remedies short of substantial community and social development. These basic social disadvantages lie at the heart of the digital divide. As a means of bridging this divide greater Internet access is a necessary, but not totally sufficient, condition.

A common open space: social barriers removed by the Internet

To examine if the use of the Internet can overcome barriers that exist in the social environment and in turn enhance social networks (see Figure 1), respondents' social interaction before and after using the Internet is compared.

The Internet can reduce physical barriers

In China, many public accommodation and transportation facilities are not accessible to persons with disabilities, thus creating major environmental obstacles to disabled people's social participation. With a new medium for communication mediated by the Internet, the constraints imposed by the poor accessibility of physical facilities are substantially reduced or eliminated. Moreover, compared with the telephone, Internet-based communication is low cost, which can greatly reduce physical barriers in social interaction.

The rapid expansion of disabled persons' geographically dispersed social networks is a key aspect of the Internet's advantages in overcoming physical barriers. According to our survey data, 62.1% of respondents claim that most of their friends contacted via the Internet are distant, while only 2.5% of respondents report that most of their friends were distant before they became Internet users. It suggests that Internet-mediated communication has greatly expanded disabled persons' social interactions in their geographical scope.

One respondent couched this geometric expansion of social networks in almost poetic terms:

> The Internet has greatly extended my social network. It is exciting and interesting to know various people across the country. With the Internet, disabled people have their wings. When on the Web, I feel like an angel freely flying.

The effect of the Internet on reducing physical barriers is also reflected by the percentage of respondents having received long-distance education on the Web. The data show that 23.5% of respondents participated in long-distance education programmes. Because there are very few institutes in China providing online education services for people with disabilities, this percentage is expected to increase as long-distance education programmes multiply in China. The Internet on the one hand can be useful in long-distance education; on the other hand, due to the lack of education programmes, the Internet's effects on reducing physical barriers in education are limited by concrete social conditions.

The Internet can reduce barriers in social attitudes

Fifty-four percent of respondents agree that there is less discrimination towards disabled people on the Web whilst 35.3% neither agree nor disagree, and only 10.6% disagree. It has been observed by the US National Council on Disability (NCD, 1996) that the Internet allows individuals to interact with others in such a way that their disability becomes invisible or irrelevant. Bowker and Tuffin (2002) found that in online communication disabled users have a 'choice to disclose' their disability information and therefore are more likely to achieve equality. Users are free to 'position' their identity in accord with their own wishes (Bowker & Tuffin, 2002). Therefore, a direct benefit of online interaction is that impairment is concealed or revealed at will.

Several respondents averred this new-found freedom to 'position' their identity:

> If there is any difference between the Web and the real world, it should be this: I can freely decide what information to be exchanged in online communication and how to tell the information (related to my impairment).

> On the Web, I can be whatever person I want to be without caring too much about what others think of me.

In many instances, disabled users are assumed or imagined to be non-disabled inasmuch as the Internet effectively hides their impairments from detection by others. In other words, discrimination does not come into effect on the Web, not because discrimination itself has vanished from social reality but because it is suppressed in cyberspace. As one respondent notes:

> Many of my online friends were very glad to talk with me before they know the truth (I am a disabled person). Things completely changed after I told them that I am blind.

The Internet's potential to eliminate discrimination exists in the context of a real-world social environment in which discrimination still prevails. In this regard, the Internet's optimum effect on reducing social discrimination toward people with disabilities is limited to that of a temporary suppressor; the Internet cannot, by itself, forge fundamental change in social attitudes.

The Internet increases opportunities for social interaction

The Internet has the potential to bring disabled people out of isolation and into greater social integration (NCD, 1996). This is because the Internet not only

Table 3. T-test statistics (N=122)

Variable	Mean		t-value
	Before	After	
Participation in public affairs	1.87	2.92	−9.46***
Participation in group activities	1.73	2.58	−8.41***
Number of friends	2.96	3.66	−8.06***
Satisfaction with social relationships	3.17	3.59	−5.25***
Satisfaction with friendships in general	3.50	3.75	−4.24***

***p<.001

reduces barriers that exist in the physical environment and social attitudes, but also because it increases interactive 'social' opportunities. According to our survey data, 76.2% of respondents agree that they have more chances to make friends and participate in public affairs and self-support groups (see Table 3). Directly related to greater interactive opportunities is a significant increase in the number of friendships that many respondents have experienced. In the words of one respondent:

> I have many more online friends to talk to. I feel like the Internet suddenly opens a door in front of me, through which I can see the outside world and get to know many things.

It is conceivable that online involvement could lead to less communication with family members due to excessive preoccupation with the Internet. Indeed, there is a burgeoning literature identifying two variants of Internet addiction, one of which is 'cyber-relationship addiction' (Hansen, 2002). Although our study participants might seem susceptible to such an addiction, it is not supported by our survey data. Only 13.1% of respondents report that online involvement has resulted in less communication with their family and only 13.2% think that the use of the Internet has reduced their participation in local community activities.

Can the Internet promote the quality of social interaction?

Respondents' overall satisfaction with social relationships and friendships increases significantly after using the Internet. Fifty-four percent of respondents agree that the Internet plays an important role in their social interaction; 75.4% agree that to use the Internet makes them feel meaningfully occupied; 71.3% feel happy when online. All these indicators suggest that the Internet promotes a higher quality of social interaction for disabled persons.

When the three aspects of social interaction—friendships, social participation and social support—are examined respectively, the impact of the Internet on social interaction can be seen more clearly. First, seven indictors of intimacy, including three positively worded indicators (e.g.: 'I feel close to my online friends.') and four negatively worded indicators (e.g.: 'it is unlikely to form intimate friendships online.') are combined to create an intimacy index.[1] The average of this intimacy index turns out to be 3.6 on a five-point scale, which indicates that respondents generally develop intimate friendships on the Internet.

Regarding social participation, there is some inconsistency in our findings. On the one hand, 66.1% of respondents agree that the Internet can promote social participation, and increase the mutual understanding between the disability community and society at large. On the other hand, there is some doubt among participants about the extent to which online social participation can lead to real-world outcomes. For instance, respondents who think that their online participation can enhance societal concern for the disability community (32%) are in a minority. Respondents who do not believe that their online advocacy has the potential to reduce social discrimination toward disabled people (33.6%) outnumber those who believe that it does (21.3%). More than three quarters of respondents (78.5%) have never or seldom used online services provided by the government. Given the doubts cast on real-life, societal effects of the Internet, a strictly quantitative approach to understanding the meaning of Internet use and its portends for decreasing social disadvantage and social exclusion is inadequate. Internet users with disabilities are in the best position to make connections between their online and offline experiences and aspirations. Whether online participation can yield actual benefits for disabled people remains an open question, beyond the scope of the current study.

Interestingly, half of respondents believe that the Internet makes it easier for them to get help from friends and organizations, but 55.4% of respondents never or seldom pursue any help through the Internet. There is a large proportion of users who think the Internet an effective means of information diffusion, but only 24.2% agree that Internet is helpful for job searching and only 17.3% believe that online dating services can help them find a boy/girlfriend. These findings suggest that respondents do not think that Internet-based social interactions or networks can take the place of real-life social networks. Rather, Internet-based social interactions or networks appear to be ancillary, or at best complementary, which is not to diminish their importance to a population that regularly confronts social exclusion and isolation.

The Internet clearly has the properties of a common open space for social exchange, discourse and information gathering. In this 'free' space, characterized by less perceived biases and discrimination, disabled persons have more opportunities for social integration. By virtue of this fact, disabled persons' overall quality of social interaction is also promoted, with some degree of variation depending upon the dimension in question. Generally, intimate online friendships are more likely to be developed than social participation and social support. The Internet is clearly beneficial in terms of providing a space for communication, yet it does not invariably lead to real-world gains in social interaction. A respondent notes the limited real-world effects of virtual world social interactions:

> Of course, the Internet can bring me out of the isolated world and let me know more people. But it is just a tool, a way of communicating, and a complementary of real life. The online world seems not so much different from the real world. Online friends can be

real or not real, can be intimate or superficial. I was very excited at the very beginning, but the excitement disappeared soon. Nothing has been changed. Everything remains the same.

Comparison of heavy and light users groups

Finally, we sought to compare the heavy and light users groups on the grounds that whatever effects Internet use might produce would be most pronounced for those who are most involved with the medium. For this portion of the analysis, the sample is divided along a mathematical combination of two dimensions: time since the first exposure to the Internet and time spent daily on the Internet. A new variable was created by multiplying these two variables, followed by a log transformation aimed at equilibriating the variables' disparate distributions. Upon finding the median of this new variable, the sample was divided into two groups: the heavy users and the light users. Table 4 presents the relevant t-test statistics.

Before using the Internet, although both groups had very few opportunities to participate in public affairs, the light users group had marginally more such opportunities than the heavy users group. This group difference, however, disappears after Internet use commences. Before using the Internet, the two groups did not differ in terms of satisfaction with friendships or overall social relationship; in contrast, after using the Internet, the heavy users group tends to be more satisfied with friendships and overall social relationship than the light users group. The two groups did not differ from each other in terms of number of friends before using the Internet;

Table 4. Heavy users (n=54) vs. light users (n=68)

Variable	Group (mean)		t-value
	Heavy	Light	
Chances to discuss public affairs before using the Internet	1.70	2.00	1.81[a]
Chances to discuss public affairs after using the Internet	2.94	2.90	−0.23
Satisfaction with social relationships before using the Internet	3.21	3.14	−0.40
Satisfaction with social relationships after using the Internet	3.81	3.42	−2.81**
Number of friends before using the Internet	3.07	2.87	−1.13
Number of friends after using the Internet	3.85	3.51	−2.33*
Satisfaction with friendships before using the internet	3.59	3.42	−1.07
Satisfaction with friendships after using the internet	3.94	3.60	−2.39*
Online friends are mostly disabled	2.55	3.15	2.89**
Feeling close to online friends	3.35	3.07	−1.91[a]
Online friends are willing to share their deep feelings	3.42	2.87	−3.10**
Online friends are not real	2.65	2.91	1.84[a]
Contact online friends through traditional media (e.g., mails)	2.57	2.15	−2.25*
Participation in online discussion	3.44	2.85	−2.71**

*p<.05,   **p<.01,   [a]p<.10

however, after using the Internet, the heavy users group has significantly more friends than the light users group. Heavy Internet use appears to be associated with a more satisfying and expansive social life, a strong finding in light of pre-Internet use equivalency of the two groups.

Another important finding is that the use of the Internet appears to influence friendship structures. For instance, the light users group is more likely than the heavy users group to have online friends with disabilities. In other words, the more frequently they use the Internet, the more likely it is that they will develop friendships with non-disabled individuals. Moreover, the heavy users group is more likely than the light users group to report having intimate friends online, to exchange deep feelings, and to contact online friends through traditional ways whilst the light users group is more likely than the heavy users group to perceive that online friends are not real. Compared with the light users group, the heavy users group is more likely to participate in online discussion. In other words, heavy users appear to have a greater level of investment in their online exchanges, altering their perceptions about the meaning and import of online relations. The greater investment by heavy users also appears to influence their online behavior to the extent of expanding the circle of their online friendships to non-disabled persons.

In summary, the above evidence supports the proposition that the Internet provides an open space for people with disabilities to increase communication, social networks and enhance the quality of social interaction. More intensive use of the Internet appears to yield greater benefits for people with disabilities than less intensive use.

Conclusion

For the Chinese disability community the Internet appears to be both a 'commons' and a manifestation of a 'digital divide'. It is a commons insofar as the virtual space for discourse and information encompassed by the Internet is, for the most part, unregulated and freely accessible once entered (e.g., Brin, 1995). For persons with disabilities this openness, combined with the possibility of near instantaneous communication across the globe, provides both a forum for discussion and a vehicle for new social relations unlike that found in the real world where issues of accessibility and discrimination constrain social participation. These benefits are borne out by the participants in this study who reported numerous benefits to their social life, particularly if their use of the Internet was heavy.

The 'good news' of the commons, is, however, mitigated by the harsher reality of the digital divide. As Stephen Graham notes in his incisive analysis of the urban digital divide, ICT have not produced the promised 'death of distance' nor the 'end of geography'; rather, the economic polarization of haves and have nots is reified in the technological gap between the privileged and the disadvantaged (Graham, 2002). In this study we found that Internet users with a disability were not representative of most Chinese with disabilities, owing to the privileges stemming from their high level of education, relatively high levels of socio-economic support, and their access to computer equipment and Internet services.

For the silent majority of Chinese with disabilities to engage in Internet-based discourse and information-seeking will require social development in tandem with greater access to computers and Internet service. As a number of investigators have noted, closing the digital divide will require more societal resources for the disadvantaged, including literacy programmes, education, health care, food, and other basic needs (e.g., Charp, 2001; Warschauer, 2003). Mark Warschauer (2003) links closing the digital divide with increasing social inclusion; a critical connection, reminding us that the Internet cannot by itself remedy the social exclusion faced by persons with disabilities, but must instead be part of a larger programme fueled by social development.

Having said that, China, no less than other developing nations, faces limited resources for social development, lending credence to an argument made by the editors of the Far Eastern Economic Review (FEER, 2001) that bridging the digital divide must fall low on the priority list for aiding Asia's poor and disadvantaged. Perhaps it is not a matter of exclusive choices: basic social development to the exclusion of Internet development, or Internet development to the exclusion of social development. To the extent that Internet development can be shown to spur social development it can piggyback on broader development efforts, not as a magical lever for progress, but rather as part of an infrastructure for positive change.

Note

1. First, the three negatively worded items were reversely coded. Then, the sum of all the seven items was divided by seven to create the intimacy index.

References

Asch, A. (2001) Disability, bioethics, and human rights, in: G. L. Albrecht, K. D. Seelman & M. Bury (Eds) *Handbook of disability studies* (Thousand Oaks, CA, Sage Publications).

Aspinall, A. & Hegerty, J. R. (2001) ICT for adults with learning disabilities: an organisation-wide audit, *British Journal of Educational Technology*, 32(3), 365–372.

Birnie, S. A. & Horvath, P. (2002) Psychological predictors of Internet social Communication, *Journal of Computer-Mediated Communication (online)*, 7(4). Available online at: http://www.ascusc.org/jcmc/vol7/issue4/horvath.html (accessed 7 January 2004).

Blasiotti, E. L., Westbrook, J. D. & Kobayashi, I. K. (2001) Disability studies and electronic networking, in: G. L. Albrecht, K. D. Seelman & M. Bury (Eds) *Handbook of disability studies* (Thousand Oaks, CA, Sage Publications).

Bowker, N. & Tufflin, K. (2002) Disability discourses for online identities, *Disability & Society*, 17, 327–344.

Bricout, J. C. (2004) Using telework to enhance return to work opportunities for individuals with spinal cord injuries, *NeuroRehabilitation*, 19(2), 147–159.

Brin, D. (1995) The Internet as commons, *Information Technology and Libraries*, 14(4), 240–242.

Charp, S. (2001) Bridging the digital divide, *Technological Horizon in Education*, 28(10), 10.

China Disabled Persons' Federation (1998) *A survey report of disabled people living in poverty*. Available online at: http://www.cdpf.org.cn/fupin/fp0006.htm#2 (accessed 7 January 2004).

China Disabled Persons' Federation (2002) 2002 *China disability statistics*. Available online at: http://www.cdpf.org.cn/shiye/sj-02.htm (accessed 7 January 2004).

China Internet Network Information Center (CNNIC) (2003) *The twelfth survey report on the Internet development in China.* Available online at: http://www.cnnic.net.cn/html/Dir/2003/11/05/1210.htm (accessed 7 January 2004).

Coles, J. (2001) The social model of disability: what does it mean for practice in services for people with learning disabilities? *Disability & Society,* 16, 501–510.

Cummings, J. N., Sproull, L. & Kiesler, S. B. (2002) Beyond hearing: where real-world and online support meet, *Group Dynamics: Theory, Research, and Practice,* 6(1), 78–88.

Danforth, S. (2001) A pragmatic evaluation of three models of disability and special education, *Journal of Developmental and Physical Disabilities,* 13(4), 343–357.

Davis, J. J. (2002) Disenfranchising the disabled: the inaccessibility of Internet-based health information, *Journal of Health Communication,* 7(4), 355–367.

Disabled People's International (DPI) (1982) *Proceedings of the First World Congress* (Singapore, Author).

Far Eastern Economic Review (FEER) (2001) The 'digital divide' (Editorial), *Far Eastern Economic Review,* 164(14), 6.

Goodley, D. (1997) Locating self-advocacy in models of disability: understanding disability in the support of self-advocates with learning disabilities, *Disability & Society,* 12, 367–379.

Graham, S. (2002) Bridging urban digital divides? Urban polarization and information and communication technologies, *Urban Studies,* 39(1), 33–56.

Hansen, S. (2002) Excessive Internet usage or 'Internet addiction'? The implications of diagnostic categories for student users, *Journal of Computer Assisted Learning,* 18(2), 232–236.

Hughes, B. & Patterson, K. (1997) The social model of disability and the disappearing body: towards a sociology of impairment, *Disability & Society,* 12(3), 325–340.

Law of China on the Protection of Disabled Persons (1990). Available online at: http://www.cdpf.org.cn/zhengce/fl-ool.htm (accessed 7 January 2004).

Marks, D. (1997) Models of disability. Who needs models? *Disability & Rehabilitation,* 19, 492–495.

National Bureau of Statistics of China. (2000) 2000 *China population census: Population by education.* Available online at: http://www.stats.gov.cn/ (accessed 7 January 2004).

Noble, S. (2002) Web access and the law: a public policy framework, *Library Hi Tech,* 20(4), 399–405.

Ritchie, H. & Blank, P. (2003) The promise of the Internet for disability: a study of on-line services and web site accessibility at centers for independent living, *Behavioral Sciences and the Law,* 21, 5–26.

Roulstone, A. (1998) *Enabling technology: disabled people, work and new technology* (Philadelphia, PA, Open University Press).

Siminski, P. (2003) Patterns of disability and norms of participation through the life course: empirical support for a social model of disability, *Disability & Society,* 18, 707–718.

Tregaskis, C. (2002) Social model theory: the story so far, *Disability & Society,* 17, 457–470.

The U.S. National Council on Disability (NCD) (1996) *Access to the Information Superhighway and Emerging Information Technologies by people with disabilities.* Available online at: http://www.ncd.gov/newsroom/publications/superhwy.html (accessed 7 January 2004).

Yu, H. (2002) Web access and the law: recommendations for implementation, *Library Hi Tech,* 20(4), 406–419.

Warschauer, M. (2003) *Technology and social inclusion: rethinking the digital divide* (Boston, MA, MIT Press).

Zheng, W. (2002) *Chinese disabled people and information technology* (in Chinese). Available online at: http://www.2000888.com/jujiao/200301025153008.htm (accessed 7 January 2004).

Increases in wheelchair use and perceptions of disablement

Bob Sapey,[a] John Stewart[a] and Glenis Donaldson[b]

[a]*Lancaster University, UK;* [b]*Manchester Metropolitan University, UK*

Between 1986 and 1995, there appeared to be a 100% increase in the number of wheelchair users in England and Wales. This article reports some of the findings of a study designed to explore the social implications of this increase. Specifically, it examines the various explanations for the increases and concludes that whilst demographic changes or research methodologies are not responsible, the more likely causes are changing prescription practice, medical advances and changing attitudes to disablement. The article then explores the latter explanation by examining perceptions of wheelchair use, contrasting clinical and user views gained from in-depth interviews. It also reports findings from part of a large-scale postal survey of wheelchair users, which examined their attitudes toward different models of disability. It concludes that the responses of a large majority of wheelchair users of all ages are better explained by the social model of disability than any other.

Introduction

In 2001 we were given funding by the NHS Executive North West R & D Directorate to undertake a study into the social implications of the increases in wheelchair use in the north-west of England. Between 1986 and 1995, there appeared to be around a 100% increase in the numbers of wheelchair users in England and Wales. Little was understood about why the increase had taken place, or what the social implications were.

Our research study comprised three phases. First, we analysed the available data from a local DSC (Disablement Services Centre), which gave us some basic demographic information about the population of wheelchair users. Second, we carried out semi-structured, in-depth interviews with 33 wheelchair users in the region in order to access their privileged knowledge, gained from their experience of wheelchair use. Interviewees were selected to reflect the available demographic data from the DSC. We then used our analysis of these interviews to produce a postal questionnaire which was sent to nearly 5000 people from the patient database of the DSC, stratified by location, age and sex. The survey resulted in a response of 1226 people, which we believe to be one of the largest surveys of wheelchair users to have been carried out in the UK. Amongst other things, this survey attempted to quantify the way wheelchair users perceived disablement. We have drawn on this aspect of the survey, our review of the literature and an examination of images of wheelchairs on the World Wide Web in order to offer some conclusions about the relevance of different models of disability to the population of wheelchair users.

The evidence for the increase in wheelchair use lay primarily in two national studies. In 1986 the OPCS disability surveys estimated there were 360,000 wheelchair users in England and Wales (Martin *et al.*, 1989). Ten years later Aldersea's (1996) investigation into the NHS Disablement Services showed that the number of wheelchair users in England was then approximately 710,000. At that time, wheelchair users would have constituted almost 10% of the 7.2 million disabled people identified by the *Follow-up to the Family Resources Survey* (Grundy *et al.*, 1999). While the number of wheelchair users appeared to have doubled over the previous decade, this was in contrast with a lower increase (38%) in the total numbers of disabled adults in Great Britain between 1986 and 1996–7.

Secondary evidence that these changes were occurring, but may have been patterned in a complex way, came from discussions with local providers and purchasers. In 1996 the Morecambe Bay Health Authority had experienced a 15% increase in the number of people issued with wheelchairs, whereas by 1999 the Preston DSC believed that their out-turn figures would show this increase to have ceased. Further data, obtained from Wirral Health Authority as part of an initial survey of all AHAs and CHCs in the north-west region, indicated a similar trend of referrals increasing at the rate of 50% over the five years from 1995 to 1999, but that this had slowed down considerably since 1997.

Explanations for the increase in wheelchair use

There appeared to be no one satisfactory explanation of what had caused this increase, and in reviewing the literature we found five possible contributing factors.

1. Demographic change

A Department of Social Security study of all disabled people suggested that the rising numbers were linked to the increasing population of older people (Craig & Greenslade, 1998), but that study made no attempt to look specifically at wheelchair users. Our examination of Aldersea's study showed increases across the age range, hence – in addition to demographic changes – there must have been other explanations. Grundy *et al.* (1999) also showed increases across the age range, lending support to this interpretation. We also examined this explanation in more detail by comparing two datasets that we had obtained 8 years apart. As Table 1 shows, the

Table 1.   Age of wheelchair users

	Plymouth DSC (Cornwall only) April 1993 (Sapey, 1995)	Preston DSC July 2001	Survey sample 2003
Valid cases	4728	23216	1192
Mean	67.9	67.61	67.92
Median	74	74.00	72
Mode	85	81	80
Standard Deviation	23.19	22.154	19.371

examination of these different DSC datasets indicates no significant change in the distribution of wheelchair users by age between 1993 and 2001.

Certainly the older population of wheelchair users has been increasing, but so too have the numbers of younger wheelchair users. During this period, the overall increase in the number of people over the age of 65 in the UK was 202,000 (2.2%), while there was a decrease in the number of people under 16 years old of 51,000 (0.4%) (Social Trends, 2004, Figure 1.3). The overall population change between 1991 and 2002 was a net increase of 163,000 (Social Trends, 2004, Figure 1.7). Thus, any change in wheelchair use that could be accounted for solely by the increase in the ageing population should increase the average ages of wheelchair users, yet the two datasets show a slight decrease in both the mean and mode. This may be accounted for by the different sizes of the data sets, but what is clear is that there is no significant increase in the average age of wheelchair users during a period in which their total numbers did increase.

2. Changing prescription and allocation practice

It is also possible that the increase was a result of changes in the prescription and allocation procedures within the NHS. In the past, institutional practices in the allocation of wheelchairs had led to such increases. For example, in Canada in the 1940s, a change to allocating wheelchairs to individuals rather than hospital wards not only led to an obvious increase in the numbers of wheelchairs in use, but also to the presence of wheelchair users in Canadian social and economic life (Tremblay, 1996). In this way, a relatively simple change in prescription practice brought about significant social change. Woods and Watson (2002a) point to a similar rise in wheelchair use following the establishment in 1948 of the National Health Service, with its universal provision in Britain. However, they also describe how this increase, which was managed by the Ministry of Pensions, resulted in the standardization and mass provision of inappropriate wheelchairs. The Ministry Model 8 which came into service in 1951 was designed for the occasional, older user and fashioned to be amenable to the standardized production process favoured by the Ministry. Woods and Watson (2002a) argue that this was 'a wheelchair designed for the service, rather than the wheelchair user'.

During the 1986–1995 period of increase, there was a change in prescribing practice for wheelchairs, with the Disablement Services Centres training therapists and nurses to undertake this task, and it may well have been that the different perceptions of need by health professionals other than doctors could have accounted for some of the increase. Our survey was of the wheelchair users rather than of NHS personnel and, as such, it was not possible to quantify the effect of changing prescription practice. We considered a question in the survey about who had 'prescribed' the respondent's first wheelchair and when, but from analysis of our interviews we doubted our ability to make this reliable. However, many discussions with various therapists over the course of the study did indicate that change in prescription practice was a contributing factor to the increase.

3. Changes in medical and social care practice

A different, but related explanation is that changes in medical practice and health behaviours resulted in the delayed mortality of sick people and, hence, a larger proportion were surviving to become disabled people (Grundy *et al.*, 1999), of which a sizeable minority may well be wheelchair users. Also, the recent developments in care in the community resulted in fewer younger disabled people living in institutions in this period, and whilst the numbers of older people in such homes have increased (Oliver & Sapey, 1999), there may have been changes in their social behaviour, such as their getting out and about more often. In such circumstances, people may be less willing to rely on wheelchairs owned by institutions and therefore they would have been referred to their DSC for equipment of their own.

Although some data was gathered in our survey about the medical causes of people's impairment, the accuracy of this is far from that which would be required to make any firm claim for this cause. Our only evidence here is anecdotal from those involved in the provision of wheelchairs and it is clearly supportive of this explanation for the increase in relation to younger people, especially children.

4. Methodological differences

A further possibility was that the changing figures may have been partly the result of better research methods, with Aldersea's study being more accurate than the OPCS survey. However, this would not have accounted for the increases that were being reported to us by various DSCs and health authorities. While we have confidence in Aldersea's figures, we should note that the Audit Commission (2000) reported the total number of wheelchair users for the UK to be only 640,000. That data was provided by the Royal College of Physicians, with Aldersea herself being a member of the Audit Commission's external advisory group. There is no further information from them about how they calculated this figure.

This means there are two competing figures for the number of wheelchair users: Aldersea's (1996) figure of 710,000 wheelchair users in England and the Audit Commission's (2000) figure of 640,000 for the UK. While these differ quite widely, they are both considerably larger than the 1986 OPCS figure of 360,000 and, as we noted in the background to our study, local health trusts were themselves reporting increases of around 15% per year in the late 1990s. Artefact of measurement may well be an issue, but not to such an extent that it can account for the increase.

See Addendum.

5. Changing attitudes towards disablement

Craig and Greenslade (1998) also suggested that changing attitudes towards disablement may have contributed towards the increased numbers of people counting themselves as such, but again the authors did not specifically consider whether there was such a link to wheelchair use. Their proposition would suggest that wheelchairs have become more socially acceptable and people are not so self-conscious of being seen in them. In the absence of any clear evidence that conditions leading to ambulant immobility were increasing at a greater rate than other impairments, the validity of this explanation must be seriously considered.

We found a level of assertiveness amongst both our interviewees and survey respondents which would support this hypothesis, but it is not possible to say whether this accounts for all of the increase. The overwhelming majority of wheelchair users view wheelchairs as potentially positive rather than as undesirable clinical equipment, despite criticisms of the lack of choice and certain design failings.

Our studies of the various explanations put forward for the increase in wheelchair users suggest therefore that the more probable causes lie in changes in medical practice, prescription practice and in attitudes of disabled people toward wheelchair use. The ageing of the population does not account for the increase and, while measurement reliability is an issue, it affects only the recorded volume of the increase, not the fact that there is one. In our survey and interviews, we explored the issue of changing attitudes in more depth.

Perceptions of wheelchair use

The wheelchair has long been viewed as a necessary, but undesirable piece of clinical equipment. It is the symbol of disability, despite the fact that only a minority (less than 10%) of disabled people are wheelchair users. Wheelchair users have often been treated as patients who are subject to expert assessment and prescription, rather than as people with preferences and the right to choose. While much may have changed in recent years, a dominant image of a wheelchair user is as someone dependent on others, especially within the medical care services. When we viewed images on the web as part of this study, we found that wheelchair users were often depicted as happy and contented in a 'sick role'. In some instances the two dependencies – wheelchair and medicine – would certainly go hand in hand, but this is not always the case. Indeed, for many wheelchair users, their immobility is as the result of impairments which are not treatable and therefore they may have little contact with doctors and nurses. We found that interviewees' experiences of health professionals which should by now be anachronistic are still prevalent:

> It's like when you go to the hospital or the doctors, if you go with anybody because you're in a wheelchair they don't address you, they look over you and that really infuriates me.

Although there may be much contact with rehabilitation personnel, especially occupational and physiotherapists, the story is often the same:

> I felt as if the occupational therapist especially, she just treated me like, she saw the wheelchair and she didn't see me as a person.

Oliver (1993) has argued that the efforts of the rehabilitation industry to make non-walkers walk again places a negative value on the use of a wheelchair. He links these efforts to the assertion of power:

> In terms set by the rehabilitation enterprise, walking is rule-following behaviour; not-walking is rule-ignoring, rule-flouting or even rule-threatening behaviour. Not-walking can be tolerated when individuals are prepared to undergo rehabilitation in order to nearly walk or to come to terms with their non-walking. Not-walking or rejecting nearly-walking as a personal choice is something different however; it threatens the power of professionals, it exposes the ideology of normality and it challenges the whole rehabilitation enterprise. (Oliver, 1993, p. 16)

This threat to the power of rehabilitation professionals is a central issue in the study of wheelchair use, and the role of the health and welfare services. While the study of wheelchairs and their use has been dominated by medical, managerial and technical considerations, the challenge from the disability movement has been to view the wheelchair user as the person who has the expertise. Not-walking ceases to be a medical condition, rather, it becomes a normal part of the range of human diversity. To conceptualize not-walking as normal is a significant challenge to the socialization of rehabilitation professionals, yet for many wheelchair users it is an important aspect of gaining a positive identity, as one of our interviewees commented:

> I've actually gained more out of life since I've been in a wheelchair than I did before my accident, I've certainly achieved so much.

The social model of disability, which is a central principle of the disability movement, argues that the limitations faced by disabled people result not from their impairment, but from the social responses to impairment. The social model makes a clear distinction between meanings of impairment and disability. Confusing the two terms results in a misunderstanding that is unhelpful to any discussion or analysis of disability problems. Impairment refers to the physical problems that may give rise to a person's immobility, while disability refers to the limitations that are caused by the failure of a society to take into account the presence of wheelchair users within it. At a simple level this may be illustrated by steps rather than ramps into buildings, thereby excluding anyone who is unable to negotiate the steps. However it is more complex than this, as there is a widespread belief that people who use wheelchairs may be unable to undertake a range of other physical and intellectual tasks.

The accounts of two of our interviewees, reflecting on their childhood as wheelchair users, sheds some interesting light on the ways in which their perceptions of the wheelchair were changed by the attitudes of adults in their lives.

> I'll tell you when I realised for the first time that being disabled wasn't necessarily a good thing, it was, believe it or not, when I was 11. And it was the last year of junior school. The kids went on a holiday. I just assumed that I'd go and I was absolutely devastated when my Mum and Dad said, 'No' and I said, 'Well why not' and they said, 'Because the teachers will have to help'. By that time as far as I was concerned I was physically independent, … but what I hadn't taken into account was that if I couldn't get somewhere in my wheelchair, I would have to be physically carried. … Up to that point it had not been a problem. If I needed carrying an adult lifted me up and carried me so I didn't see it as somebody doing anything that they shouldn't do, or extraordinary.

> My wheelchair was a good cop car and we used to play cops and robbers and the kids, especially the boys, used to love chasing up and down with me. … [Some] people are afraid of using a wheelchair and I know that my Mum, and I've never really understood her for this, my Mum hates my wheelchair.

Both interviewees draw a clear distinction between the views of children and of adults towards wheelchairs and their use. While in these cases, wheelchairs are seen as positive by the children and negative or limiting by the adults, a contradictory message is given in the case of other clinical equipment as the many attempts to replace the missing limbs of Thalidomide children with hideous mechanical prostheses testify. Alison Lapper, whose statue will grace the 'vacant plinth' in Trafalgar Square, describes the attempts to fit her, when a child at residential school, with metal legs and arms with hooks powered by a canister of compressed gas:

> I hissed whenever I moved. (The Independent, 17 March, 2004)

This contradiction can only be explained by reference to Oliver's (1993) analysis of rehabilitation professionals and their insistence on walking or nearly-walking rather than non-walking. To many rehabilitation professionals it may appear a sacrilege to challenge the aim of helping children to achieve some form of ambulant mobility, yet for many children such rehabilitation teaches them that to use a wheelchair is undesirable.

Sayce (2000) discusses what she terms a 'disability inclusion' model in relation to countering the stigma associated with mental ill-health. This model is based upon having strong anti-discrimination legislation to prevent people and organizations from being oppressive, but also on saying 'no to shame'. The disabled people's movement has long been concerned with promoting a positive image of disability. Many people have written about the way they can incorporate their disablement within a strong self-identity and reject the notion that they are either ill or weak. While there is some public acceptance of this view, typically portrayed by strong images of wheelchair users involved in sporting activities, it is also a view that may be shared by people who would usually be termed as frail and dependent. Wheelchairs no longer need to be seen as symbols of failure, but merely as a means of mobility used by disabled people in a variety of roles, as one of our interviewees commented:

> I just see it as a chair with four wheels and I think that's how it should be seen, but I do know that able bodied people or more able people see it differently, and when I'm on my scooter I'm treated differently.

Despite the fact that many wheelchair users are actively taking part in everyday situations, it is likely that rehabilitation staff are going to focus more on their incapacity. The majority of people who are likely to attend a disablement services centre will be over 50 years of age, with their mean age being almost 68 years. That is how some of our interviewees saw it, until it happened to be oneself:

> I always thought somebody who was in a wheelchair was always old or you had severe learning disabilities to be in a wheelchair until I ended up in a chair myself.

Two-thirds of wheelchair users are women and two-thirds are part-time users (Aldersea, 1996, p. 15). So the typical wheelchair user will be an elderly woman, probably impaired by arthritis, who is able to walk to some extent indoors, but is reliant on someone else to push her around out-of-doors. She is also likely to be issued with a Remploy attendant controlled wheelchair.

This typical chair not only conveys an image of dependency, but creates it due to a design which makes it impossible for the wheelchair user to propel him/herself. However, the women who make up the majority of wheelchair users are not necessarily content to accept this dependent image. As Ann Begg, MP, says,

> Walking is not the be all and end all, but merely one method of movement, but this is hard to convey to people when it is obvious that there are still too many physical barriers making life for those of us in wheelchairs unnecessarily difficult. (Reilly, 2002, p. 14)

The wheelchair has not always been a piece of clinical equipment. According to Cooper:

> In ancient times, dependence characterised the lives of those who were disabled. Fortunate people relied on servants or family members to carry them on litters. Being carried on a litter was not necessarily stigmatising since it was the preferred mode of transportation for the wealthy and well-born. (Cooper, 1998, p. 2)

Cooper goes on to give a brief history of the wheelchair:

> The earliest record of a wheelchair was incised in stone on a sixth century AD Chinese sarcophagus. By the European Middle Ages, the litter had been supplanted by the wheelbarrow. The wheelbarrow, while rather undignified and still requiring another's power was convenient. The rolling chair was developed during the Renaissance as a heavy cushioned armchair with a reclining back and front legs equipped with casters. ... Later, Louis XIV used a roulette (a wheelchair of the period) while recovering from an operation. This popularised the roulette among the French court. (ibid)

The modern wheelchair, like much else, is a creation of the Enlightenment; as the 18th century progressed, various governments began to finance the development and provision of wheelchairs, especially for war veterans. The disabled survivors of successive major conflicts have prompted advancements in technology through their campaigning for inclusion in mainstream society (Cooper, 1998). The main advances in the technology of the wheelchair appear to have been led by disabled people, many of whom have set up the companies that produce wheelchairs today. The principal advances brought about by such companies have been in creating lighter and more portable wheelchairs, while over time even standardized designs such as the Ministry Model 8 have become cheaper and more affordable.

Woods and Watson (2002b) argue that there is a need to take a social constructionist approach to understanding the relationship between the wheelchair as a technological product and disabled people. Different groups of actors will have different perceptions of the same objects. Ann Begg MP views her wheelchair positively and calls it her 'liberator' because it freed her from pain and the risk of fracture (Reilly, 2002). Philip Olds however, an ex-police officer who killed himself, believed his wheelchair disqualified him from his male identity (Morris, 1992). Woods and Watson conclude that:

> a wheelchair is not merely a medical device, nor is it just a means of mobility. Wheelchairs are political. This political nature goes beyond the public into the realm of the private. Wheelchairs are highly personal devices. (Woods & Watson, 2002b)

Attitudes to disablement

A significant criticism made of the social model of disability is that whilst such theorizing may be relevant to disabled activists and academics, it does not equate to the experiences of the majority of disabled people. This is distinct from the criticisms of the social model that have been made by feminist scholars (for example Morris, 1989; Thomas, 1999) whose objective was to expand and strengthen a social analysis of disablement. The criticism we refer to is that put by people working with disabled people, usually from an individual model perspective, who wish to maintain that the problems people experience arise from their impairments. This approach is reinforced by medical, rehabilitation and social welfare professionals, and as a result disabled people may themselves be coerced into viewing their situation in terms of an individual model.

In our survey we posed a series of statements that were designed to elicit the orientation of respondents to models of disability, the first two of which were deliberately provocative. Respondents were invited to express their attitude to the statements on a 5-point scale, from 'strongly agreeing' to 'strongly disagreeing', or to indicate that the statement did not apply to them. These statements in their original wording, along with the number of respondents, head the bar charts shown in Figures 1 to 8, which give the percentage distribution of responses.

As we noted above, Ann Begg MP refers to her wheelchair as 'the liberator'. This very positive view of wheelchairs formed the basis of our first two statements ('Wheelchairs can be liberating for disabled people' and 'My wheelchair has liberated me'). Given the criticism that wheelchairs are clinical equipment associated

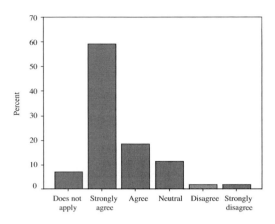

Figure 1.   Wheelchairs can be liberating for disabled people (N=1093)

with the failure to walk, we expected that respondents who see their disablement in a negative light would also view their wheelchair negatively, and would hence disagree with these statements. As Oliver (1993) has argued, the rehabilitation industry contributes to this negative view of not-walking or nearly-walking.

However, respondents to our survey showed such a strength of agreement that 'Wheelchairs can be liberating for disabled people', that only 3.5% demurred. On the face of it, this can be seen as a rejection of the wheelchair as symbolic of the failure to treat and cure. It also suggests that a significant majority of wheelchair users, those who actively agreed with the statement (77.9%), may have developed a positive identity of themselves as wheelchair users. This statement came first in the attitudinal section of the questionnaire, following two pages of demographic and technical questions, and hence respondents were not primed to answer this in any particular way. The high level of agreement to this statement illustrates a strong concordance between the experience and attitudes of wheelchair users and the social model analysis of disablement.

When applied to oneself, the situation becomes more complex (Figure 2). The proportion of respondents agreeing that they have personally experienced liberation falls to 62.9%, whilst those who actively disagree, which means that they have not found their wheelchair liberating, rises to 9.1%. We examined variables which could be associated with this distribution and there is a strong association here with being in institutional care and lack of independent living. Only half of respondents in residential care agreed that their wheelchairs had liberated them, whereas nearly two-thirds of wheelchair users living independently agreed with this statement. Living alone was not a significant variable for this attitude, however, age is significant. The youngest respondents (or their carers filling in the questionnaire for them) do not support this statement strongly, but support increases through middle age and then declines again in extreme old age, with which there is clearly a connection with being in institutional care.

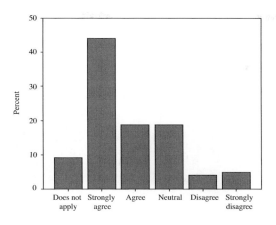

Figure 2. My wheelchair has liberated me (N=1057)

Despite the fall in agreement with the second statement, this first group of state-ments confirms the value which the social model of disability has as a means of understanding and explaining how wheelchair users experience the world. However, it is also clear that in practice many people are experiencing some form of barriers to gaining advantage from this equipment. The next group of statements attempted to explore the nature of these barriers.

The first of this next group required respondents to consider whether it was their wheelchair that prevented them from doing things that they would like to do (Figure 3).

The distribution here shows the least variation of any of our attitudinal state-ments, with 32.3% in agreement and 34% in disagreement. We could presume that this relates to factors such as the range of activities that people wish to undertake, their location, medical condition, age and so forth. In examining this distribution we found that the sex of respondent was irrelevant. However, age did appear to have an influence, with the youngest respondents (under 10 years old) being more likely to disagree, or to regard the statement as not applying to themselves, as was also the case for the oldest respondents. The middle aged and older respondents (up to 70 years) were more evenly distributed. We think it is fair to conclude that the very young and very old are probably making lifestyle decisions that do not include aspi-rations beyond what can be achieved using a wheelchair, and that as such they may perceive the equipment they are using is appropriate to their need.

Tenure did seem to have some significance with higher proportions of respon-dents in owner occupation agreeing with the statement. This was rather surprising given that social rented tenants were more likely to be dissatisfied with access within their home. We might have expected them to be more likely to agree with this state-ment, as they would presumably encounter more environmental barriers in using their wheelchairs. This adds some weight to the conclusion that the responses to this statement are referring to the wheelchair itself, rather than to its utility in a particular environment.

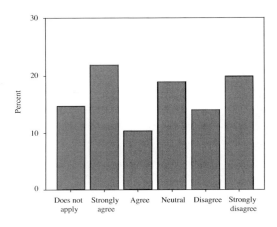

Figure 3.   My wheelchair stops me from doing many things I want to do (N=1015)

In contrast with the last statement, where responses were the most evenly distributed, agreement with 'My illness/condition stops me from doing many things I want
to do' (Figure 4) was the strongest of all the attitude statements. The level of agreement with the statements on the liberating potential of the wheelchair, which we
associate with a valuing of the social model, has to be balanced with this clear statement about the illness or condition that a respondent has: it is that condition or
illness which is seen as unequivocally limiting. The level of agreement with this
statement could be claimed to support an individual model of disability, and yet
elsewhere we found strong evidence that respondents are aware of the social
construction of barriers to their independence. However, the response to this statement supports the arguments of feminist theorists such as Morris (1989) and
Thomas (1999) for the need to include impairment effects in a social model of

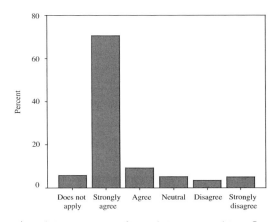

Figure 4.   My illness/condition stops me from doing many things I want to do (N=1140)

disability, or maybe for a return to *The fundamental principles of disability* (UPIAS, 1976). Thomas (2004), herself a material feminist, argues that UPIAS's original concept of disablement was one that argued that people whose lives were already affected by their impairments were further oppressed by the limitations imposed on them by their relationship to the rest of society. Disability is therefore a social relationship similar to other oppressions such as patriarchy or racism. The social–relational model of disability helps us to make sense of what may appear from either a strictly materialist, or indeed a medical perspective, to be the contradictory character of the responses to these four statements.

The only key variables of social division showing a slight positive correlation with those respondents who disagreed with this statement were sex (males), tenure (council tenants) and age (respondents in their 30s), though given the relatively small numbers involved, this could be entirely idiosyncratic.

Nearly two-thirds more of the people surveyed disagreed (38.1%) with the statement that 'Other people's attitudes towards me using a wheelchair stop me from doing many things I want to do' (Figure 5) than agreed (23.6%). However, this still means that one in four wheelchair users are experiencing limitations caused by other people's attitudes. Sex and whether someone is a full-time wheelchair user shows a weak correlation with agreement to this statement: 25.4% of males agreed compared with 22.7% of females; 25.5% of full-time users compared with 21.1% of part-time users. However, when we looked at age there were some very much stronger correlations with agreement: 54.2% (age group 10–19 years); 38.6% (age group 40–49 years); and 43.3% (age group 50–59 years). This fits the profile of the people at the top of a hierarchy of wheelchair users which interviewees suggested had been constructed by DSCs. This will be the topic of our second paper, but suffice to say here that our study shows that a hierarchy exists and is identifiable by those who receive better quality wheelchairs.

There are several issues like this one where a significant minority of wheelchair users appear to be dissatisfied or experience oppression. We are carrying out further

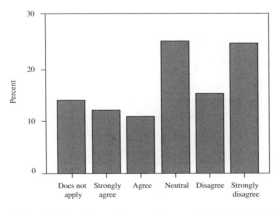

Figure 5.   Other people's attitudes towards me using a wheelchair stop me from doing many things I want to do (N=1041)

investigations into the hypothesis that certain groups of wheelchair users are pushing the boundaries of social expectations and as such they tend to experience a greater level of oppression. It may be, therefore, that those disabled people who are most actively attempting to participate in mainstream society are more likely to experience negative attitudes from other people, whilst simultaneously establishing themselves at the top of the DSC hierarchy.

Our respondents viewed the environment around them as the second most significant barrier in this group of statements (Figure 6). While not as strong a limiting factor as impairment, their environment was significantly more problematic than either the attitudes of others or their wheelchairs. Environment in this statement could mean many things to each respondent; doorsteps, kerbs, busy roads or hilly area. So, one might expect respondents on the Fylde coast (a very flat area including Blackpool) to disagree, and those people living in the foothills of the Pennines and Cumbrian Lake District to agree more strongly. Equally, those living in towns might fare better than those in rural areas. However, an analysis of this statement by postcode showed no significance in geographical location.

From these first two groups of statements we can conclude that wheelchair users do not feel that using a wheelchair is necessarily negative, indeed it can be liberating, and that while they clearly relate their own limitations to their impairment, they also strongly identify with environmental, design and attitudinal barriers around them. We would argue therefore that the individual model of disability is not adequate to explain their experience of disablement.

We also sought to ascertain whether our respondents identified with the need for legislation to counter the discrimination disabled people faced (Figure 7), as this could act as a further indicator of whether they saw their disadvantage as having a social or medical causation.

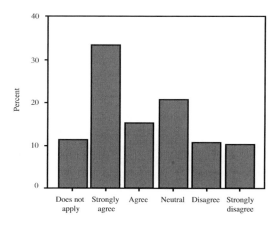

Figure 6.   The environment around me makes it hard for me to do many of the things I want to do in my wheelchair (N=1065)

The responses to the statement 'Discrimination against wheelchair users should be dealt with strongly under the law' suggested a strong identification with the need for anti-discrimination legislation, which is probably much greater than in the population as a whole, with just over two thirds of respondents (67.7%) agreeing with this statement and only 7.9% disagreeing (Figure 7). The affiliation respondents have to the social model is affirmed again, though here in the context of a rights-based approach to reducing the exclusion of wheelchair users.

Despite many criticisms of the Disability Discrimination Act, 1995 – that it is either too weak or inappropriate – just over half of our respondents did have faith in this legislation (Figure 8). However, compared with the belief in the value of legislation exhibited in Figure 7, this result suggests a drop in confidence in the power of our present UK law to change attitudes, but perhaps a belief in its potential.

Conclusions

It was clear from our survey that the majority of respondents identify both positive and negative aspects of social life that are consistent with the analysis provided by the social model of disability. We think there are three major implications that we might draw from this strength of identification with the social model. The first implication is that the social model is more than a tool for a minority of disabled people, activists and academics; rather, it provides an analysis of disablement that is relevant to the lived experience of wheelchair users.

Second, for many health and welfare professionals, the social model of disability has become synonymous with a simplistic and inaccurate analysis of the limitations disabled people face. Such opposition is often based on a partial understanding of the social circumstances of disabled people. On the one hand, it is argued that the material basis of the social model excludes explanations involving impairment, and on the other, that an appropriate regime of rehabilitation can overcome barriers. The first of those positions fails to appreciate the complexity and sophistication of the

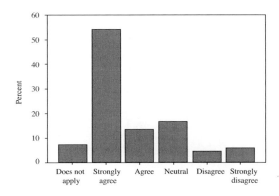

Figure 7.   Discrimination against wheelchair users should be dealt with strongly under the law
(N=1097)

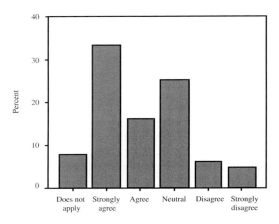

Figure 8.   The Disability Discrimination Act will help to change attitudes towards wheelchair users (N=1079)

social model of disability, whilst the second fails to accord with the experience and aspirations of disabled people. Thomas (2004) makes the case that since the original discussions of the Union of Physically Impaired Against Segregation in the early 1970s, the reformulation of disability was based upon a social–relational approach, meaning that disability results from a relationship between people with impairments and the social world. This does not deny the effects of impairment; instead it reconstructs disability as a form of social oppression that is additional to the limitations arising from impairments.

Third, as Oliver (1993) argues, disabled people become the subjects of rehabilitation professionals who, in devaluing the status of non-walking, also devalue the lives of their patients. It is necessary for all professionals involved with wheelchair users to recognize that impairment and wellness can and do co-exist. If disabled people are treated as unwell, they are then expected to occupy a particular role as a patient – one that is usually associated with being cured, despite there being no cure on offer.

This implies a considerable change in professional practice from a clinical to a social orientation. Our respondents believed that their disadvantages could be overcome with the help of anti-discrimination laws. The Department of Health and the Disability Rights Commission have recently drawn up a Framework For Partnership Action On Disability, which amongst other things recommends disability equality and disability awareness training for NHS staff. We recommend that a shared commitment to a rights-based approach would assist disabled people to achieve independent lives.

Addendum

Since acceptance of this paper, the Department of Health (2005) have given yet a further estimate of 1.2 million wheelchair users in England. Although it is important to note this figure it does not affects our argument or conclusion other than to cast doubt on the idea that the increase in wheelchair users was slowing down. See Department of Health (2005) *Improving Services for Wheelchair Users and Carers: Good Practice Guide* (London, Department of Health).

References

Aldersea, P. (1996) *National Prosthetic & Wheelchair Services Report 1993–1996* (London, College of Occupational Therapy).

Audit Commission (2000) *Fully equipped: the provision of equipment to older or disabled people by the NHS and social services in England and Wales* (London, Audit Commission).

Cooper, R. (1998) *Wheelchair selection and configuration* (New York, Demos).

Craig, P. & Greenslade, M. (1998) *First findings from the Disability Follow-Up to the Family Resources Survey* (London, DSS Social Research Branch).

Grundy, E., Ahlburg, D., Ali, M., Breeze, E. & Sloggett, A. (1999) *Disability in Great Britain* (London, DSS Social Research Branch).

Martin, J., White, A. & Meltzer, H. (1989) *Disabled adults: services, transport and employment* (London, HMSO).

Morris, J. (1989) *Pride against prejudice: transforming attitudes to disability* (London, Women's Press).

Morris, J. (1992) *Disabled lives: many voices one message* (London, BBC Education).

Oliver, M. (1993) *What's so wonderful about walking?* (Leeds, University of Leeds Disability Archive). Available online at: http://www.leeds.ac.uk/disability-studies/archiveuk/index.html (accessed 3 June 2005).

Oliver, M. & Sapey, B. (1999) *Social work with disabled people* (Basingstoke, Macmillan).

Reilly, G. (2002) The Gerald Reilly interview, *Access Journal*, 5, 14–15.

Sapey, B. (1995) Disabling homes: a study of the housing needs of disabled people in Cornwall, *Disability & Society*, 10(1), 71–85.

Sayce, L. (2000) *From psychiatric patient to citizen: overcoming discrimination and social exclusion* (Basingstoke, Macmillan).

Social Trends (2004) *Social trends, no 34* (London, National Statistics Online). Available online at: http://www.statistics.gov.uk/downloads/theme_social/Social_Trends34/Social_Trends34.pdf (accessed 3 June 2005).

Thomas, C. (1999) *Female forms: experiencing and understanding disability* (Buckingham, Open University Press).

Thomas, C. (2004) An examination of sociological approaches. How is disability understood? *Disability & Society*, 19(6), 569–583.

Tremblay, M. (1996) Going back to civvy street: a historical account of the Everest and Jennings wheelchair for Canadian World War II veterans with spinal cord injury, *Disability & Society*, 11(2), 149–169.

UPIAS (1976) *Fundamental principles of disability* (London, Union of Physically Impaired Against Segregation).

Woods, B. & Watson, N. (2002a) A concise history of the wheelchair under the British state: part 1, the rise of the model 8 and the pursuit of standardisation, paper presented to the *Society for the History of Technology Annual Meeting*, Toronto, Canada, 17–19 October.

Woods, B. & Watson, N. (2002b) *Towards a sociology of the wheelchair* (Leicester, British Sociological Association Conference, Reshaping the Social).

Back to the future, disability and the digital divide

Stephen J. Macdonald and John Clayton

Social Sciences, University of Sunderland, Sunderland, UK

The aim of this article is to explore disability and the digital divide using a quantitative methodology. The research investigates what impact digital technologies have had in improving the life-chances for disabled people from deprived neighbourhoods in the northeast of England. The study explores how disabled people engage with digital and assistive technologies in order to overcome disabling barriers and social exclusion. Unfortunately, the analysis found no evidence that digital and assistive technologies had any impact on reducing social exclusion for disabled people. In fact, the research discovered that these technologies seemed to construct new forms of disabling barriers as a consequence of the digital divide.

Points of interest

- This article explores how disabled people engage with digital and assistive technologies compared with a general (socially excluded) population.
- The article develops a statistical approach to explore whether technology plays a significant role in reducing disabling barriers.
- The paper concludes by investigating the impact that technology has in improving the life-chances for disabled people in areas such as education, employment and health services.

Introduction

The aim of this article is to examine disabled people's experience of social exclusion and how this correlates to the digital divide within the United Kingdom. Previous studies examining this area have applied a qualitative perspective to conceptualise the relationship between disabling barriers and new forms of technology (Roulstone 1998, 2007; Goggin and Newell 2003; Sheldon 2004; Harris 2010; Watling 2011). This study endeavours to examine the digital divide using a quantitative methodology, based upon an evaluation of digital inclusion in the city of Sunderland. The article examines the relationship between disabled people's engagement with digital technologies and how digital exclusion might construct new forms of disabling barriers. In doing so this will discover whether disabled people are less likely to engage in new forms of technology compared with the general (non-impaired) population in socially excluded neighbourhoods.

Digital inclusion in the city of Sunderland

Sunderland is a city located in Tyne & Wear, which is a metropolitan county of the northeast of England. It is situated on the River Wear and was historically celebrated for its shipbuilding, glass-making and coalmining industries. With the decline of heavy industries in the 1980s, shipbuilding and coalmining have completely disappeared leading to high levels of unemployment. Since the 1990s, despite efforts of regeneration, deprivation and poverty remain an entrenched issue for the city. Eighty-two of the city's 188 Lower Super Output Areas (LSOAs)[1] are ranked among the 20% most deprived in England and 41 of those are ranked within the 10% most deprived nationally (Indices of Deprivation 2007).

In March 2006 the city of Sunderland (Sunderland Local Strategic Partnership) became the recipient of £3.5 million from the Department of Communities and Local Government (plus additional investment from the private sector). This was provided to implement Sunderland's proposal of delivering technological solutions to socially excluded individuals and communities within the city (Sunderland City Council 2007). One of the key groups identified within Sunderland's socially excluded remit were disabled people (Tunstall 2008). Disability has been a major concern in terms of digital inclusion, both by Labour and the recent Tory-led government. As the Department of Work and Pensions states:

> Digital inclusion provides people with wider choice and empowerment around the major areas of their lives. By ensuring that disabled people have access to technologies ... digital inclusion opens up many social, financial and entertainment benefits of the internet. Digital inclusion can also improve: employment and learning opportunities [and] access to services and information, including public services. (Department of Work and Pensions 2011)

There has been a recent move in terms of government policy and private industry in developing inclusive technology aimed at people with a range of abilities and impairments. Owing to the Equalities Act 2010, places of business, educational institutions and public spaces must be accessible for people with a range of impairments. In terms of government discourse, the ideology of inclusion has become central to technological innovation (Goggin and Newell 2003).

Definition of digital exclusion/inclusion

Digital exclusion is a lack of access to and use of information and communications technology (ICT) resources. By ICT the study refers to a range of technologies, including, but not limited to, desktop and laptop computers, Internet connections, mobile telephones, digital and interactive television, health-monitoring equipment and assistive technology for those with impairments. As with UK Online Centres (2007), the research emphasises the importance of the *availability* of ICT resources, whilst also acknowledging the significance of the various *motivations* that drive *use* and the *skills* needed for initial and continuing engagement. There is also a recognition that technology is increasingly used by individuals and agencies (particularly those delivering public services), which may well have a discernible indirect impact upon the quality of life of those in socially excluded groups (Department for Communities and Local Government 2008).

The government's objective of greater digital inclusion is directly related to the goal of improved lives and life-chances – what is seen as a more socially inclusive society. For disabled people the use of digital technologies, particularly with reference to assistive technologies, is destined to enable new ways of engagement with local services, education and the workforce, which would have been restricted previously due to the nature of certain impairments. UK Online Centres (2007) have identified a correlation between those who are socially excluded and those who are digitally excluded. Those who remain disconnected from technology are more likely to also remain excluded from mainstream social, economic and political activities. Therefore, greater access to and use of technology is positioned as a key tool for addressing such social problems. What is at stake here is not, then, just the importance of use and access to technology, but the socio-economic benefits this may bring. From the government's perspective, digital technologies might assist disabled people to confront and overcome many of the barriers they face in order to prevail over social exclusion.

Disability studies and new technologies

As disability is one of the targeted groups where digital technologies are considered useful in removing disabling barriers, it should be noted that in the literature on disability a number of conflicting discourses have emerged in contrast to the official government stance (Roulstone 1998, 2007; Oliver, Barnes, and Thomas 2001; Goggin and Newell 2003; Harris 2010). To comprehend the relationship between technology and disability, it is important to understand how disability and technology have been interconnected within a historical context from a disability studies perspective. Watson and Woods (2005) suggest that technological advances have been the foundation of the development of disability activism and the political movement.

Watson and Woods (2005) use the wheelchair as an example to demonstrate the importance of technological development. Before the emergence of the wheelchair in 1916, people with physical impairments were very rarely seen by the public owing to a lack of mobility. Watson and Woods (2005) suggest that, in post-war society, access for disabled people, especially people in wheelchairs, became a central point in the negotiation for the disability movement. This was due to architectural features that excluded individuals with physical impairments who needed the assistance of certain technologies. This became the focal point for the disability movement in relation to disabling barriers, thus establishing a separation between disability (disabling barriers) and impairment (biology).

However, the idea that technology can somehow overcome issues of impairment, and include individuals who had been previously excluded, has been somewhat rejected from within disability studies (Oliver 1978; Roulstone 1998; 2007; Oliver, Barnes, and Thomas 2001; Goggin and Newell 2003; Harris 2010). Oliver, Barnes, and Thomas (2001) imply that it was the 'old' technologies of the industrial revolution that previously excluded people with impairments from society and are critical of why the 'new' technologies of the twenty-first century will subsequently include disabled people. Roulstone (1998, 2007) further dismisses the government's idea that disability can be entirely overcome by technological advances. He suggests that digital technologies do not change the relationship between individuals with an impairment and society. What they have the potential to do is to assist in the reduction of disabling barriers presented in the environment, education and the workforce. Roulstone (1998, 2007) states that it is important to recognise that digital technologies can only assist in changing the social environment and are not the ultimate answer to overcoming disablement and social exclusion.

This is supported by Goggin and Newell (2003), who suggest that the promise of digital technologies to overcome issues of impairment and disability have been greatly exaggerated and have not materialised. They suggest that digital technologies, rather than create a system of inclusion, have the opposite effect and in many cases have further isolated people with a range of impairments. Goggin and Newell (2003) propose that the reason for this is that technology designers seek to 'normalise' disabled people. One of the key barriers they illustrate is that technologies are often too expensive and ineffective for most disabled people. This is illustrated by Harris (2010), who studied how effective assistive technologies are for many disabled people. He discovered that the fundamental barriers people experience when using assistive technologies were due to financial cost, poor design and poor training from providers. Harris discovered that for people who have access to assistive technologies they often go unused due to a lack of knowledge and training. Furthermore, many of these technologies are not adequately designed for disabled people (Harris 2010). In order for assistive technologies to be affective, Borg, Larsson, and Östergren (2011) imply that affordable digital technologies must be seen as a basic human right. From this perspective, access to digital technologies should be seen as a 'right of assistance' for disabled people rather than a 'commodity'.

The digital divide and disability

The consensus is that in the coming decades of technology, adoption will continue apace alongside growing expertise and continuing processes of globalisation (Harvey 1990; Bauman 1998), transforming the way individuals live, work, play and communicate (Bradley and Poppen 2003). The use of technology is not without its drawbacks and disadvantages, but for the majority who have access to ICT (in particular, computers and the Internet) there are a number of clear economic, educational, social and health-related advantages. However, those who remain excluded from the opportunities such technologies provide in a 'network society' (Castells 1996) are increasingly at risk of being left behind.

As more everyday commercial and public services, which were once conducted through face-to-face interactions, become transferred online, there is a danger that those who are not accessing such channels will become further excluded. From the government's (individual model) perspective, digital technologies have the potential to enable disabled people to overcome 'limitations' of their body in order to improve their life-chances. Unfortunately, there is also a recognition for disabled people who are not engaging in digital technologies that these individuals have the potential of becoming further excluded and experience more disabling barriers significantly reducing their life-chances (Goggin and Newell 2003; Harris 2010).

This gap that exists between those who have access to and use of ICT and those who do not has become known as the *digital divide* (National Telecommunications and Information Administration 1995). We also know that those on the wrong side of this divide are characterised by their already disadvantaged positions (UK Online Centres 2007). In particular, non-users of ICT indicate that financial situations and social class positions heavily influence access to what Selwyn (2003) calls the 'opportunity structure' of ICT. Those who suffer deep social disadvantage are up to seven times more likely to be disengaged from the Internet than those who are more socially advantaged (Helsper 2008). Within these digitally excluded groups, it has been suggested that disabled people are overly represented within the digital divide (Harris 2010; Watling 2011). There is then a fundamental inequality in the current levels of access to ICT (Graham 2002), which favours more advantaged social groups and more affluent and connected localities (Russell and Stafford 2002). Poor levels of access to technology arguably both reflect and exacerbate these existing divisions.

Online resources, assistive technology and disability

The government suggest that there are some clear benefits of recent technological advances that can be found in terms of improving the quality of life of disabled people (Digital Inclusion Task Force 2009). These allow individuals to carry out tasks and activities that they would have otherwise been unable to do on such an independent basis. However, whilst those with such conditions may rely upon forms of assistive technology, it has been suggested that the Internet in particular remains '… inaccessible or difficult to access by people across a spectrum of impairments and this may have serious implications for the potential use of the Web for increasing social inclusion' (Adam and Kreps 2006, 217). Sheldon (2004, 158) emphasises this point by stating 'discriminatory Web design creates major barriers which prevent disabled Internet users from accessing information'.

Yet it may be suggested that it is not the Internet that is generally inaccessible for disabled people, but particular online resources which affect people with impairments in different ways (Haywood 1998). From this point of view, it is not useful to refer to disabled people as a generic group in terms of ICT design, but there should be a focus on designing assistive technologies around issues of impairment. For example, an individual with a learning impairment will experience different difficulties to someone with a hearing impairment (Gregor, Sloan, and Newell 2005). Although this might be a significant point at an individual level, as the Disability Rights Commission demonstrated in their 2003/04 review of website accessibility, there are key structural barriers that affect disabled people in general. These structural barriers include issues of affordability, a lack of knowledge and skills, ineffective assistive technologies, and poor design of online resources (Disability Rights Commission 2004, 2006). Even when disabled people have access to assistive technologies to support online use, these are often not compatible with particular web-browser design (Disability Rights Commission 2006). The Disability Rights Commission (2004) draw attention to the fact that disabled people are not generally consulted within the process of commercial and public online design. Hence, Glesson (1999) advises against an uncritical approach to technology for disabled people as this constructs a technological determinist approach to impairment. These issues are summarised by Alan Sheldon, who implies:

> Technology is not neutral. It is created by the same oppressive society that turns those with impairments into disabled people. … It is no surprise then that disabled people have a complicated relationship with technology. We are often excluded from mainstream technology, a factor said to have contributed to our current labour force exclusion. (Sheldon 2004, 155–156)

In the United States, Dobransky and Hargittai (2006) also found that disabled people are less likely to live in households with computers, are less likely to use computers and are less likely to be online. It has also been identified that those living with such conditions that are also in lower socio-economic groups are often unable to access the technology that is needed, while for others dependency and isolation is actually increased through their use of technology (Sheldon 2004). Hence, it seems that disabled people are excluded in their own homes from accessing technology due to lack of funds, lack of state provision, lack of support or lack of skills to access resources in different ways to a non-disabled population (Allen 2005; Oliver 2009). They are also excluded from more public spaces providing ICT, such as community centres, libraries and colleges for a number of reasons including physical inaccessibility, inability to travel, resources in place and provision of support – and not all these spaces are open – for example, to access post-compulsory educational space is both an achievement and an expense. Both poverty and disability then intersect to exclude from both these types of spaces (Allen 2005).

By drawing on a social model approach, not only does this article look to address the concept of the digital divide, but it examines how digital exclusion impacts on disabled people from more deprived socio-economic areas. In the finding section, the study explores disabled peoples level of usage of digital technologies and its impact in reducing disabling barriers for people living in deprived areas of Sunderland. The study sets out to explore the impact that digital/assistive technologies have had in assisting disabled people to improve their life-chances and reduce social exclusion.

Methodology

Over recent years criticisms have been made of disability studies due to a lack of quantitative research examining the effectiveness of the social model of disability (Shakespeare 2006). This study has attempted to quantitatively assess the value of the social model in relation to a correlation between 'disability' and the 'digital divide'. The data in this study were obtained through a quantitative survey completed by local residents in socially excluded areas in the city of Sunderland. A questionnaire gathered basic demographic data, information concerning usage of various technologies, involvement with digital inclusion activities and the discernible impact and benefits upon living circumstances, quality of life and life-chances.

The purpose of the survey was to access the opinions, experiences and behavioural patterns of a range of residents from a range of social groups at different stages of the 'digital spectrum'. This allowed an assessment of the reach of digital activities, and the benefits of engagement with technology. People were classified as disabled in this study through self-identification, where respondents specified their impairment(s). These ranged from mobility impairments, hearing impairments, brain injuries and learning difficulties to mental health problems. The study recognises the possibility that some respondents who have an impairment that affects their ability to use technology might not identify themselves as disabled. This is a general limitation to this study and questionnaire based surveys on disability in general.

Our definition of 'socially excluded' geographical areas was based upon the 'Indices of Deprivation' (Department for Communities and Local Government 2007) and those LSOAs in Sunderland that fall within the '10 per cent most deprived nationally' category in this index. When developing a quantitative study, the Indices of Multiple Deprivation is viewed as one of the most reliable measurements of deprivation, which includes data from domains such as income; employment; health and disability; education, skills and training; barriers to housing and services; living environments; and crime (Conrad and Capewell 2012). However, the study recognises its limitations, which include; the fact that it is not necessarily a direct measurement of poverty and exclusion but a relative scale (i.e. most through to least deprived); it can be described as over simplistic due to the complex nature of deprivation and exclusion; and the measurement is based on geographical concentration that excludes scattered deprivation and poverty. Yet in order to develop a large-scale study of disability, the Indices of Multiple Deprivation were viewed as more reliable compared with its alternatives.

Given that 61, 171 (21.8%) of the city's 280,600 population in 2007 lived in those LSOAs classified as amongst the 10% most deprived LSOAs nationally, the initial postal questionnaire aimed to be sent out to at least 6117 residents (10% of the socially excluded population). In order to access the sample frame of addresses we matched the LSOAs with corresponding post codes using the National Post Code Directory and then used the Electoral Roll (for 2009) to locate the most current registered addresses in these areas. According to this register, the number of residential addresses currently found in these areas totals 26,443. We took a 25% sample of this population, providing a total of 6610 addresses (a total in excess of the 6117 figure mentioned above and therefore a representative sample). This sample was then systematically and randomly selected by beginning with a random number and then selecting every third address within the frame (Dane 1990).

In total 811 residents responded to the questionnaire. The survey represents a response rate of 12.7% and a sampling error of below 4% at a 95% confidence level (de Vaus 1993). From the 811 respondents included in this study, 38&% ($n = 300$) classified themselves as having some form of impairment. A number of cross-tabulation tests were used to examine frequency distribution of cases (respondents) when examining the correlation between two or more variables. This shows the distribution of cases by their values. Two or more variable frequency distributions were analysed using a chi-square statistic (χ^2) to discover whether variables (i.e. disability×digital exclusion) are statistically independent or whether they are associated. The null hypothesis classification (p) is either independent (i.e. no relationship between variables exist) or the p classification is dependent (i.e. that a relationship exists between variables).

In the social sciences a statistical relationship exists if a χ^2 statistic is equal to or below 0.05 (<5% chance). The data from this survey were subsequently analysed and only data were used that were calculated to be of significance ($p < 0.05$). The data were analysed using SPSS in the form of single variable analysis, and where data were calculated to be of significance ($p < 0.05$), bivariate (comparing two variables) and multivariate analysis was also applied (comparing three or more variables). The key areas of concern in this analysis were ownership and use, engagement with digital inclusion initiatives and online public services, skills, learning and employment opportunities as well as benefits and drawbacks to the use of technology. This analysis was particularly interested in examining the use of technology in relation to the key social groups identified (age, gender, disability, employed/unemployed).

In relation to multivariate analysis, disability and digital technological interaction was compared with age, gender and employed/unemployed variables to investigate the intersectional nature of the disability variable in this study (D ↔ A,

G, E, $\leftrightarrow$ DT [where D=disability; A=age; G=sex, E=employment, DT=digital technology]). Based on the chi-square statistical data, the multivariate analysis was rejected and it was only the bivariate analysis that confirmed a significant dependent correlation between the disability and digital technology variables (D $\leftrightarrow$ DT) It is this statistical relationship which might imply that the key factor in this study is how disabled people experience technology due to macro (disabling) barriers of poverty and inaccessibility, rather than restrictions because of other social factors such as gender, age and social class.

For the purpose of this article only significant data collected on disability will be used. The aim was to make a comparison between a disabled population ($n = 300$) and a non-disabled population living in deprived areas of Sunderland ($n = 511$). The non-disabled, socially excluded, population will be referred to as the 'control group' in this article. This article employs the social model of disability to the data analysis; hence 'disability' refers to disabling structural barriers and 'impairment' to biological/neurological variations.

Findings: disability and the use of digital technologies

The UK government has maintained that technology plays a crucial part in their national and local commitment to improve social inclusion and foster independence for disabled people (Digital Inclusion Task Force 2009). Based on the assumption that Sunderland has made significant investment in reducing digital exclusion within its local population, it would be probable that the data analysis would reveal that technology played a vital role within the lives of disabled people. Unfortunately, this does not seem to be the case as the data present no evidence of greater technological usage by disabled people compared with the control group (see Figure 1). When studying the data, the reverse seems apparent, as disabled people were less likely to use forms of digital technologies compared with the control group.

Hence, 42% of people with impairments ($n = 127$) reported never having used a mobile phone, computer or having accessed the Internet. This is compared with 28% ($n = 140$) of the control group, revealing a 14% difference ($p < 0.00$). As Roulstone (1998, 2007) notes, technologies have the potential in assisting people overcome some issues of impairment and reducing some barriers. In order for technology to have any impact on disabling barriers, people must first have access to it (Goggin and Newell 2003; Harris 2010; Watling 2011). These data seem to reveal that the principal barrier illustrated by respondents was not having immediate, or any, access to digital technologies.

Yet it is important to examine issues of usage in more depth, as the potential for specific technologies seems particularly relevant for some disabled people. The data revealed that 71% of disabled people had never used a laptop or personal computer compared with 48% of the control group (see Table 1). These findings were extremely surprising as they reveal that only 29% of disabled people had used a computer. The lack of technological usage is also confirmed when examining Internet use: 73% of respondents with an impairment reported having never connected to the Internet, compared with 49% of the control group.

Again this indicates that only 27% of disabled people have access to Internet services. Mobile phone usage was also extremely low for this group as 50% of disabled people reported using a mobile phone. This is compared with 61% of the

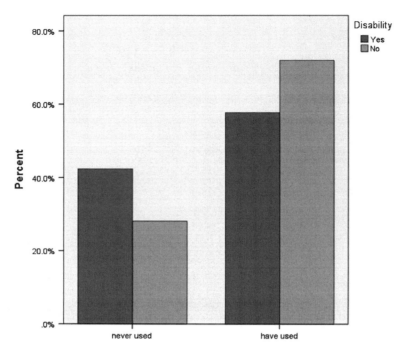

Figure 1. Usage of digital technologies, comparing disabled people with the general population.

Table 1. Reported usage of digital technologies.

Digital technology	Response	Persons with a disability (frequency)	Persons without a disability (frequency)	Persons with a disability (%)	Persons without a disability (%)
Notebook/laptop/PC	No	212	237	71	48
	Yes	88	261	29	52
Mobile phone	No	150	196	50	39
	Yes	150	302	50	61
Internet connection	No	220	242	73	49
	Yes	80	256	27	51
Digital television	No	163	231	54	46
	Yes	137	267	46	54

control group. These data findings indicate that disabled people in this study were far less likely to use digital technologies than people in the control group (see Table 1). Again this reinforces Roulstone's (1998, 2007) and Goggin and Newell's (2003) claim that the potential of digital technologies is not being achieved as disabled people are not accessing basic technologies.

When examining barriers of access to ICT, both the disabled group (58%) and the control group (71%) implied that these were due to financial constraints. The specific problem for disabled people, at 18%, was having no confidence in their skills/knowledge when using ICT ($p < 0.01$); which was not the case for the control

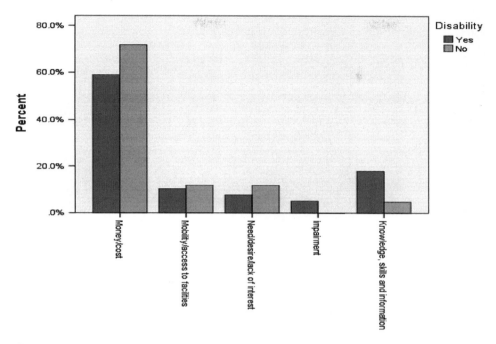

Figure 2. Barriers preventing access to technology, comparing disabled people with the general population.

group at 5% (see Figure 2). Furthermore, only 5% of the disabled group suggested that it was impairment that prevented access to digital technologies. Hence, barriers preventing disabled people from accessing technologies were primarily financial limitations, but specifically a lack of skills/knowledge of ICT. These data strengthen Harris's (2010) qualitative study suggesting that it is knowledge and cost that are barriers to engagement. It should be noted that ownership is particularly important for disabled people as access to technologies in public places (i.e. libraries) is often restricted through disabling barriers such as inaccessible buildings or PCs without the appropriate assistive software, which again restrict usage (Oliver 2009).

Disability and assistive technologies

Although the majority of respondents defined digital technologies in terms of computer/Internet and mobile phones, it should be noted that assistive technologies were also acknowledged. Although it would be expected that disabled peoples' level of engagement with technology would be higher than the control group, due to assistive technologies, this was not the case. The data analysis revealed that disabled people in this study did not engage with assistive technologies to any great extent. Very few reported using technology to assist them in medical support or to enable independent living (7% of the impaired population, $n = 23$). Within this analysis it was the Telecare service (at 17%), and the use of chair and bath lifts (at 17%) that were most commonly used (see Figure 3). Again these data suggest that this group of people are not engaging in the use of digital technologies, even ones that are specifically design for particular impairments.

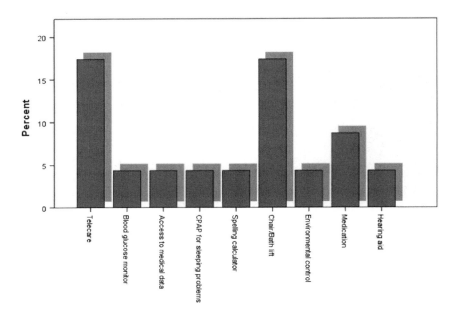

Figure 3.   Assistive technologies.

Again, referring to Harris (2010) or Adam and Kreps's (2006) research, this could be due to other barriers disabled people face when accessing these forms of technologies. With an emphasis on independent living it would be expected that many disabled people will be accessing digital technologies through local government social services or National Health Service healthcare services. This does not seem to be the case in this sample, as for many people who might benefit from these technologies access seems to be denied. Hence, one of the key barriers experienced by respondents in this study is a lack of access to recent technological advances to assist people with different types of impairment.

Technology and improvements in life quality

As Goggin and Newell (2003) state, the idea that disabled people are being socially included due to technological advances seems to be a misconception. This point is illustrated within the study as 57% ($n = 145$) of disabled people did not consider that technology had improved the quality of their lives (see Figure 4). This was compared with 42.9% ($n = 109$) who agreed that some improvement had taken place ($p < 0.00$) due to recent advances in digital technology. When comparing this with the control group 64% ($n = 301$), agreed improvement had been made to their lives. Hence, the control group were far more likely to agree that technology had improved their quality of life.

Disability and domains of social exclusion

When this research was conducted, the UK government had targeted five domains of social exclusion (education, employment, social networking, independent living and healthcare) that they would improve with the assistance of new/digital technologies. As disabled people were defined as a digitally excluded group, there was an

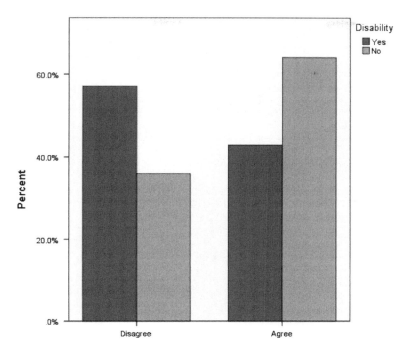

Figure 4.   Long-term health condition and quality-of-life benefits from use of technology.

aim to enhance inclusion by improving access to these domains (Prime Ministers' Strategy Unit/Department for Trade and Industry 2005). The research discovered no statistical evidence to suggest that digital technologies had improved in any of these domains for disabled people in Sunderland. A significant (but negative) relationship was discovered between disability and improved healthcare ($p < 0.01$), disability and education ($p < 0.00$) and employment and disability ($p < 0.00$).[2]

When examining whether digital technologies enhanced access to healthcare, the data revealed little evidence of improvement. Only 41% ($n = 65$) of disabled people reported that technology had any impact on their general health or have made an improvement to their local healthcare services (see Figure 5). This is compared with 56% ($n = 184$) of the control group who acknowledged some benefits in their healthcare service and overall health. This is surprising given the potential benefits that some of this group could gain from greater and more effective use of assistive technologies in terms of healthcare. These findings reinforce data in Figure 3 that illustrated barriers relating to access of assistive technology for disabled people. These data are particularly concerning as disabled people could be one group who might need quick and easy access to healthcare depending on their particular impairment. Hence, this might indicate that the digital divide constructs a new layer of social barriers, where people become further excluded from their health service compared with the control group who have increased access to technology (see Table 1).

When examining the data on the relationship between technology and enhanced access to education, no evidence could be found in order to support any positive improvements for disabled people. The data revealed that 66% ($n = 95$) of disabled people did not consider that digital technologies improved educational attainment

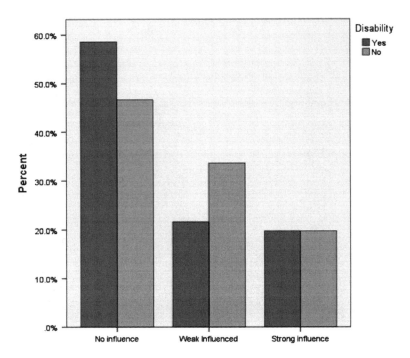

Figure 5.   Social inclusion and health.

($p < 0.00$). This was reversed when examining the control group, as 64% ($n = 225$) of non-disabled respondents felt that digital technologies did in fact improve access to education. Furthermore, only 16% ($n = 23$) of disabled people reported that digital technologies had strongly influenced their educational achievements compared with 41% ($n = 144$) of the control group. As with the data analysis on healthcare, these findings illustrate that digital technologies appear to have a greater impact on the educational achievements of the non-disabled group compared with the disabled population in Sunderland (see Figure 6). Hence, the analysis seems to suggest that digital technologies do not appear to have an impact on improving access to education or the general educational experiences of disabled people in this study.

Finally, when examining the relationship between digital technologies, enriched employment opportunities and income improvement, again there were significant differences between disabled people and the control group. As we can see in Figure 7, 73% ($n = 102$) of this group reported that they felt technology had not improved their life-chances in relation to employment and income ($p < 0.00$). This was compared with 62% ($n = 223$) of the control group who felt technology had made some improvement to their employment chances. These data illustrate that although the government and local agencies in Sunderland have developed a number of initiatives in supporting disabled people back into work with the aid of digital technologies, these projects seem not to have played a significant role in improving the employability of the disabled group.

These data reveal that there has been a general failure in improving employability for people with disabilities within Sunderland using digital technologies. Again this reinforces the idea that digital technologies play only a partial role in improving access to the job market, as other disabling barriers such as social stigma,

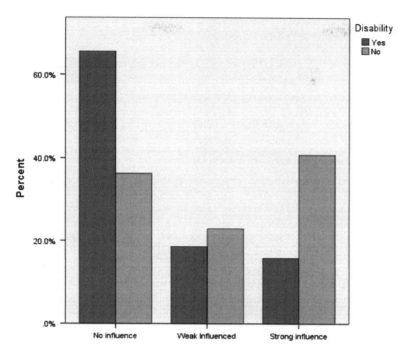

Figure 6.   Social inclusion and education.

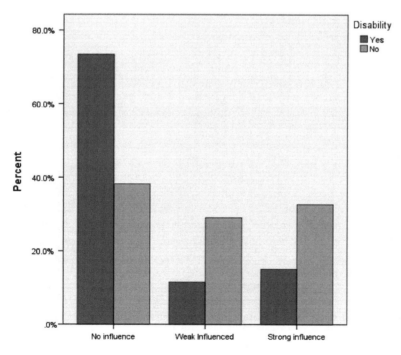

Figure 7.   Social inclusion, employment and income.

environmental issues, education, and so forth, all restrict access to the workforce (Goggin and Newell 2003; Roulstone 2007; Oliver 2009). For disabled people in this study, the findings seem to reveal that these respondents are still excluded within their local communities. These data might reveal that, due to a polarised view of what disability means, digital technologies rather than improving life-chances, in reality, add an extra layer of exclusion by means of the digital divide for some disabled people (Goggin and Newell 2003).

Conclusion: barriers to digital and social inclusion

A criticism of this study, from an individual model perspective, might suggest that the ability to use ICT depends on impairment (i.e. visual, hearing, motor and cognitive, etc.). Someone with no functional vision is more likely to experience difficulties using the Internet than someone with restricted lower body movement – yet both appear under the same general category of 'disabled' in this study. From this individual model perspective, barriers to technology relate directly to impairment, and analysis should attempt to segregate respondents based on disclosed impairment in order to understand emerging patterns and barriers.

The response to this criticism is that although impairment impacts on how individuals use technology, the authors have presented evidence that there are structural barriers, such as poverty, skills/knowledge and inaccessibility, which prevent disabled people in this study from using a range of digital technologies. Hence, digital technologies are designed for people without impairments (Borg, Larsson, and Östergren 2011) and in order to make them accessible for disabled people additional technologies need to be purchased. This constructs barriers of usage as ICT design is directed towards a non-impaired consumer group, and extra financial burden falls on the disabled population.

The aim of this article is not to suggest that digital technologies cannot improve the lives of people with impairments. Digital technologies might have the power to include some groups of people with impairments; however, access must be improved to all members of society rather than to the few who can afford these digital technologies. The data have illustrated that investment by both local and national government in terms of reducing social exclusion in areas of healthcare, education and employability has not yet been successful for disabled people in Sunderland. This paper has presented (some) statistical evidence that it is poverty, a lack of ownership, restricted knowledge and inaccessible ICT that construct new forms of barriers for disabled people in this study. Furthermore, it could be suggested that barriers to digital inclusion also relate to the under use of already existing public facilities in the city due to issues of disabling technologies/public environments (Oliver 2009).

These data might indicate that disabling barriers cause aspects of digital exclusion for disabled people rather than micro issues resulting from an individual's impairment. This study has revealed that there is still a long way to go before digital technology successfully impacts on the lives of disabled people in order to reduce social exclusion. Therefore, if access to digital technologies is only for people who can afford them, then digital and assistive technologies, rather than benefit disabled people, will create a new level of social inequality reinforcing the digital divide within the United Kingdom. This study concludes by reinforcing Borg, Larsson, and Östergren's (2011) claim that access to digital technology that helps remove barriers of exclusion for disabled people should be seen as a 'right' rather than a privilege for disabled people. Designers should be encouraged to develop inclusive ICT, and, where this is impossible, disability funding should be made available for assistive ICT support. Unfortunately, with the new Tory-led government and the focus on local cuts to services and benefits, disabled people seemed destined to a new level of exclusion for the foreseeable future.

Notes

1. The smallest area measurement of deprivation in England.
2. When examining the relationship between social networking and disability ($p < 0.07$) and independent living and disability ($p < 0.28$) it should be noted that the data analysis was not significant in our study. Hence, this study is unable to comment on improvement or failure by Sunderland to improve access to social networking and independent living with the use of digital technologies.

References

Adam, A., and D. Kreps. 2006. Web accessibility: A digital divide for disabled people. In *Social inclusion: Societal and organizational implications for information systems*, ed. E. Trauth, D. Howcroft, T. Butler, B. Fitzgerald, and J. DeGross, 217–28. Boston: Springer.

Allen, C. 2005. Bourdieu's habitus, social class and the spatial worlds of visually impaired children. *Urban Studies* 42, no. 7: 487–506.

Bauman, Z. 1998. *Globalization: The human consequences*. Oxford: Polity.

Borg, J., S. Larsson, and P. Östergren. 2011. The right to assistive technology: For whom, for what, and by whom? *Disability & Society* 26, no. 2: 151–67.

Bradley, N., and W. Poppen. 2003. Assistive technology, computers and Internet may decrease sense of isolation for homebound elderly and disabled persons. *Technology and Disability* 15, no. 1: 19–25.

Castells, M. 1996. *The rise of the network society*. Oxford: Blackwell.

Conrad, D., and S. Capewell. 2012. Associations between deprivation and rates of childhood overweight and obesity in England. *British Medical Journal* 2: e000463. doi: 10.1136/bmjopen-2011-000463.

Dane, F.C. 1990. *Research methods*. Pacific Grove, CA: Brooks Cole.

de Vaus, D.A. 1993. *Surveys in social research*. 3rd ed. London: UCL Press.

Department for Communities and Local Government. 2007. *The index of multiple deprivation*. London: The National Archives, DCLG.

Department for Communities and Local Government. 2008. *Delivering digital inclusion: An action plan for consultation*. London: HMSO.

Department of Work and Pensions. 2011. Digital inclusion: Office for Disability Issues – ODI projects. http://www.dwp.gov.uk/odi-projects/digital-inclusion (accessed May 9, 2011).

Digital Inclusion Task Force. 2009. *Champion for digital inclusion*. London: Pricewaterhouse Coopers LLP.

Disability Rights Commission. 2004. *The Web access and inclusion for disabled people*. London: The Stationery Office.

Disability Rights Commission. 2006. *Disability briefing March 2006*. Leeds: Disability Archives.

Dobransky, K., and E. Hargittai. 2006. The disability divide in Internet access and use. *Information, Communication and Society* 9, no. 3: 313–34.

Gleeson, B. 1999. Can technology overcome the disabling city? In *Mind and body spaces: Geographies of illness, impairment and disability*, ed. R. Butler and H. Parr, 98–118. London: Routledge.

Goggin, G., and C. Newell. 2003. *Digital disability. The social construction of disability in new media*. Oxford: Rowman & Littlefield Publishers.

Graham, S. 2002. Bridging urban digital divides? Urban polarisation and information and communications technologies (ICTs). *Urban Studies* 39, no. 1: 33–56.

Gregor, P., D. Sloan, and A.F. Newell. 2005. Disability and technology: Building barriers or creating opportunities? *Advances in Computers* 64: 283–346.

Harris, J. 2010. The use, role and application of advanced technology in the lives of disabled people in the UK. *Disability & Society* 25, no. 4: 427–39.

Harvey, D. 1990. *The condition of postmodernity*. Oxford: Blackwell.

Haywood, T. 1998. Global networks and the myth of equality: Trickle down or trickle away? In *Cyberspace divide: Equality, agency and policy in the information society*, ed. B.D. Loader, 19–34. London: Routledge.

Helsper, E. 2008. *Digital inclusion: An analysis of social disadvantage and the information society*. London: Department for Communities and Local Government.

Indices of Deprivation. 2007. *The index of multiple deprivation*. London: The National Archives, Communities and Local Government.

National Telecommunications and Information Administration. 1995. *Falling through the Net: A survey of the 'haves' and 'have-nots' in rural and urban America*. New York: US Government Printing Office.

Oliver, M. 1978. *The misuse of technology: Walking appliances for paraplegics*. Leeds: Disability Achieves.

Oliver, M. 2009. *Understanding disability from theory to practice*. 2nd ed. Basingstoke: Palgrave.

Oliver, M., C. Barnes, and C. Thomas. 2001. *Disability and the sociological imagination*. Sheffield: Teaching and Learning Network.

Prime Ministers' Strategy Unit/Department for Trade and Industry. 2005. *Connecting the UK: Digital strategy digital strategy*. London: Strategy Unit.

Roulstone, A. 1998. *Enabling technology: Disabled people, work and new technology*. Buckingham: Open University Press.

Roulstone, A. 2007. The role of assistive technology in the lives of disabled adults. Outlines. Vol. 5. Research into Practice for Adults. http://www.ripfa.org.uk/publications/outlines/outlinesPDF/5.pdf (accessed March 2, 2011).

Russell, N., and N. Stafford. 2002. *Trends in ICT access and use*. London: Department for Education and Skills.

Selwyn, N. 2003. ICT for all? Access and use of public ICT sites in the UK. *Information, Communication and Society* 6, no. 3: 350–75.

Shakespeare, T. 2006. *Disability rights and wrongs*. London: Routledge.

Sheldon, A. 2004. Changing technology. In *Disabling barriers, enabling environments*, ed. J. Swain et al, 155–60. London: Sage.

Sunderland City Council. 2007. *Vision statement for digital challenge: Final draft*. Sunderland: Sunderland City Council.

Tunstall. 2008. *Sunderland City Council: Fair access to care services eligibility criteria application*. Whitely Bridge: Tunstall. http://www.tunstall.co.uk/assets/literature/SunderlandCaseStudy.pdf (accessed September 5, 2009).

UK Online Centres. 2007. *Digital inclusion: A discussion of the evidence base*. London: Fresh Minds.

Watling, S. 2011. Digital exclusion: Coming out from behind closed doors. *Disability & Society* 26, no. 4: 491–5.

Watson, N., and B. Woods. 2005. The origins and early developments of special/adaptive wheelchair seating. *Social History of Medicine* 18, no. 3: 459–74.

Disability, identity and disclosure in the online dating environment

Natasha Saltes

Department of Sociology, Queen's University, Kingston, Canada

This paper examines how disabled people construct self-identity and negotiate disclosure of impairment in the online dating environment. Grounded theory was used to code and analyze 108 responses to an online open-ended questionnaire completed by disabled people who engaged in online dating. Findings reveal that while the body and impairment may not be present in digital space, it plays an important role in how disabled people present themselves online. This paper suggests that the embodied/disembodied dichotomy that has been traditionally used to distinguish offline and online interaction is blurred in the online dating environment.

Points of interest

- This article provides first-hand accounts of disabled people's experience constructing and presenting self-identity and negotiating disclosure of impairment in online dating sites.
- Findings reveal that, despite the Internet's capacity to facilitate disembodied anonymous interaction, the body and impairment play an important role in how disabled people construct their self-identity and interact with others.
- The suggestion for extending the parameters of the social model to reflect the sociology of impairment and the 'lived body' is raised in an attempt to apply the social model in digital environments.

Introduction

The Internet has added a new dimension to the way people find and cultivate romantic relationships. In a digital environment characterized by disembodied interaction, online dating provides disabled people with the option to conceal impairment and engage with others anonymously. In addition to the countless general online dating sites that exist, there are currently over a dozen online dating sites designed specifically for disabled people. While the opportunities to engage in online dating have increased, little is known about disabled people's experience.

The impetus for this study stemmed from the dearth of literature on the experiences of courtship and dating among disabled people and in response to the growing popularity of online dating. This study also emerged out of the recognition that while much has been written about the technical aspects of computer accessibility, little consideration has been given to investigating the types of online interaction that occur and how disabled people present themselves in digital environments.

One of the few studies to examine disability within the context of online interaction looked at the type of relationships disabled people seek out and the role that the body plays in online interaction. Seymour and Lupton (2004) found that, even in the online environment, an emphasis on the body and physical appearance was present. Rather than taking advantage of the anonymity that the Internet provides, participants sought ways to reinstate the body online. This study builds from that of Seymour and Lupton and looks at how disabled people present themselves in online dating sites where the purpose of interaction is to develop a romantic relationship.

Empirical research on online dating has shown that developing intimacy in digital space is facilitated through the building of trust and through self-disclosure (Hardey 2004; Lawson and Leck 2006). The absence of conventional social 'rules' for online mediated courtship requires online daters to develop and understand for themselves a set of rules that shape how they should interact (Hardey 2008). For disabled people, the lack of interactional rules and the desire to establish 'trust' raise important questions about disclosure. This paper explores how disabled people navigate through the online dating environment where the rules of interaction are unclear, and argues that the embodied/disembodied dichotomy that has been traditionally used to distinguish offline and online interaction is blurred in the online dating environment. The desire to develop an intimate relationship that can extend to the offline environment means that disabled people are confronted with difficult decisions regarding how to present themselves in 'disembodied' digital space. The issue of disclosure prompts disabled people to determine the extent to which the embodied characteristics of impairment are part of their self-identity and how this influences the type of information they include in their online dating profiles.

Anonymity and self-disclosure in the online environment

The popularity of social networking sites such as *Facebook*, through which individuals rarely disguise who they are, suggest that online interaction is no longer primarily characterized by anonymity in the way it perhaps once was (see Miller 2011). Yet there are circumstances, such as online dating, where issues of anonymity and disclosure are still highly significant aspects of social interaction. It is therefore worth revisiting some of the literature that has examined anonymity and self-disclosure.

According to Rheingold (2000), the online environment is ideal for developing meaningful relationships because it is a space where people disclose more intimate information than they would without anonymous features such as pseudonyms and lack of visual presence. A study on visual anonymity and self-disclosure conducted by Joinson (2001) found that participants were likely to disclose more personal information during online interaction compared with face-to-face interaction. Joinson (2001) also found that visual anonymity during online interaction resulted in greater disclosure and that the presence of images significantly reduced self-disclosure. This last observation is interesting given that, in the online dating environment, photographs play an important role in attracting people to view and respond to profiles.

While the Internet may encourage self-disclosure, a recent series of four studies conducted by Rosen et al. suggest that self-disclosure may not necessarily yield desired results. While men were found to be accepting of either high or low levels of self-disclosure as opposed to moderate levels of self-disclosure, women tended to prefer lower levels and were less likely to respond to an initial email if there was a high level of self-disclosure (Rosen et al. 2008). Self-disclosure may signify that a relationship has reached a certain stage. For instance, it may suggest that a level of intimacy and trust has been established to enable someone to feel comfortable revealing personal information. This suggests that, for first encounters, self-disclosure might be viewed as impersonal. When people meet face to face they tend to be cautious about revealing too much information. Personal information is usually revealed after establishing an emotional connection. However, in the online environment, people have less inhibition and are more likely to disclose personal information and deeper feelings sooner and, according to Rosen et al. (2008), often within the first few correspondences. While existing research shows that in the online environment anonymity actually encourages self-disclosure, and often earlier than in offline encounters, it is important to consider that the impact of self-disclosure may ultimately depend on the type of information that is revealed and how receptive the person who is receiving this information is. For instance, the self-disclosure of one's personal dreams and aspirations may receive very different reactions from the self-disclosure of impairment.

Contrary to existing research that suggests anonymity promotes self-disclosure, Dobransky and Hargittai adopt a different perspective and contend that 'the most striking aspect of online communication for people with disabilities is the ability it affords the user to hide aspects of him or herself' (2006, 316). They explain that in allowing disabled people the option to remove their impairment from the forefront of interaction, the Internet enables disabled people to escape the isolation and stigma they may encounter offline. They state:

> Unlike communication in the offline world where the stigma of disability or one's impairment itself may at times prevent one from venturing into the world freely and interacting with others, online communication allows the individual with disability to encounter and interact with others to a degree that may not be possible offline. (Dobransky and Hargittai 2006, 316)

Barney lends support to Dobransky and Hargittai's point, noting that 'the dislocation, disembodiment and opacity of network communication can enable a high degree of anonymity and fluidity in the social construction of our selves …' (Barney 2004, 152). Barney adds that the Internet enables people to construct identities they choose, rather than having their identity assigned to them based on prejudicial characteristics (2004, 152). Yurchisin, Watchravesringkan, and Brown McCabe suggest that anonymity afforded by the Internet enables people to re-evaluate their identity and try out new aspects of identity, which they refer to as 'possible selves' (2005, 737). They contend that the creation of online dating profiles may help individuals to 'explore and recreate their self-identities' (Yurchisin, Watchravesringkan, and Brown McCabe 2005, 737). In the context of online dating, the question of anonymity is less about projecting a false representation of self and is more about having the control to decide which aspects of self will be revealed and when. While the absence of bodies online removes physical attributes as a marker of identity, it calls into question whether and to what extent impairment is considered part of one's identity. This paper aims to shed light on how disabled people perceive and construct identity and how this influences disclosure of impairment and self-presentation in online dating sites.

The social model and digital environments

As new information and communication technologies increasingly become part of the infrastructure of daily life, the distinction between online and offline environments begins to blur. This, in turn, raises important questions about the boundaries of the social model of disability when the distinction between 'embodied' (offline) and 'disembodied' (online) interaction no longer holds. The social model separates impairment from disability by locating disability as a consequence of social barriers that limit and exclude disabled people. According to the social model, people with impairments become 'disabled' when society fails to accommodate for their difference (Oliver 1990). The medical model, by contrast, considers disability to be the consequence of impairment. By pathologizing disability, the medical model assigns disability to the body. The social model's recasting of disability from the body to the social has underpinned the politics of disablement. While this has been effectual in advancing an agenda of disability rights, it has also produced a paradox; in that while it argues for a sociology of disability, it does so by situating and understanding impairment within a biomedical framework.

While acknowledging the merits of the social model, scholars have sought to expand its parameters to reflect 'an embodied, rather than disembodied notion of disability' (Hughes and Paterson 1997, 326). Hughes and Paterson argue for a sociology of impairment, noting that while the social model offers a viable theoretical framework for emancipatory politics by understanding impairment through a biomedical lens, it is unable to provide a theoretical basis for an emancipatory politics of identity. According to Hughes and Paterson, the social model's reduction of impairment to medical discourse diminishes the 'lived body' and is consequently unable to consider and account for the 'bodily point of view of disabled people or the embodied experience of prejudice and oppression, disadvantage and discrimination' (1997, 337). This becomes evident in disembodied digital spaces where impairment may be felt and experienced, but not seen by others.

The divide between the medical and social models can be bridged by conceptualizing disability through the perspective of actor network theory (Galis 2011). Galis situates the enactment of disability within a discourse of performative agency, and argues that disability is not reduced to impairments or social constructions, but rather is simultaneously experienced through 'symbolic, material physical and cultural practices' (2011, 835). Galis' perspective contributes to a sociology of impairment advocated by Hughes and Paterson by recognizing the bodily point of view of disabled people. The social model examines the ways in which disability is socially constructed by looking at, for instance, attitudinal, architectural, structural and systemic barriers present in physical space. With information technology emerged a sort of digital space, which has enabled individuals to be simultaneously present and interacting in both the physical and digital environment. Mobile technology have made it possible for people to be in transition from one physical space to another while being present in digital space and interacting with others both physically and digitally. In order to gain an understanding of how disability may be constructed in digital space, it is crucial that we recognize the 'physical' boundaries of the social model and work toward extending its parameters. The simultaneous experience of disability that Galis raises is important to consider in light of the way in which people coexist and simultaneously interact within digital disembodied spaces and embodied offline environments.

In the context of online dating, the goal in meeting an intimate partner means that the interaction that takes place in the online environment is often carried over to the offline environment. Moving beyond thinking about the social model in terms of accessible technology to thinking about the 'lived body' and how it is constructed and presented in digital space is helpful for recognizing how offline embodied experiences of impairment emerge online.

Methods

Ethics, recruitment, sample, demographic and data collection

Ethical approval was granted by the Sociology Ethics Committee at the University of Cambridge, where this research was carried out. Recruitment occurred over a two-month period beginning in November 2009 and ending in January 2010 and consisted of two Internet-mediated approaches. In the first approach, over 300 calls for participants were emailed to disability organizations, disability resource centers in universities and disability related academic programs located in Canada, the United States and the United Kingdom. The second approach in recruitment incorporated online social networking and included posting the call for participants on disability and online dating discussion forums as well as in related groups on social networking sites. Calls for participants were also emailed to over 500 members of various online disability dating interest/support groups.

Purposive sampling was used to generate a repertoire of participants. The key criteria of the sample were individuals who identified themselves as living with an impairment who were former users or current users of an online dating site and 18 years of age or older. A total of 108 participants ranging in age from 18 to 75 responded to the calls for participants. The most common age group that participants fell within was 36–45 (32%), followed by 26–35 (26%), 18–25 (15%), 46–55 (11%) and 66–75 (1%). The representation of gender was fairly evenly balanced, with females representing 51% of participants and males representing 49%. Participants represented a range of impairments, with the majority indicating that they had mobility impairment (63%). The majority of participants (57%) had used an online dating site for less than one year, followed by one to three years (21%), four to seven years (13%) and eight years and over (9%). By far the most common online dating sites that participants reported using were general dating sites (65%) and disability dating sites (59%). Participants also reported using 'other' dating sites (18%), gay/lesbian dating sites (12%), religious dating sites (8%), race/ethnic dating sites (4%), single-parent dating sites (2%) and senior dating sites (1%).

Data were collected using an open-ended questionnaire that was completed online by anonymous participants. The open-ended questions were designed to gain a better understanding of factors that influenced an individual's decision to disclose their impairment, how they constructed their self-identity, and the self-presentation strategies they used in creating their online dating profile. Data were analyzed within the framework of grounded theory and followed in the tradition of Strauss and Corbin (1998).

Findings and discussion

Constructing self-identity

Symbolic interactionists such as Cooley and Mead have argued that the self is primarily socially constructed through interaction with others and the attitudes that become apparent during these social exchanges (Harter 1999; Cooley 1998; Mead 1967). Hall's concept of identity operates more on a comparative framework and is based on the notion that individuals define their identity based on what they are not. He claims that identities are 'constructed within and not outside discourse' and that they are 'constructed through and not outside difference' (Hall 1996, 4). For disabled people, the concept of identity can be a source of contention in that it is based on social norms that others impose.

According to Watson (2002), the agency to reject the identity of a disabled person is achieved by separating impairment from self-identity. Watson suggests that, for some disabled people, physicality is not considered 'an essential biological determinant of the self' (2002, 524) and that self-identity therefore is not constructed from biological features. Watson (2002) indicates that because the presence of impairment becomes part of a disabled person's day-to-day experience, it is normal for them to have impairment and that the presence of impairment therefore becomes part of their ontology rather than part of their self-identity. Within this study there was some evidence of this. According to one participant: 'I feel my disability is as natural as my height, weight, hair colour and other physical attributes.' However, others felt differently and considered their disability to be a part of their self-identity. When responding to a question that asked participants to describe their feelings about disclosing their impairment, one participant illustrated this with the following response: 'I feel very comfortable because this is part of who I am.'

While the presence of impairment may be accepted as a natural attribute that does not alter one's sense of self-identity, or as a significant part of one's self-identity that is embraced, for others it is an attribute from which they wish to disassociate. Some participants expressed a desire to be known for other attributes besides their impairment. As one participant wrote: 'I don't like my disability to be more important than who I am.' The separation of impairment from self-identity could be attributed, in part, to how disabled people perceive others will view them in relation to their impairment. For example, one participant wrote that 'how they react, or what they may think' was an influential factor in determining whether to withhold or disclose their impairment.

The notion that an individual develops a sense of self from the perceptions of others was introduced by Cooley in his concept of the *looking-glass self*. This social psychological concept rests on the idea that one's perception of their self-identity is arrived at through a process of imagining how they appear to others and how others will judge or perceive that appearance followed by an associated feeling such as pride or shame (Cooley 1998). In the words of Cooley: '... the character and weight of that other, in whose mind we see ourselves, makes all the difference with our feeling. ... We always imagine, and in imagining share, the judgments of the other mind' (1998, 164–165). In the context of disability, it is through interactions with others that disabled people become aware of their differences. To refer back to Hall's definition, identity is 'constructed through and not outside difference' (1996, 4). Thus, it is the recognition of difference that often influences perception of self. The idea that the self exists in relation to others often means that those with whom we expect to encounter and interact with play a vital role in influencing how we present ourselves whereby the extent to which information is disclosed is adjusted according to the anticipated or imagined reactions of others, or to avoid the reactions we anticipate and imagine.

Self-presentation

Self-presentation can be understood as the packaging of information to others (Schlenker and Pontari 2000). It is the idea that through our behavior and appearance we project an identity to those with whom we interact (Goffman 1959). In *The Presentation of Self in Everyday Life,* Goffman uses a dramaturgical analogy to illustrate how impressions of self are managed in face-to-face interaction. Within his analysis, he argues that individuals are concerned with presenting themselves in a favorable light. In doing so, they project a desired self-image onto others. In presenting a dualistic conception of the self, Goffman (1959) likens the individual to a performer and their presentation of self as the performance.

Since Goffman's analysis is constructed around face-to-face interaction, applying his theory to online interaction requires some repositioning. To begin with, we might consider that one way of exploring an aspect of self-presentation in the online dating environment is to look at how individuals construct their dating profiles. Deciding what information to include about themselves, how much information to include, whether to use a photograph, how many and which one(s) are ways in which individuals exercise some control over their self-presentation. Self-presentation is especially important in online dating sites when profiles have a significant impact on first impressions. A study conducted by Whitty (2008), which examined how individuals present themselves in online dating sites, found that crafting an attractive profile was considered important by nearly all of the participants and that presenting an attractive physical image was more important than any other characteristic.

For disabled people, the question that arises when attempting to present an attractive self-image is whether to reveal or conceal their impairment. The type of information that participants in this study included in their profiles varied from information about their impairment to other attributes, interests, activities, educational background and what they were looking for in a partner. In response to a prompt that asked participants to describe the type of information they typically include in their online dating profile, one participant provided the following:

> a little humor, try to throw in some of my personality. I tell what I spend most of my time doing, and some of the things I'd like to do. Also, I give a little history & info about my accidents. I include fav music, videos, books and tv shows.

This quote indicates how information about impairment can be balanced with other information. However, it is important to note that even if one's impairment is revealed in the profile, it can be overlooked by other online daters – as one participant explains: 'I met a man who hadn't read my profile. When he found out I was in a wheelchair he stopped talking.' In addition to illustrating the superficial form of interaction that can occur when impairment is concealed, this response suggests that the question of presenting impairment may not be the only issue, but that how it is presented might also be an issue.

Participants that disclosed their impairment in their dating profiles often found different ways of doing so. One participant, for instance, reported that he always includes at least two photographs of himself in his wheelchair. Another participant avoided using medical terms and the word 'disability' or 'impairment' and provided a description of her attributes in her own words: 'I usually mention that I'm "oddly brained" or make a vague reference to my shyness or lack of eye contact. I also talk about how to talk to me.' What sets this participant's response apart from some of the others is that, in addition to indicating the presence of impairment, information about how to communicate and interact with her was also provided.

The self-presentation strategies of participants reveal various levels of disclosure from no mention of impairment to providing indirect statements with the intent of alluding to impairment to more detailed information. Some of the participants were quite direct with how they presented their impairment in their profile. For instance, one participant reported mentioning that she is a post-polio quadriplegic and uses a ventilator. Others indicated that in presenting themselves they too provided a description of their impairment with an explanation of how it affects them. For some participants, self-presentation is adjusted according to the type of dating site used as one participant explains: 'It depends upon the type of site. On a disabled dating site, I do not mind disclosing my disability, as I figure that most people on the site likely have a disability of their own.' According to another participant: 'On general online dating sites, I do not disclose my disability, as I figure that it would turn off most potential mates.' These responses suggest that, in the absence of the physical presence of others, some disabled people engage in a process of imagining how their dating profile will appear and how other online daters will judge that appearance. Because disabled people are routinely stigmatized in the offline environment, the anticipation for rejection carries over in the online environment and the evaluative pressure intensifies.

Negotiating disclosure

According to Giddens, the self is 'constantly "on display" to others in terms of its embodiment' (1991, 57). He elaborates on the role that the body plays in constructing identity suggesting that 'routine control of the body is integral to the very nature both of agency and of being accepted (trusted) by others as competent' (1991, 57). For disabled people, negotiating disclosure involves consideration of how impairment will be received by others. Concern that the body would become more important than the self came through in the data, as did the issue of whether the impaired body would be accepted. Consider the following quote in response to a prompt asking participants what influenced them to withhold or disclose their impairment: 'that people would only look at my handicap and forget to look at me and my personality.' Another participant shared a similar view: 'being judged for my disability. I always worry that people see a wheelchair instead of a true person.' One participant summarized this sentiment by stating the following: 'I want people to know me, not a label.'

When prompted to describe how they feel about disclosure, a number of participant responses included the following words: weird, strange, uncertain, embarrassed, ashamed, annoyed, uncomfortable, obligated, nerve racking, apprehensive, and afraid. What was striking was that a number of participants associated their impairment as something that was 'wrong' with them or a problem that others needed to be informed about. They viewed themselves as different from others and feared that because they did not fit the socio-cultural standards of 'normal' then others would not be interested in dating them. Consider the following responses: 'If I don't disclose my disability how would they know what's wrong with me'; 'I have trouble ... being motivated to pursue relationships. I often feel like I don't have as much to offer as normal people'; and 'There aren't that many people who can deal with all the cons of my disability. Not only looks wise, but I'm talking about all the work involved also.'

Negative feelings about the idea of disclosing impairment online stem from a fear of rejection. When asked to describe how they feel about disclosing their impairment on dating sites, one participant summed it up: 'afraid of rejection.' Those who opted against disclosure at the outset reported negative outcomes when their online partner later learned of their impairment: 'when I disclosed my disability, some people stopped talking to me'; 'once I've disclosed my disability men run'; and 'I once hid the fact that I have a disability and when I felt the time was right, most of the times the results were disastrous.' Others revealed how negative experiences from withholding impairment in the past could have an influence on their decision to disclose in the future:

> I am sometimes hesitant to disclose this information, but do find that I would rather have that information be in what the other potential person is reading so they can either self select themselves as to whether they're interested in getting to know me. When I haven't included this information or it's been missed in the profile, and as we get to know each other, I find that it's harder to disclose the information because then I run the risk of never hearing from them again, or the interaction becoming different as a result.

In her work on the self in a social context, Harter (1997) suggests that the consequence of the self being ignored, rejected or devalued encourages the suppression of the true self in an attempt to gain approval and avoid rejection. This could help to explain the reluctance that a number of participants had toward disclosure. The option to conceal impairment means that disabled people must engage in an intricate decision-making process that involves imagining how others would react and respond and whether the response would be accepting or rejecting.

Contrary to the notion that concealing impairment offers an elevated form of interaction, some participants were of the view that revealing their impairment in their dating profile would enable them to avoid rejection. As one participant explains:

> I include what I do for a living and even put out there that I have a disability only because if I didn't and then mentioned it to them, I would think they weren't getting to know me because of my disability.

Another participant explains how he feels about disclosing his impairment in online dating sites: 'It's a lot easier than going to a bar or a social mixer because those whom respond to you know your disability and haven't rejected you because of it.' One participant indicated that meeting others who would be accepting of impairment was a motivating factor for engaging in online dating: 'to meet people where you are accepted for who you are, whatever your disability.' Other factors that influenced disclosure included beliefs in being honest and positive feelings about their impairment in relation to their sense of self. Consider the following quotes: 'I believe in honesty and have no problem whatsoever disclosing my disability'; and 'I don't mind because I am very confident. I'm beautiful, educated, independent, and very humorous.'

While some were confident and had a positive view of self-identity, others felt compelled to disclose their impairment online because it was apparent offline. Consider the following quotes: 'My disability is obvious to anyone that meets me so I see no point in not disclosing'; 'I'm a quad. I cannot hide that fact'; and 'I have CP. My right side is affected and so is my speech. I have always been honest so not have someone say that I didn't disclose that info at the start.' In responding to a prompt that asked participants to describe what influenced them to withhold or disclose their disability, one participant explained: 'if the interaction moves from initial inquiry to possible meeting.' Despite having the option to conceal their impairment, these responses indicate that some disabled people with visible impairments feel compelled to disclose on online dating sites, especially if there is a possibility of meeting offline. These responses resonate with Seymour and Lupton's findings about the importance of reinstating the body online and suggest that online interaction does not occur independently from offline experiences. While the body may be absent in digital space, consideration for extending interaction offline prompted a number of participants to reveal and situate the embodied aspects of themselves. These responses challenge Dobransky and Hargittai's view of anonymity by alluding to the importance of meaningful interaction in which impairment is an accepted attribute as opposed to superficial interaction that is only sustained as long as impairment is concealed.

Contested bodies desired: the devotee phenomenon

While the question of what to reveal and conceal presents an issue for all online daters, for disabled people disclosing impairment can raise unique issues and challenges. For a number of female participants in this study, a barrier cited concerned encounters with devotees. In describing the barriers she encounters in online dating sites, one female participant wrote the following:

> Men who say they are divorced, but are not. Running into a lot of devotees, there are no men in my area, the response is low and I think that is because the disability; the men who respond are often devotees.

While those who mentioned devotees indicated that they are a barrier to online dating, one female participant implied that they could be a last resort to avoid loneliness: 'I've met devotees. They like women who can't move. They are strange but if you have no one they are better than nothing I guess.' This response alludes to the notion that disabled people, like non-disabled people, desire companionship and seek to avoid being alone.

Among the male participant responses there was no mention of devotee encounters. However, for one male participant who used a disability dating site, the question of whether he considered himself a devotee or whether others considered him a devotee presented an issue:

I have disclosed the matter of my recently diagnosed chronic illness in some of the sites, but the data I find most difficult to disclose is actually the question of whether to call myself a 'devotee' or not, since I do not think it fairly describes me and it lends itself to most stereotypical and unfair characterizations, not to mention terrible prejudice on occasion.

This quote illustrates the social tensions surrounding devotees. The devotee phenomenon has stirred much debate among the disabled community. Some women consider devotees 'disgusting fetishists', while others welcome the sexual way in which their bodies are desired (Solvang 2007, 51). The devotee desire is a complex phenomenon, but one that is important to consider in the context of disability and online dating. The Internet provides greater opportunity for devotees to connect with disabled people, especially those who use disability dating sites. Depending on their level of disclosure and how they feel about devotees, this can have a profound impact on their online dating experience. Taken together, the participants' responses about devotees shed light on how disclosing impairment and re-instating the 'lived body' in disembodied digital space influences the types of encounters that occur and how one experiences online dating.

Overall experience dating online

Despite encountering barriers including cost, geographic distance, and lack of face-to-face interaction, participants reported several advantages to online dating, which included privacy, ability to communicate more effectively, feeling more at ease, and finding people more accepting of their impairment. According to one participant: 'meeting online is sometimes much easier to start a conversation. It is less intimidating to some degree and allows you to speak freely and let your guard down.' Another participant shared a similar view and explained that, when engaging in online dating, 'you open up more to the other person and you get to know them quite quickly.' These responses resonate with Joinson's argument that the Internet facilitates disclosure, suggesting that for some disabled people online dating may enable a level of interaction with others to a degree that is not possible offline not because the Internet enables them to conceal their impairment, as Dobransky and Hargittai suggest, but because it enables them to feel more comfortable disclosing their impairment.

When asked to describe their overall experience dating online, participant responses reflected a wide range of views from frustration and disappointment to satisfaction and success. Several participants claimed that they developed a committed relationship with someone they had met online and credited online dating for their success in finding a partner. One participant compared his online experience to his offline experience:

I'm 45 years old and I've had a few offline dating experiences. The internet was a godsend. Offline I was rejected 99.9% of the time, except in bathhouses where men only wanted sex and didn't ask questions. Online I was able to find a partner whom I've been with for the past 4 years.

Others who were less successful in finding a partner expressed frustration and attributed their lack of success to their impairment:

I always say that I have a disability and I have been unsuccessful in this search for a date for 8 years now. So I say I feel that my disability is a put off, but I can't change the fact that I have a disability.

While it is unclear from this response whether impairment was a factor that contributed to lack of success, the participant's perception that it was seems to suggest that the embodied experiences of prejudice which occur offline can emerge in the online environment. In digital space, where the body is absent, the question of how much to reveal and conceal presents an issue. While disabled people vary in their views on disclosure and in how they disclose impairment to other online daters, the rationale behind these choices are guided in the hope of achieving meaningful relationships and acceptance.

Conclusion

Traditionally, the body has represented a fixed basis of identity (Barney 2004). Barney (2004) suggests that a medium that facilitates interaction without the presence of the body diminishes physical attributes as a marker of identity. This paper has attempted to illustrate that the embodied/disembodied dichotomy that has been traditionally used to distinguish offline and online interaction is blurred in the online dating environment, especially for disabled people. In the online dating environment, disabled people are forced to confront their impairment and self-identity in a manner that is atypical in offline interaction. For those with visible impairments, especially, the opportunity to project any other identity than that which is perceived and determined by others seldom occurs during initial face-to-face interaction. Despite the Internet's capacity for concealment, the embodiment of impairment does not vanish in digital space. Rather, it often becomes a source of anxiety whereby the individual is confronted by a heightened sense of awareness of their impairment at a time when they most want to appear desirable in order to attract a partner.

This paper suggested that expanding the parameters of the social model is important as information technology is altering how we interact with others as well as how we conceptualize spatial environments. Thinking about the social model in relation to the 'bodily point of view' of disabled people is helpful for understanding how disabled people perceive and construct their self-identity online. The emergence of mobile digital devices in recent years has altered the way people access information, and how technology and space intersect to create information environments (Baym 2010; Elliott and Urry 2010). The recognition that wireless technology reconfigures particular spatial constraints and boundaries means that interactions which take place both online and offline are no longer separate and distinct but mutually shaped. Thinking about impairment within the context of the 'lived body' and of disability as simultaneously experienced is necessary for thinking about the politics of identity and how it is constructed and presented in digital space.

The encounters occurring in 'disembodied' digital space signal a shift in how people are pursing intimate relationships and how they situate and present themselves in digital environments. An emerging trend in online dating is virtual dating. Virtual dating advances beyond the conventional textual and image-based dating sites in that they are designed to enable users to interact through avatars (digital representations of self) in computer-simulated environments that resemble typical dating venues. For disabled people, the use of avatars may further highlight the embodiment of impairment, calling into question the process involved in reinstating the 'lived body' online by constructing an aesthetic and digital representation of self. The scope of this study examined how disabled people construct and present their self-identity and negotiate disclosure of impairment within conventional online dating sites. Future research that continues in this tradition might extend this study on disability and online dating to examine disability and virtual dating.

Acknowledgements

The author wishes to thank John Thompson and Martin Hand for their helpful comments on earlier drafts.

References

Barney, D. 2004. *The network society.* Cambridge: Polity.

Baym, N. 2010. *Personal connections in the digital age.* Cambridge: Polity.

Cooley, C.H. 1998. *On self and social organization.* Ed. H.-J. Schubert. Chicago: Chicago University Press.

Dobransky, K., and E. Hargittai. 2006. The disability divide in Internet access and use. *Information, Communication and Society* 9, no. 3: 313–34.

Elliott, A., and J. Urry. 2010. *Mobile lives.* London: Routledge.

Galis, V. 2011. Enacting disability: How can science and technology studies inform disability studies? *Disability & Society* 26, no. 7: 825–38.

Giddens, A. 1991. *Modernity and self-identity: Self and society in the late modern age.* Cambridge: Polity.

Goffman, E. 1959. *The presentation of self in everyday life.* New York: Penguin Books.

Hall, S. 1996. Who needs identity. In *Questions of cultural identity,* ed. S. Hall and P. du Gay, 1–17. London: Sage.

Hardey, Mariann. 2008. The formation of social rules for digital interactions. *Information, Communication & Society* 11, no. 8: 1111–31.

Hardey, Michael. 2004. Mediated relationships: Authenticity and the possibility of romance. *Information, Communication & Society* 7, no. 2: 207–22.

Harter, S. 1997. The personal self in social context. In *Self and identity: Fundamental issues,* ed. R.D. Ashmore and L. Jussim, 81–105. Oxford: Oxford University Press.

Harter, S. 1999. Symbolic interactionism revisited: Potential liabilities for the self constructed in the crucible of interpersonal relationships. *Merrill-Palmer Quarterly* 45, no 4: 677–703.

Hughes, B., and K. Paterson. 1997. The social model of disability and the disappearing body: Towards a sociology of impairment. *Disability & Society* 12, no. 3: 325–40.

Joinson, A.N. 2001. Self-disclosure in computer-mediated communication: The role of self-awareness and visual anonymity. *European Journal of Social Psychology* 31: 177–92.

Lawson, H.M., and K. Leck. 2006. Dynamics of internet dating. *Social Science Computer Review* 24, no. 2: 189–208.

Mead, G.H. 1967. *Mind, self and society: From the standpoint of a social behaviorist.* Ed. C.W. Morris. Chicago: University of Chicago Press.

Miller, D. 2011. *Tales from Facebook.* Cambridge: Polity.

Oliver, M. 1990. *The politics of disablement.* London: MacMillan.

Rheingold, H. 2000. *The virtual community: Homesteading on the electronic frontier.* Cambridge, MA: MIT Press.

Rosen, D.L., N.A. Cheever, C. Cummings, and J. Felt. 2008. The impact of emotionality and self-disclosure on online dating versus traditional dating. *Computers in Human Behavior* 24: 2124–57.

Schlenker, B.R., and B.A. Pontari. 2000. The strategic control of information: Impression management and self-presentation in daily life. In *Psychological perspectives on self and identity*, ed. A. Tesser, R.B. Felson, and J.M. Suls. Washington, DC: American Psychological Association.

Seymour, W., and D. Lupton. 2004. Holding the line online: Exploring wired relationships for people with disabilities. *Disability & Society* 19, no. 4: 291–305.

Solvang, P. 2007. The amputee body desired: Beauty destabilized? disability re-valued? *Sexuality and Disability* 25: 51–64.

Strauss, A., and J. Corbin. 1998. *Basics of qualitative research: Techniques and procedures for developing grounded theory*. 2nd ed. London: Sage Publications.

Watson, N. 2002. Well, I know this is going to sound very strange to you, but I don't see myself as a disabled person: Identity and disability. *Disability & Society* 17, no. 5: 509–27.

Whitty, M.T. 2008. Revealing the 'real' me, searching for the 'actual' you: Presentations of self on an Internet dating site. *Computers in Human Behavior* 24: 1707–23.

Yurchisin, J., K. Watchravesringkan, and D. Brown McCabe. 2005. An exploration of identity re-creating in the context of internet dating. *Social Behavior and Personality* 33, no. 8: 735–50.

'I know, I can, I will try': youths and adults with intellectual disabilities in Sweden using information and communication technology in their everyday life

Rebecka Näslund[a] and Åsa Gardelli[b]

[a]Department of Business Administration, Technology and Social Sciences, Luleå University of Technology, Luleå, Sweden; [b]Department of Arts, Communication and Education, Luleå University of Technology, Luleå, Sweden

This study introduces how technology and humans are part of relationships that influence agency among people with disabilities. It aims to focus attention on the use of, and access to, information and communication technology (ICT), and agency among youths and adults with intellectual disabilities. The study draws on empirical research conducted with youths and adults with intellectual disabilities, as well as staff at a day centre. It shows that by drawing upon interests, previous experiences, and cooperating in ICT activities the participants' agency changed. Also, it shows how disability is relational and how it can be influenced by ICT. An interdisciplinary approach is adopted to interpret the findings and to explore: How do people of different ages with intellectual disabilities experience the use of ICT in their everyday lives? Are people with intellectual disabilities able to influence their level of activity by using ICT? And if so, in what ways?

Points of interest

- This article deals with use of, and access to, information and communication technology (ICT), and agency among youths and adults with intellectual disabilities in Sweden.
- Additionally it illustrates how disability is influenced by ICT; and with ICT being used as an example, it shows how people with intellectual disabilities can develop agency through support from others during sessions with ICT.
- It also introduces how people with intellectual disabilities are able to influence their levels of activity and agency by using ICT, and the ways in which this is done.
- By working with ICT tools and relating it to their own interests, the agency of the participants was further developed.
- Another importance issue for agency to develop by using ICT is to relate the use to the experiences of the participants.

Introduction

The focus of this article is on how technology and humans are part of relationships that influence agency among people with disabilities. Extensive research exists that focuses on how, from various perspectives, information and communication technology (ICT) is used by adults, youths, and children. Some of this research deals with disability and ICT, and focuses on online community discussions among people with disabilities (Anderberg 2007), while other research explores Internet use among people with mobility/physical disabilities who are familiar with computers (Anderberg and Jönsson 2005). Harris (2010, 429) conducted research that aimed: '… to explore the challenges, barriers and facilitators to acceptance and acceptability of advanced technological devices designed to assist and support independent living'. When it comes to research focusing on the use of ICT among adults and young people with disabilities, some of it focuses on the digital exclusion (Watling 2011), the circumstances that causes ICT to be socially inclusive or exclusive, and equally on the relation between ICT, identity and social relations for youths with blindness and partial sight and youths with mobility disabilities (Söderström 2009, vii). Still other research focuses on ICT and children with disabilities, the experiences, and expectations of ICT of the parents of children with disabilities (Lindstrand 2002, abstract), ICT, children with disabilities, and equal opportunities in school from the perspective of parents and children with disabilities (Brodin 2010, abstract), social relations, ICT and empowerment among people with intellectual disabilities (Renblad 2003, abstract), differences in impressions of the meaning of mobile phones in everyday lives among young people with mobility disabilities and young people without disabilities, and mobile phones' influence on youths' lives (Söderström 2011, abstract). Research also exists, such as that carried out by Moser (2003), which focuses on adults with disabilities (relating to traffic accidents), and how they become disabled and live with disability.

Compared with previous research, our study aims to focus attention on the use of, and access to, ICT, and agency among youths and adults with intellectual disabilities. Defining disability is a bit complicated according to Vehmas, Kristiansen, and Shakespeare (2009). In this article the young and adult participants are presented as people with intellectual disabilities. By wording the participants in this way, there is a risk of categorising people as belonging to a special group based on some intrinsic factor such as their individual characteristic (in this case, intellectual abilities). However, in our definition of the participants as people with intellectual disabilities, all of the participants are active agents who encounter with intellectual disabilities in their everyday lives. We take the everyday practices of their lives as the starting point rather than locating them as people with a characteristic of being intellectually disabled.

The article focuses on how technology and humans are part of relationships that influence what access to and use of ICT becomes as well as opening up for ways to talk about the relation of ICT, disability, and agency from the viewpoint of the user's everyday life. The research draws on empirical research through observations, diary notes, video recordings, photographs, drawings, and interviews among youths and adults with intellectual disabilities, as well as staff at a day centre. An interdisciplinary approach is adopted to interpret the findings and explore the research questions: How do people of different ages with intellectual disabilities experience the use of ICT in their everyday lives? Are people with intellectual disabilities able to influence their level of activity by using ICT? And if so, in what ways?

ICT, disability, and agency

The current study draws on work within disability studies, science and technology studies, pedagogy, and health sciences. More specifically, it relates to disability as the interrelation between the individual and the wider society. Thus, we are interested in what Gustavsson, Tøssebro, and Traustadóttir (2005, 33) regard as a relational model of disability. This implies that disability is seen as a social construction which gets life in relationships between individuals, as well as in interactions between the individual and the wider society (Gustavsson, Tøssebro, and Traustadóttir 2005, 33). This suggests, as Shakespeare (2006) explains, that impairments and disability are relational rather than dichotomous. More specifically he says: 'By relational, I mean that the disability is a relationship between intrinsic factors (impairment, etc.) and extrinsic factors (environments, support systems, oppression, etc.)' (Shakespeare 2006, 57). The relational model can be seen as evolving from the earlier debates around the meaning of disability. Disability was earlier seen as caused by medical or psychological limitations and as such located within the individual, leading to the medical model of disability (Vehmas, Kristiansen, and Shakespeare 2009). In relation to this way of thinking, the social model evolved. It regards disability as having come into existence by the wider environment (Oliver 1996, 32). The relational model is a further development around the concept of disability. According to Shakespeare, it is difficult to draw a clear boundary between impairment and the disability (Shakespeare 2006, 36). It is of importance to take bodily differences and limitations as well as the surrounding environment into consideration when one explores disability.

Additionally, as a way to explore the relation between agency, disability, and technology, we strive to bring together the relational model of disability (Shakespeare 2006) with the actor-network theory (ANT) approach (Galis 2011; Law 1992, 1999; Moser 2003; Söderström 2009, 2011). For Shakespeare, disability cannot be separated as belonging to any inner or other characteristic but gets its life in the encounter between the human and the surrounding environment. This in turn is also in line with ANT, which is a theoretical approach that evolved as part of the research field of sociology of science and technology during the early 1980s (Galis 2011, 830; Law 1992, 381). According to Söderström (2011, 94): 'This perspective refuses to make *a priori* distinction between entities and actors, or define in advance what kind of entities might be granted agency and explanatory force'. For advocates of ANT, agency, for instance, gets its life as consequences of relations between the individual/society, and humans/non-humans (cf. Law 1999). Thus, according to Law, entities take shape as consequences of their associations with other entities (Law 1999, 3–4).

By working with Shakespeare's definition and ANT, it is possible to explore everyday experiences of disability, impairments, and interactions of the body with the wider environment (cf. Galis 2011). The relation between ICT and disability is not a given but is a consequence of encounters, relationships between humans and non-humans. This means that the researcher is interested in the ways disability is enacted in everyday practices of life, by interactions between the body, technology and the wider society, and as such the body, technology, and the surrounding play mutual parts (Galis 2011). This way of exploring disability and ICT can also be related to the concept of agency. Remember that when one works with these approaches, one as a researcher does not either focus solely on the body nor solely on technological artefacts, nor on the wider society. Instead, the analysis is on situations in which encounters between bodies, artefacts and culture enables or disables the ways agency gets its life (Galis 2011, 830). Thus agency is similarly to disability, a simultaneously biological, material, and semiotic phenomenon. It gets enacted in everyday lives, in encounters between bodies, technologies, and the wider society. It is, as Moser states:

> ... agency is not a capability or property that belongs inherently in some exclusive human bodies. First, in addition to humans, many things act, and are attributed agency. And second, many things act together, as agency is made possible and emerges in practices and activities that precisely link many and heterogeneous actors and elements. (Moser 2003, 158)

In the concept of agency we include the notion of subjectivity. We are inspired by Moser, who sees subjectivity in the following way: 'Likewise, subjectivity, by which I understand a location of knowing, thinking and consciousness, is not seen as an inner essence but as a relational effect.[117] It is shaped in particular ways and made possible in local material arrangements' (Moser 2003, 31). For Moser, subjectivity is not limited to the human body and mind. Instead, it comes into existence as part of relationships between various kinds of actors, practices, technical aids, carers, and policy documents, and so forth (Moser 2003, 181). For us, agency and subjectivity are created as part of people's interaction with other humans, technology, and various practices. Thus, the relation between ICT and disability is not given but is a consequence of encounters, and relationships between humans and non-humans. So, in summary, it is in everyday practice that the actors (the participants, the surrounding environment, the staff, and ICT) encounter and it is in these encounters that disability and agency get their lives.

We also argue for the fruitfulness of using the salutogenic theory and the construction 'sense of coherence' as developed by Antonovsky (1987) when tracing agency and subjectivity. The salutogenic perspective recognises the world as meaningful and predictable, and focuses on wellness factors that cause good health rather than on risk factors that cause illness or disease. Sense of coherence includes three components: comprehensibility, which refers to a belief that that life is consistent and makes sense; manageability, which is a belief that you have the ability to take care of things and that things are under your control; and meaningfulness, which is a belief that life is emotionally worthwhile and meaningful.

As a way of exploring agency and subjectivity we also work with the concept of the level of 'the zone of proximal development' as developed by Vygotsky (1978). This concept can be explained as the distance between the actual development level the person is in and the level of the possible development that could be activated through problem-solving, during the guidance in collaboration with more capable people. It is about developing abilities that have not yet matured but which are in a process of maturing. Vygotsky contends that people live in a context and that knowledge is developed in relationship to our social surroundings. A central argument of Vygotsky is that all people are active and creative and that all people are constantly developing and changing.

Moreover, we are interested in tracing how access and use come into existence and what is involved in order for them to appear. Technology is part of our everyday lives and can, in various ways, affect disability (Brodin and Lindstrand 2003; Harris 2010). Gardelli's research shows that, for the person with disabilities (the participants in her study), use of ICT was a way '… to be someone, to tell, to be seen, to mean something for someone else, to be important and to have a task …' (Gardelli 2004, 220; our translation). Her research also shows that it was not primarily disability, but rather '… technological problems around aids, economic causes, absence of support, problems with authorities and to have enough of time in everyday life as disabled …' that influenced whether the participants continued or discontinued their use of ICT (Gardelli 2004, 223; our translation). Research carried out by Näslund (2009, abstract) highlights, among other things, how pupils with intellectual disabilities live with disabilities and their consideration of disabilities and technology. Another focus of Näslund's research is on how disability becomes entangled with technology and the wider society.

Besides exploring the relation between access and use of technology, we focus on the attitudes and expectations of the surrounding having meaning for people's development (Rosenthal and Jacobson 1968). If one does not put demands on or expect something from a person, it can become a self-apparent prophecy (Merton 1968) and the person is taught to become passive. Brodin (1991) shows how important it is as to what kind of expectations the surrounding has on people with disabilities; and, according to her, expectations on people with disabilities are often low.

Methods and materials

This article is based on a secondary analysis of already collected data that have been previously presented in Gardelli and Johansson (2008) and Näslund (2009). From a re-reading of the studies we became interested in exploring: How do people of different ages with intellectual disabilities experience the use of ICT in their everyday lives? Are people with intellectual disabilities able to influence their level of activity by using ICT? And if so, in what ways?

The sample for this study is based on six youths aged 15–20 years and five adults aged 40–60 years. These two groups were chosen due to research earlier presented in this article, which has omitted a discussion of the relationship between ICT and disability and agency. The youths consisted of five boys and one girl: all of them went to special schools designed for pupils with intellectual disabilities; and they all had access to ICT in various forms, mobile phones, computers, and the Internet (Näslund 2009). All of them participated in various social activities. The youths all lived at home at the time of the study. The adult participants consisted of three men and two women: all of them had a severe intellectual disability; some of them were unable to communicate verbally, while others could. Some of the adults additionally had difficulties with mobility (Gardelli and Johansson 2008).

We were aware, similar to other researchers, of the importance of ethics when conducting social research (Codex 2011; Hammersley and Atkinson 1995; Kvale 1997; Miles and Huberman 1994). When the studies among the youths were set up, the researcher contacted the teachers and the headmasters of the school, and informed them and the other members of staff about the study (Näslund 2009, 47). People with intellectual disability and with difficulty to communicate verbally can often have problems themselves to give their consent to participate in a project.

From an ethical standpoint, this was solved in each case by informing the parent/ trusteeship about the project objectives and training purposes. The school distributed a letter with information about the study and a form of letter of consent to the parents and the pupils (Näslund 2009, 47). Parent/trusteeship of the adults was also giving their oral and written consent for participation. In order to avoid the participants being identified, they were presented in the final report by fictitious names, and their ages were given to the nearest even decade. With regard to staff participation, they had the choice to do so or not. The studies have been evaluated by ethical reviews.

The materials and methods drawn upon in this article are based on observations, diary notes, video-recordings, photographs, drawings, and interviews with youths and adults with intellectual disabilities, as well as staff at a day centre. As a way to get more knowledge of the youths' access and use of ICT, field notes from participant observations and semi-structured interviews were used (Adler and Adler 1994; Flick 2002; Fontana and Frey 1994; Mason 1996; Yin 1994). Additionally, during the interviews with the pupils, they also drew pictures (Näslund 2009, 55). When talking about their pictures, the pupils' views of the computer were linked to the use of technology since most of them talked about using computers for entertainment (playing games), writing, retrieving information, and interacting and communicating with others in virtual ways (Näslund 2009, 85).

The adults' activity ability was documented during the project by the staff, who had responsibility for the respective participant (Gardelli and Johansson 2008). In order to be able to compare the possible development of abilities over time, an estimation of the level of performance of the activity with a computer, both at the start of the project and subsequently, was conducted. A template created by the project leader was used in the actual project as an additional aid. The staff's own observations were documented in diary notes after the training sessions, with descriptions and interpretations of the participants' levels of activity, together with possible signs of development. Video-recordings were conducted at the first training session and continuously during the project time. A digital camera was used in order to photograph the participant in various situations and settings. Photographs were also taken of the staff and other people who the participants were familiar with. The documentation formed a basis for the description of a participant's activity ability at the end of the project.

The analysis of the empirical material was inspired by a qualitative approach. Additionally, the analysis draws upon the relational model of disability (Gustavsson, Tøssebro, and Traustadóttir 2005; Shakespeare 2006). Also, as a way of exploring disability and agency, we analysed our material in relation to the work done by Shakespeare (2006) and by scholars following the ANT approach (Galis 2011; Moser 2003; Söderström 2009, 2011). The analysis is inspired by the work of Galis (2011), Moser (2003) and Söderström (2009, 2011) concerning the relationship between the body, technology and the wider surrounding's interactions and its relation to agency. As a way to trace changes in activity levels, the analysis is inspired both by the work of Antonovsky (1987) (the salutogenic theory) and Vygotsky (1978) (theory about the zone of proximal development). The analysis was based on a secondary analysis of already collected data. We read our previous analysis with the purpose of finding some common text units. Structural themes were then subsequently analysed by applying a thematic approach, evident in the material, as well as methodological and theoretical approaches from the study. We returned to our own individual analysis and consideration of the material, followed by a conversation about themes, in which we differentiated between those that related to each other and those that differed. The themes we drew upon were: how people of different ages with intellectual disabilities experience the use of ICT in their everyday lives and the ways in which they are able to influence their levels of activity and agency by using ICT.

Results and concluding discussion

Agency and its relation to experiences of ICT

Agency became visible throughout the study in various ways. One instance was when we explored the previous experiences of ICT among the participants. All of the participants had various experiences of using ICT in their everyday lives before as well as during the studies. For the younger participants, their previous experience mostly involved playing games and communicating; whereas for the adults who had no previous experiences of ICT, the study increased their ways of communicating and their level of activity. Most of the youths used the Internet and mobile phones while some of them had virtual friends who they communicated with via chatrooms (Näslund 2009). For Anders, who was in his 20s, previous experience played an important part in his interaction with the computer. While having difficulties with using the mobile phone based on limited experience, he liked to work with pictures and change their settings in various ways when he worked with the computer (Näslund 2009, 74). Thus, he expressed that while interacting with mobile technology he felt he needed more practice, but when interacting with computers he felt more confident.

The experiences also became related to disability. For instance, the young participants' disabilities interacted with their ways of using and accessing ICT in the sense that they used, for instance, specific functions (the spelling function) in Word as a way for them to write correct Swedish (Näslund 2009, 79). All of the youths used software such as Word, Internet Explorer, and Windows media player. All of the youth participants had previous experiences of computers and as such no problems could be seen with the applications and programs. This was related to their interest in and experiences of technology generally. As mentioned previously, all of them also had experience of technology (computers, mobile phones) at home. Many of the educational programs that the adult participants used were not designed for adults with intellectual and perceptual disabilities (Gardelli and Johansson 2008, 25). They were designed for children, with pictures of children and with childish voices. Thus, a need exists for the programs to be developed and take into consideration the age of the users. The programs should be created with adult voices, have short clear instructions and simple adult symbols with clearly defined motifs and clean backgrounds.

The staff also contributed to the software that was used and enabled the students with possibilities to work with the computer. They supported the participants in their use of ICT by allowing them to dwell deeper into their own interest when interacting with the technology (Näslund 2009, 77). For instance, one of the youths had a special interest in subways. With teachers supporting him in his interest, drawing upon previous experiences, he started to send emails to people working with subways in the capital area and corresponded with them about his interest.

Five adults with disabilities participated in the project, during which they had the opportunity of learning to use computers (Gardelli and Johansson 2008). None of the adult participants had used a computer before the project started. They all had difficulties with communication and some of them behaved somewhat passively; they also often rejected interplay, and some of them often gave the impression of being insecure. During the study the adults, in cooperation with the staff, acquired tools for increasing their level of activity and communication by using ICT. Some of them, who often wanted to do the same things and were reluctant to try new activities, found a new interest by using a computer. The activity with the computer supported their ability to act and express themselves. Their understanding of images developed as well as the understanding of the use of images in general for communication purposes. In the interaction with ICT, the adult participants gained tools to communicate with, where they could express their thoughts and emotions through images. Through the use of digital images, the aim was to raise the awareness of the participants and to show emotions without destructive manifestations.

As the results show, drawing upon previous experiences and creating experiences are a way to support agency to come into life among people with disability. Similarly to Galis (2011), Moser (2003), Shakespeare (2006), and Söderström (2009, 2011), our study has shown that agency and disability come to life in everyday practices. The result shows that technology, individuals, and groups are part of the construction of the perceived social realities. ICT, disability, and agency are part of constant ongoing processes, reproduced by people who act on their interpretations and their knowledge of such processes in relation to technology. As mentioned previously, the result highlights the importance of drawing upon the users' experiences when using ICT. We recommend that using computers and supporting the participants to use it in a way that is part of their everyday lives will enable it to be used more frequently.

Agency and its relation to level of activity

The results additionally show that, besides drawing upon experiences when using technology, ICT enables changes in the level of activity to take place. There was hope in the project for the adults that their interaction with ICT would increase their degree of alertness and arouse their interest and willingness to be active (Gardelli and Johansson 2008). The sessions with ICT were used to try different methods to develop understanding of the relationship of cause and effect. Through computer use, the participants got the opportunity to improve their sensory-motor skills through the use of different methods that required precision. Furthermore, the use of the computer increased their motivation to try new techniques. By using ICT in the project, the adults also increased their self-esteem, belief in themselves, and their abilities.

While most of the youth participants used the computer on their own, all of the adult participants learned how to use the computer with the assistance of staff and all of them also developed their abilities during the duration of the project. They developed a goal-oriented use of the hands, with a control mode she/he was comfortable with. For example, Mikael's ability to take initiatives regarding activities, answering, and asking for help when not being able to solve a task improved. He started to take initiative, showed what he wanted to do, and showed what kind of control mode he wanted to use. He began to use both hands in a more varied manner. Per, another of the adult participants, also increased his ability to take initiative, and improve self-confidence through at each session, choosing control mode, games, programs, and pictures. The awareness of his own ability was increased by being able to perform more tasks on his own, such as switching on the computer, printer, headphones, and inserting CDs as well as choosing the right symbol on the desktop. By using different control modes and gradually increasing the degree of difficulty from the touch screen to control mode, his functioning and the ability to control his arm with precision improved. When the participants gained control of their actions and revealed an increased understanding of the technology, the motivation and the urge to act increased. For example, Kalle, another of the adults, started to take initiative and make his own choices. Before the project, when Kalle was offered to try out new things and the staff asked if he wanted to do an activity, he often said: 'do not know, cannot, have never tried' (Gardelli and Johansson 2008, 18). During the project he became more secure and dared to give expression to his frustration. He developed a strong interest in exploring things and increased his desire to find strategies and solutions. His concentration, awareness and strength were noticeably increased. At the beginning of the sessions he had the strength to be active for about 15–20 minutes, but after the project he had the ability to be active for an hour or longer. The staff, who were familiar with each of the participants, considered that the result of the ICT project exceeded their expectations.

Our study shows that the participants' activity level increased in relation to ICT and social actors such as friends, family, and staff. Thus, people with intellectual disabilities experience the use of ICT in their everyday lives as part of relationships to other humans and to technology. Moreover, disability is also part of relations between humans and technology. In line with Gustavsson, Tøssebro, and Traustadóttir (2005), Moser (2003), and Shakespeare (2006), our study illustrates that disability is relational. Thus, when using ICT with the right tools, some of the participants' abilities were altered. While previously having limitations in communication abilities, ICT tools and relationships with the staff enabled changes in ways of expressing oneself. It is important to stress that all actors involved (the participants, ICT, and staff and other actors) are all mutually important for this to take place. Similar to an ANT approach, our study illustrates that agency gets its life in everyday lives, in encounters between bodies, technologies, and the wider society (cf. Galis 2011; Moser 2003). Similarly to Moser (2003), we argue that agency as well as disability is not something that is located solely in the human body. Thus, all the participants in our study were able to act in various ways due to them being part of human and non-human relations represented in various forms of practices.

The study illustrates that people with intellectual disabilities are able to influence their abilities by using ICT. They were using ICT to study, communicate, and have fun as well as for developing their inner capabilities. Thus when the participants used the computer they were able to see that they could predict what was going to happen and were also able to understand what was happening around them. They additionally showed that when using technology they had the necessary abilities to take care of communicating, searching for information, and thus things were manageable and within their control. Another aspect for the participants was that the computer encouraged them to believe that things in life are interesting and that using computers is worthwhile and that there is a good reason to care about what happens when using computers. These findings are in line with Antonovsky's

(1987) and Vygotsky's (1978) work concerning how the level of activity can change and that it is important to search for ways to develop one's abilities. Thus, we would like to stress the importance of using ICT as a way to take advantage of the various levels of activity.

Agency as networking and cooperation

Besides drawing upon previous experiences and using ICT as a way to develop levels of activity, networking and cooperation also played a vital part. The computers for the youngsters were related to having fun and as something with which to occupy oneself during spare time (Näslund 2009, 77). However, for some the computer was also used as a means for communicating, writing, and searching for available occupations on the Internet as well as searching for information about particular interests (Näslund 2009). So, in a way, the computer enabled them to network with the wider society.

The cooperation between the adult participants and staff in interaction with ICT were of central importance to the project, as was the sense of security the participants felt when they received help (Gardelli and Johansson 2008). Each session with ICT was built on communication and interaction with new technology, and this inspired and motivated the participants to act and use their abilities in meaningful way. Britta, one of the female adults, experienced an increased awareness of her abilities and started to make her own decisions regarding what kind of control mode she wanted to use, such as the touch screen, operator mode, and keyboard. A central factor for a positive development was that the participants could experience meaning and mutual trust through cooperation (cf. Gunnarsson 1990; Reilly 1974). In the cooperation between participants and staff it was also important for the staff to believe that the participants were capable, and to distribute that sense to her or him (cf. Brodin 1991; Merton 1968). Anna, another of the female adults, started to make her own decisions to talk about what she wanted to do and in what order (Gardelli and Johansson 2008). She increased her concentration and patience.

The attitudes and expectations of the social environment are important for people's development (cf. Rosenthal and Jacobson 1968). The results of our study show that it is important to explore the kind of expectations one has regarding people with disabilities. If one does not put demands or expect something from a person with or without disabilities it can lead to a self-fulfilled prophecy, and the person is thereby taught to become passive. The expectations regarding people with disabilities are often low. Sandvin et al. (1998) argue that it is vital that the social environment allows people with intellectual disabilities to try out alternative strategies to master their lives.

During the ICT sessions it was important that the staff could reflect over their ways of meeting the participants as well as the way they acted (e.g. to give the participants time to think and wait for a reply and not to do things for the participants that she/he herself/himself could perform). This could also depend on observation, providing attention, stimulation, motivation, encouragement, and guidance in the activity. In the interplay between Britta and the staff, her understanding of taking turns was developed and she could wait both for her turn and assistance (Gardelli and Johansson 2008). Her patience increased considerably; for instance, her ability to wait while the computer and programs started. She became more aware of what happened on the screen and improved her ability to coordinate her eye and hand movements. As a way of capturing the interplay, video documentation became important. Each part of the filming was studied in the project group with an analysis and interpretation of changes in the abilities in order to support the participant at all times regarding the right level of development. The video documentation captured the staff's way of instructing and teaching, and could make them aware of different ways of acting. When watching the video documentation it became apparent to the staff that they sometimes were too quick to help, gave too much information or repeated an instruction rather than wait for a reply or an initiative from the participant.

The development of people with intellectual and multiple disabilities might imply that they can need several years of training to become independent in their use of ICT. It became apparent that the pedagogy and the ways of interaction used by the staff with the participants had a great influence on the latter's development and ways of acting. That the participants developed alternative ways of interacting with the ICT was most probably due to the fact that the staff supported and encouraged it. The results show that accessing and using the computer does not mean that one is sitting solely alone in front of the computer. Instead, by interacting with other people, staff, classmates, and other adults in the peer group, the use of computers becomes part of a community project. The importance of cooperation and networking is very vital to develop agency by the use of ICT.

Conclusion

ICT has meaning for the everyday lives of people with and without disabilities. In this paper we have opened up possibilities of talking about the relationship between ICT, agency, and disability from the perspective of interplay with youths and adults with disability. Moreover, we showed how technology and humans are part of relationships that influence access to, and use of, ICT, disability, and agency. The article shows how people of different ages with intellectual disabilities experience the use of ICT in their everyday lives. This study showed that ICT can make a contribution to the development of agency for people with intellectual disability. More specifically, it was shown by working with ICT tools and relating it to their own interests and previous experiences that the participants' agency was influenced. It was also shown how people with intellectual disabilities were able to influence their levels of activity, their agency, by using ICT, and the ways that this was done. Finally, our study has shown how agency among the participants was developed by support from others, through cooperation, and networking during ICT activities.

References

Adler, P.A., and P. Adler. 1994. Observational techniques. In *Handbook of qualitative research*, ed. N.K. Denzin and Y.S. Lincoln, 377–92. Thousand Oaks, CA: SAGE Publications.

Anderberg, P. 2007. Peer assistance for personal assistance: Analysis of online discussions about personal assistance from a Swedish web forum for disabled people. *Disability & Society* 22, no. 3: 251–65.

Anderberg, P., and B. Jönsson. 2005. Being there. *Disability & Society* 20, no. 7: 719–33.

Antonovsky, A. 1987. *Unraveling the mystery of health: How people manage stress and stay well*. San Francisco, CA: Jossey-Bass.

Brodin, J. 1991. *Att tolka barns signaler: Gravt utvecklingsstörda flerhandikappade barns lek och kommunikation* [To interpret childrens' signals: Play and communication in profoundly mentally and multiply disabled children]. PhD diss., Univ. Stockholm.

Brodin, J. 2010. Can ICT give children with disabilities equal opportunities in school? *Improving Schools* 13, no. 1: 99–112.

Brodin, J., and P. Lindstrand. 2003. *Perspektiv på IKT och lärande för barn, ungdomar och vuxna med funktionshinder* [Perspectives on ICT and learning for children, youths and adults with disabilities]. Lund: Studentlitteratur.

Codex. 2011. *CODEX – regler och riktlinjer för forskning. Humanistisk och samhällsvetenskaplig forskning* [CODEX – rules and guidelines for research. Humanities and Social Sciences]. http://www.codex.uu.se/forskninghumsam.shtml.

Flick, U. 2002. *An introduction to qualitative research.* 2nd ed. London: SAGE Publications.

Fontana, A., and J.H. Frey. 1994. Interviewing: The art of science. In *Handbook of qualitative research*, ed. N.K. Denzin and Y. Lincoln, 361–76. Thousand Oaks, CA: SAGE Publications.

Galis, V. 2011. Enacting disability: How can science and technology studies inform disability studies? *Disability & Society* 26, no. 7: 825–38.

Gardelli, Å. 2004. *'Det handlar om ett värdigt liv': Människor med funktionshinder införlivar IKT i sina vardagliga liv* ['It is about having a worthy life': People with disabilities use information and communication technology in their daily life]. PhD diss., Luleå University of Technology.

Gardelli, Å., and A. Johansson. 2008. *Datoranvändandets betydelse för vuxna personer med utvecklingsstörning* [The importance of using computers for adult people with intellectual disabilities]. Report FoU Norrbotten 2008:47. Luleå: Kommunförbundet Norrbotten.

Gunnarsson, S. Olof. 1990. *Kommunicera är nödvändigt* [To communicate is necessary]. Solna: Sipu.

Gustavsson, A., J. Tøssebro, and R. Traustadóttir. 2005. Introduction: Approaches and perspectives in Nordic disability research. In *Resistance, reflection and change: Nordic disability research*, ed. A. Gustavsson, J. Sandvin, R. Traustadóttir, and J. Tøssebro, 23–44. Lund: Studentlitteratur.

Hammersley, M., and P. Atkinson. 1995. *Ethnography: Principles in practice.* London: Routledge.

Harris, J. 2010. The use, role and application of advanced technology in the lives of disabled people in the UK. *Disability & Society* 25, no. 4: 427–39.

Kvale, S. 1997. *Den kvalitativa forskningsintervjun* [The qualitative research interview]. Lund: Studentlitteratur.

Law, J. 1992. Notes on the theory of the actor-network: Ordering, strategy and heterogeneity. *Systems Practice* 5, no. 4: 379–93.

Law, J. 1999. After ANT: Complexity, naming and topology. In *Actor network theory and after*, ed. J. Law and J. Hassard, 1–14. Oxford: Blackwell Publishers.

Lindstrand, P. 2002. ICT is the answer – but what is the question?: Parents of children with disabilities: Their thoughts, experiences, and expectations of information and communication technology (ICT). PhD diss., Stockholm Institute of Education.

Mason, J. 1996. *Qualitative researching.* London: SAGE Publications.

Merton, R.K. 1968. *Social theory and social structure.* New York: Free Press.

Miles, M.B., and A.M. Huberman. 1994. *Qualitative data analysis: An expanded sourcebook.* Thousand Oaks, CA: Sage.

Moser, I.B. 2003. Road traffic accidents: The ordering of subjects, bodies and disability. PhD diss., University of Oslo.

Näslund, R. 2009. Bringing actors together: ICT, disability and pupils in special school. Licentiate diss., Luleå University of Technology.

Oliver, M. 1996. *Understanding disability: From theory to practice.* New York: St Martin's Press.

Reilly, M. 1974. *Play as exploratory learning: Studies of curiosity behavior.* Beverly Hills: Sage Publications.

Renblad, K. 2003. Empowerment: A question about democracy and ethics in everyday life: ICT and empowering relationship as support for persons with intellectual disabilities. PhD diss., Stockholm Institute of Education.

Rosenthal, R., and L. Jacobson. 1968. *Pygmalion in the classroom: Teacher expectation and pupils' intellectual development*. New York: Holt, Rinehart and Winston.

Sandvin, J., M. Söder, W. Lichtwarck, and T. Magnusson. 1998. *Normaliseringsarbeid og ambivalens: Bofellesskap som omsorgsarena* [Normalization work and ambivalence: Communities as care arena]. Oslo: Universitetsforlaget.

Shakespeare, T. 2006. *Disability rights and wrongs*. London: Routledge.

Söderström, S. 2009. Ungdom, teknologi og funksjonshemming: En studie av IKTs betydning i dagliglivet til ungdommer som har en funksjonsnedsettelse [Young people, technology, and disability]. PhD diss., Norges teknisk-naturvitenskapelige universitet.

Söderström, S. 2011. Staying safe while on the move: Exploring differences in disabled and non-disabled young people's perceptions of the mobile phone's significance in daily life. *Young* 19, no. 1: 91–109.

Vehmas, S., K. Kristiansen, and T. Shakespeare. 2009. Introduction. In *Arguing about disability: Philosophical perspectives*, ed. K. Kristiansen, S. Vehmas, and T. Shakespeare, 1–11. New York: Routledge.

Vygotsky, L.S. 1978. *Mind in society: The development of higher psychological processes*. Cambridge, MA: Harvard Univ. Press.

Watling, S. 2011. Digital exclusion: Coming out from behind closed doors. *Disability & Society* 4: 491–5.

Yin, R.K. 1994. *Case study research: Design and methods*. 2nd ed. Thousand Oaks, CA: SAGE Publications.

Implants and ethnocide: learning from the cochlear implant controversy

Robert Sparrow

Centre for Human Bioethics, Faculty of Arts, Monash University, Clayton, Australia

This paper uses the fictional case of the 'Babel fish' to explore and illustrate the issues involved in the controversy about the use of cochlear implants in prelinguistically deaf children. Analysis of this controversy suggests that the development of genetic tests for deafness poses a serious threat to the continued flourishing of Deaf culture. I argue that the relationships between Deaf and hearing cultures that are revealed and constructed in debates about genetic testing are themselves deserving of ethical evaluation. Making good policy about genetic testing for deafness will require addressing questions in political philosophy and anthropology about the value of culture and also thinking hard about what sorts of experiences and achievements make a human life worthwhile.

Implants and ethnocide: learning from the cochlear implant controversy

In Douglas Adams' *Hitchhiker's guide to the galaxy* books, experienced hitchhikers make use of a remarkable invention, the 'Babel fish', to assist them in their quest to see the galaxy for less than 30 Altairian dollars a day (Adams 1979). When inserted into a person's ear the Babel fish converts sound waves to brain waves, thereby allowing its owner to understand the speech of the aliens they meet in their travels. In a characteristically jaded aside Adams observes that, by making it possible for people from different cultures to understand each other, the Babel fish was responsible for more conflicts than any other invention in human history (Adams 1979, 50). Whether Adams' cynicism about the benefits of universal communication is justified or not, the 'Babel fish' turns out to be a useful imaginary device to allow us to understand the past and present controversy over the use of a medical device – the cochlear implant (Doe 2007). Consequently, thinking about the Babel fish may also assist us in thinking through the lessons of the cochlear implant controversy for the next challenge facing health policy-makers and others concerned with the flourishing of deaf persons: the impact of genetic, and especially prenatal, testing for deafness.

Cochlear implants are medical devices designed to serve as a (partial) cure for certain types of deafness. They are distinguished from ordinary hearing aids by the fact that a portion of the device is surgically implanted into the middle ear of the recipient. This electrode stimulates nerve endings in the inner ear, allowing the implantee to perceive sound even in cases where the cause of deafness is dysfunction in the middle ear (Copeland and Pillsbury 2004; National Institute on Deafness and Other Communication Disorders 2008).

The development of the cochlear implant has been widely hailed as an example of medical progress, with its inventors receiving both public acclaim and financial rewards (Cochlear Limited 2006, 2007a, 2007b). People are therefore often surprised to learn that some people with the very condition that the implant is designed to cure greeted its invention with less enthusiasm (Barringer 1993; Doe 2007; Edwards 2005; Lane 1994; Lane and Grodin 1997). A significant portion of persons who are deaf understand themselves to be members of a minority cultural group ('Deaf culture'), defined by their use of a signed language rather than individuals defined by a disability (Davis 2007; Dolnick 1993; Edwards 2005; Kauppinen 2006; Ladd 2002, 2006; Lane 1984, 1992, 1994; Lane and Bahan 1998a, Lane, Hoffmeister, and Bahan 1996; Mundy 2002; Padden and Humphries 1988).[1] Members of various Deaf cultures have been especially critical of the implanting of cochlear implants into young deaf children (Barringer 1993; Lane and Bahan 1998a; National Association of the Deaf 1993, 2; Silver 1992) – a policy recommended by some in the medical profession in order to maximise the amount of time children have to get used to the implant and to learn to understand spoken language with it (Balknay, Hodges, and Goodman 1996; Balkany et al. 2001; Copeland and Pillsbury 2004).

I should make it clear that I am not a member of a Deaf culture and write here as a professional philosopher with research interests in the areas of multiculturalism and technologies of human enhancement. This article is, therefore, intended as a rational reconstruction and examination of an argument that might support claims that are often attributed to Deaf critics and not as advocacy for any particular position 'on behalf of' Deaf culture. In order to understand why some Deaf persons might object to the use of the cochlear implant in young children it helps to consider the following hypothetical scenario.

Imagine that you are a member of a minority linguistic community. You might think of yourself as a Native American in the USA or as a non-Han ethnic minority in mainland China. In the not-too-distant past, members of your community have been imprisoned and tortured for daring to use their own language. Perhaps in response to the persecution they have faced in the past, members of your group tend to be fiercely proud of their cultural community. Despite this, members of your community face a number of profound social and economic disadvantages. It is harder for them to complete their education, find a job or achieve the level of material success that is typical of members of the larger community. In part, this is because they are subject to morally pernicious discrimination from members of the dominant community. However, it is also the predictable consequence of being a minority surrounded by another culture whose members speak a different language.

These disadvantages seem especially disturbing when one considers the prospects of young children. Whereas older persons at least have the benefit of a cultural pride that affirms the values of the options they do have and discounts the value of the options they may have missed, young children appear to face only the prospect of a lifetime of disadvantage.

Government officials, doctors and social workers have come up with a solution for the difficulties facing these children – they will provide all the young children born into this community with Babel fish. With the fish in their ear these children will have no problem understanding and speaking the majority language. As a result, they will be able to avoid the disadvantages facing those who speak only the minority language and they may even, if they wish, become fully integrated into, and members of, the majority community. Cynics amongst your community note that those who are most enthusiastic about the Babel fish are the doctors and researchers who produced them and who stand to profit substantially from the sale of each fish.

It must be said at this point that there are three important disanalogies between the scenario I have just described and the case of the cochlear implant: existing implants are nowhere near as effective as the imaginary 'Babel fish' at facilitating cross-cultural communication; deafness is arguably an organic dysfunction of the human organism regardless of whether it is also a condition or marker of cultural identity; the next generation of potential members of the Deaf culture are born to parents who are members of another culture. These (greatly) complexify the issue in ways to which I will return in a moment.

In the meantime, I want to consider how one might feel about the government's policy in the scenario described above. The introduction of the Babel fish, even if motivated by concern for the opportunities available to the children, is likely to be extremely destructive to the culture of which they otherwise would have been members. While use of a Babel fish will not prevent these children from learning the language of their parents, it *is* likely to greatly reduce the probability that they will use it as their first language in adulthood or teach it to their children. Within two generations, then, the size of this minority culture is likely to be greatly reduced. As the community of people who use the language grows smaller, the opportunities for those within it grow fewer and the social disadvantages they face larger. This in turn increases the incentives for the next generation to learn the majority language and leave the minority culture behind. Over the longer term, this policy is likely to result in *ethnocide* – the destruction of a people's culture. This may appear as an attack on one's very identity, in so far as this is connected with one's membership of a group with a historical past and an imagined future.

Not only is this policy likely to lead to the destruction of the culture, it also seems to involve a profound lack of respect for it. Thinking that the problems facing these children can be solved by providing them with a Babel fish undervalues what they are being encouraged to leave behind and what is threatened by their doing so. It is also insensitive to the fact that the source of the 'problem' is the relative size and social power of the two groups. If history had turned out differently it might have been the (current) majority cultural group that would be facing cultural extinction. A policy of assimilation based on the use of the Babel fish seems to claim as a right for the majority group a privilege it has as a result of historical accident.

Finally, there is something disturbing about the nature of the intervention – the physical alteration of the capacities of the bodies of children through the insertion of the Babel fish – being used to promote integration into the majority culture and the role of scientists and doctors in advocating and facilitating it. A medical technology is here being used to advance a cultural agenda – a scenario that brings to mind some of the worst abuses of medical authority in the past.

Of course, with important caveats noted above, this is the likely story of the eventual impact of the cochlear implant. Deaf people use signed languages with all the complexity, structure and communicative power of spoken languages (Vermeerbergen 2006). Deaf communities around the world have their own signed languages, as well as distinct cultural institutions, such as Deaf clubs, churches, sporting groups, etc.

(Edwards 2005; Goodstein 2006; Ladd 2002; Lane, Hoffmeister, and Bahan 1996). [Some] Deaf people are proud of their heritage and very conscious that, in the past, Deaf persons have been persecuted, imprisoned and punished for using their own languages (Kauppinen 2006; Ladd 2002, 2006; Lane 1992, 1994). They are all-too-aware that a reduction in the numbers of people using signed language threatens the long-term survival of their culture. Some Deaf people have also objected strenuously to medical practitioners interfering in the bodies of young children in the service of a cultural ideal (Barringer 1993; Doe 2007, 4–5; Dolnick 1993; National Association of the Deaf 1993). It is no wonder then that some Deaf critics have been extremely critical of the use of cochlear implants in young children and have even accused advocates of implantation of complicity in ethnocide (Balknay, Hodges, and Goodman 1996, 748; Barringer 1993; Dolnick 1993; Edwards 2005; Lane and Grodin 1997; Silver 1992).

Before one might reach any conclusions about the ultimate strength of these objections, however, we need to return to consider the three disanalogies, between the imaginary scenario I have been describing and the case of the cochlear implant, to which I referred above.

The first disanalogy derives from the fact that, despite dramatic improvements in the performance of the implants since they were first developed, cochlear implants are nowhere near being a real world version of the imaginary 'Babel fish'. Outcomes after implantation vary widely, with the factors contributing to the development of high levels of speech perception and language use after implantation, other than age of implantation and mode of comunication prior to implantation, still poorly understood (Kubo, Iwaki, and Sasaki 2008; O'Donoghue, Nikolopoulos, and Archbold 2000; Taitelbaum-Swead et al. 2005). Some individuals who receive an implant may still need to rely on lip reading and clever guesswork in order to communicate with oral language users (Crouch 1997; Lane and Bahan 1998a). Moreover, there is a danger that parents of implanted children will fail to expose them to sign language after they have received an implant, either because they believe this to be unnecessary because they expect their child to become fluent in spoken language using the implant or in the belief that exposure to Sign will reduce the incentive for their children to work at the difficult task of learning to use the implant (Edwards 2005, 913). Children who do not learn to hear and speak using the implant may therefore end up deprived of the benefits that arise from exposure to sign language from an early age for deaf children (Lane and Bahan 1998a). As a result, the policy of promoting cochlear implantation in young children risks repeating the history of past policies of forced cultural integration wherein children were taken from one culture and prevented from learning its language but were also effectively denied the opportunity to assimilate into another culture (Wilson 1997). It may lead to children not becoming full members of the Deaf *or* hearing cultures. This may result in children having fewer opportunities for a flourishing life than if they had remained members of the Deaf culture.

The inability of implantation to guarantee full membership of the hearing culture greatly strengthens the case against cochlear implantation in young children (Crouch 1997). At the very least it shows that implantation must be accompanied by exposure to, and education in, signed language in order to insure against the possibility that the child will be left 'between' cultures (National Association of the Deaf 1993). If pursuing implantation reduces the exposure of children to signed languages and establishes a significant risk of their being left between cultures then this may establish an all-things-considered case against implantation. However, this argument against implantation relies on an empirical claim about the (lack of) effectiveness of the implants, which is likely to weaken as the implants improve. At some point, this argument against implantation is likely to collapse entirely.

Perversely, the limitations of existing implants have also contributed significantly to reducing the controversy about cochlear implants. A number of accounts resolve the controversy by insisting that cochlear implants are not a threat to Deaf culture because implantees will continue to sign and to participate in the social life and institutions of the Deaf (Christiansen and Leigh 2006, 368; Doe 2007; Murray 2006; National Association of the Deaf 2000; Tucker 1998). However, while this may be true as a consequence of the limitations of the current (and previous) generation of implants, again it seems unlikely to remain true as the implants improve. In the long term, this 'pragmatic' solution to the controversy is therefore likely to have significant consequences for the survival of Deaf culture.

The second disanalogy concerns the fact that limitations on the opportunities available to deaf children are not just the result of their being members of a minority linguistic culture, they are also a consequence of these children suffering from an organic dysfunction of their hearing (Levy 2002a, 2007). It might, therefore, be argued that the entire analogy with forced cultural assimilation which I have offered here is misguided (Balkany, Hodges, and Goodman 1998; Charles Berlin, cited in Barringer 1993; Davis 2007; Harris 2001; Tucker 1998). Cochlear implantation is justified not by the desire to expand the opportunities available to these children but in order to enable them to achieve 'normal species functioning' (Balknay, Hodges, and Goodman 1996).

However, this way of understanding the ethical issues around implantation in young children relies upon our being able to set out an account of 'normal species functioning' which grounds a distinction between the moral significance of illness and of suffering due to 'merely social' causes. It may well be possible to set out an account of normal human capacities or normal species functioning by drawing upon an essentially Aristotelian notion of the proper functioning of various organs and, therefore, of the capacities of a normal human organism (Cooper 2007, 569–70; Daniels 1985; Boorse 1975, 1977). What is more difficult, is to explain the moral significance of any such account, i.e. it is difficult to explain why 'normal species functioning' should function as the justification of technological intervention where other barriers to the flourishing of individuals would not. Why should the fact that the limitations on the opportunities available to children in this particular case are due to organic dysfunction justify a policy that one would not think appropriate as a response to (for instance) racism or simply membership of a minority culture (Lane and Bahan 1998a)?

One possible answer is to argue that the reduction in welfare and/or loss of opportunities associated with less-than-normal human capacities is so extensive and so resistant to amelioration by anything other than medical approaches that normal health acquires moral significance by defining a baseline of opportunity that we should attempt to ensure is available to everyone (Daniels 1985). However, if the ultimate justification for a concern for normal species functioning refers to its effects on the welfare and/or range of worthwhile opportunities available to individuals then such concern is vulnerable to the possibility that particular deviations from normal species functioning need not result in deprivations of these goods. Some Deaf persons may argue, plausibly, that they experience no negative impacts on their well-being or regrets due to the unavoidable loss of worthwhile opportunities from being deaf (Cooper 2007; Edwards 2005; Lane and Bahan 1998a). Moreover, it is clear that medical treatment is not the only way to ameliorate any negative impacts on well-being or restrictions on opportunity experienced by the Deaf by virtue of their circumstances.

Arguments for the normative force of this baseline are also undercut by the sensitivity of accounts of what is normal to historical and technological circumstances. One needs to be conscious of the fact that the idea of a 'normal human' body has often been deployed in the defence of discrimination and hierarchy in the past, around sex, race and sexuality (Gould 1981; Conrad and Schneider 1980). Of course, this doesn't mean that a distinction between normal and abnormal capacities cannot be made, or does not apply in this case, but it should reduce one's confidence in it.

Finally, it is worth noting that Deaf culturalists need not deny that deafness is a departure from normal species functioning. but only that this excludes it from also being a condition of cultural membership (Anstey 2002, 287) and that medical grounds for treatment must always trump concerns for culture (Levy 2002a). Even if one grants that deafness is an organic dysfunction and that it is normally appropriate to endorse the use of medical therapies to restore normal species functioning in cases of organic dysfunction, it is still an open question as to whether or not it is appropriate in this case, given that deaf persons are clearly capable of enjoying an adequate range of worthwhile opportunities and a high level of well-being without medical treatment and given the cultural significance that deafness has for Deaf persons.

Obviously, there is (much) more to be said on this matter; reasons of space prevent me from doing so in this context. If one is inclined to adopt a medical model of deafness then the analogy between cochlear implants and the Babel fish will inevitably appear strained. However, what I have tried to show here is that establishing that deafness is a medical condition is not itself enough to invalidate the analogy.

There is a third disanalogy involved here. Early childhood deafness has a variety of causes and many of them do not involve inheritable conditions. Approximately 90% of children who are born deaf are born to parents who are not deaf (Balknay, Hodges, and Goodman 1996, 748). Providing *these* children with implants will not remove them from their culture because in ordinary cases one would say that 'their' culture was the culture of their parents (Balknay, Hodges, and Goodman 1996, 749). Indeed, where deaf children are born to hearing parents the use of a cochlear implant may serve to facilitate their integration into their (parents') culture (Levy 2007, 140–1; Shannon 1998). In the short term, while implantation remains an unreliable method of achieving this integration, it may be possible to argue that the 'first' language of these children is a signed language and thus that they are appropriately thought of as potential members of the local Deaf culture (Barringer 1993; Dolnick 1993; Lane and Bahan 1998a, 304; 1998b, 312). However, even if one concedes this, it will still be the case that without a cochlear implant these children will not grow up as members of the culture of their parents, who will be denied the opportunity to transmit their culture to their children. The analogy with cultural assimilation of the children of a minority into a larger cultural group only seems entirely appropriate, then, in the case where deaf children born to Deaf parents are encouraged or required to undergo implantation (Levy 2002a, 2007).

Nonetheless, it remains true that the use of cochlear implants in young children threatens Deaf culture in a way which restricting their use does not threaten oral cultures. If deaf children of hearing parents grow up as members of the Deaf culture their parents will be deprived of the pleasures associated with sharing a culture with their children and of the knowledge that their children will both enjoy the benefits of their culture and contribute to its flourishing in the future. However, the parents' culture itself will not be threatened; nor will the parents' capacity to feel confident that their culture will continue to flourish in the future. In contrast, the long-term survival of Deaf culture *will* be severely threatened if deaf children born to hearing parents grow up using spoken languages as a result of the widespread use of cochlear implants (Levy 2002a). Indeed, over several generations the widespread use of cochlear implants in young deaf children is likely to result in the extinction of Deaf culture (Lane and Bahan 1998a, 305).

This asymmetry between the circumstances of Deaf and hearing cultures in relation to deafness and implantation has important implications for the relationship between these cultures. Modern multicultural societies consist of different social groups living alongside one another, as well as different individuals doing so. The interests that individuals have by virtue of membership in these groups can sometimes only be defended by policies that refer to relations between these groups. It is appropriate, then, for Deaf persons – and others sympathetic to their circumstances – to be concerned for the survival of their culture. The policy of encouraging prelinguistic implantation in deaf children, especially if promoted by the government or by members of the majority (hearing) culture, represents an attack on Deaf culture. Members of Deaf culture may have cause to wonder why they should have any loyalty to a society that is dedicated to, or at least complicit with, the destruction of their culture (Lane and Bahan 1998a, 305). If one believes that the state in a liberal society should, as far as is possible, be neutral in relation to disputes between cultural groups (Kukathas 2003; Kymlicka 1992) then this may provide grounds to be concerned about this policy, even if one is not a member of the culture under attack.

Importantly, recognising that there may be grounds for reservations about a policy of encouraging implantation arising out of a concern for relations between social groups does not itself establish that cochlear implants should not be made available to deaf children of hearing parents. The demands of the Deaf community that these children should grow to contribute to the flourishing of Deaf culture need to be placed against the desires of hearing parents of deaf children that their children should grow up within *their* culture (Anstey 2002; Levy 2002a, 2007; Shannon 1998). Resolving the conflict between these competing demands will require addressing some difficult questions in political philosophy regarding the status and moral significance of the claims of culture and their relative weight in relation to the moral demands of individuals (Davis 2007; Levy 2002a). It will also require theorising the relationship between parents, children and the wider society. These are far larger tasks than I can hope to attempt here. My suspicion, though, is that the more implants come to offer a reliable mechanism of integrating deaf children into hearing society the more difficult it will be to resist the demands of hearing parents that they should be allowed to bring their children up in their own culture (Levy 2007). I have argued elsewhere that concern for relations between social groups *might*, however, justify restrictions on the sorts of medical research that should be funded by the state in multicultural societies (Sparrow 2005).

These three disanalogies therefore complexify but do not entirely invalidate the analogy between the case of the cochlear implant and the imaginary scenario involving the 'Babel fish' described above. It remains the case that this scenario may serve as a useful illustration of the issues surrounding cochlear implantation in young children. In particular, it serves to show why a policy of encouraging implantation might be accused of advocating ethnocide and why this policy might also be thought to demonstrate a profound lack of respect for Deaf culture. Whether or not these serious challenges to policy around the cochlear implant outweigh the increased opportunities implantation may offer to deaf children and, in particular, the opportunity it allows deaf children of hearing parents to grow up in their parents' culture is, I believe, the most profound ethical question surrounding the use of cochlear implants.

To a large degree the cochlear implant controversy has been resolved in practice by the fact that large numbers of individual parents are making the decision to implant their children. Deaf institutions – and to some extent each local Deaf culture – are then faced with a choice between maintaining their opposition to implantation and thus risking becoming irrelevant to the needs of large numbers of children with hearing difficulties or welcoming implantees in the hope that they will come to identify with and contribute to Deaf culture, despite their desire to also participate in hearing cultures (Murray 2006, 351–2). Deaf culture is uniquely vulnerable to being forced to make such a choice because in order to flourish it relies on the children of parents who are typically not members of the culture becoming members of Deaf culture. As I noted above, it seems likely that the inability of Deaf cultures to successfully resist the trend towards implantation will have significant implications for the nature of these cultures in the longer term.

Given the contemporary state of the debate it might be thought that the analysis I have provided here can only be of theoretical interest. I hope it is at least that. However, understanding precisely what was at stake in the cochlear implant controversy and the relative merits of the arguments therein may also help us to better understand the issues involved in the next challenge facing the Deaf community and others concerned with health care (and other) policy around deafness – the challenge of genetic testing.

Many forms of deafness are at least partially a result of genetic factors in the affected individuals. Scientists are making rapid progress in understanding the genetic causes of deafness, a task in which they have been greatly assisted by the completion of the Human Genome Project. As a consequence, it is now possible to test individuals for various genes associated with deafness. This may assist them in managing their health care. It may also assist them in making reproductive choices with the intention of minimising – or, for that matter, maximising (see Mundy 2002) – the chance that their children will be born deaf. Genetic testing of adult individuals will allow them to determine the probability that they will conceive a deaf child in a particular relationship (Dillehay and Arnos 2006). Prenatal testing will allow them to determine if a particular pregnancy is likely to lead to the birth of a deaf child and to terminate the pregnancy if they don't like the answer. Finally, preimplantation genetic diagnosis will allow parents who are willing to conceive via IVF to choose whether they want a deaf child or not by selecting some embryos for implantation over others. Given that most prospective parents are not deaf and are likely to want hearing children, the prospect of widespread genetic testing poses a profound challenge to the continued existence of Deaf culture (Murray 2006).

The history of the cochlear implant controversy contains a number of lessons in relation to this challenge (Murray 2006).

The first, and most important, lesson relates to the urgency of the issues. As the history of the cochlear implant controversy shows very clearly, once a technology that offers apparent health benefits to children becomes available, most parents will decide to use it, regardless of subtle costs relating to longer-term considerations about how this might reshape the cultural environment in which their children grow up. The decision to make use of genetic information, once it becomes available, may be even easier to make than the decision to proceed with cochlear implantation (or not), because there is no danger of the child being left 'between' cultures as long as the parents choose a child like them. Thus, leaving the decision up to individuals or to couples is likely to result in a predictable outcome – a dramatic decline in the number of children born deaf and thus of potential members of Deaf culture(s). If Deaf activists or policy-makers want to avoid this outcome then it will be essential to contest the development of the technology or, given that it is arguably already too late to do this, at least the policy of making it available to individuals as a matter of routine (Murray 2006).

The second lesson that may be drawn from my analysis of the cochlear implant controversy is that this policy debate is, at least in part, a question of the relations between social groups and not simply an argument about the rights of individuals. It is the latter too, of course, but there are aspects of what is at stake in this debate that will be obscured if it is conducted entirely as a debate about individual liberty. Thus it is essential that one pays attention to the relationships between Deaf and hearing cultures that are both revealed and constructed in debates around genetic testing and considers the ethics and justice of those relations as well (Sparrow 2008). The force of arguments relating to these relations will depend on the extent to which deaf persons organise on the basis of a (Deaf) cultural identification and argue for respect and equality on that basis.

A third lesson of my analysis, then, is that the strength of possible Deaf objections to policies of routine genetic screening for deafness will depend in part on how one assesses arguments relating to the intrinsic worth of culture (Davis 2007). The hypothetical example of the Babel fish is extremely useful in this context, as it encourages us to imagine a scenario in which a culture is destroyed without any of its individual members being made any worse off. It seems clear to me that the world is a poorer place every time a culture disappears. However, whether the value of culture justifies turning away from policies that would benefit individuals but threaten cultures is a (much) more difficult question. Meeting the policy challenge of genetic testing, then, will require engaging in debates in anthropology and political philosophy about the value of culture, as well as in debates on medical ethics.

However, finally, the history of the cochlear implant controversy shows that the argument that one should understand debates about funding for genetic testing for deafness as a contestation between cultural groups is most compelling if one *doesn't* think that deafness is also a medical condition that restricts the opportunities and experiences open to those who suffer it (Levy 2002b). The public's enthusiasm for the cochlear implant was arguably the result of the appeal of the idea of 'curing deafness' and restoring children (and others) to normal functioning. Similarly, given current understandings about health and disease, the choice between bringing a hearing or a deaf child into the world is naturally understood as a choice between a healthy child and a child suffering from a disease or disorder (Hintermair and Albertini 2005). Ideas about 'normal human' bodies are also likely to play a central role in debates about the use of preimplantation genetic diagnosis because of the possibility that this technology might eventually be used to choose 'enhanced' and not just 'healthy' children (Silver 1999). The idea of the 'normal' has significant appeal as a way of distinguishing between legitimate therapeutic interventions and non-medical eugenic uses of this technology (Fukuyama 2003). Thus, despite the existence of the independent considerations about relations between hearing and Deaf cultures surveyed above, I suspect that it will ultimately prove impossible to resist the drive to test for and eliminate deafness without contesting the medical model of deafness. Developing good policy around genetic testing for deafness – and for other character traits – will require thinking hard about what sorts of experiences and achievements make a human life worthwhile and about the relationship between our ideas about what is normal and the availability of these goods in a world in which we have the power to shape the capacities of those we bring into the world (Hintermair and Albertini 2005; Parens 1995; Sandel 2004). Those who believe that there should be room for the Deaf in this world would therefore be well advised to play an active role in those debates (Dillehay and Arnos 2006).

As I observed at the outset of this paper, Douglas Adams quipped of the Babel fish that improved communication led to as much conflict as cooperation. The history of the cochlear implant certainly includes its fair share of conflict and controversy. My hope is that the analysis I have offered of the issues in this controversy might assist all involved to better understand what is at stake and why each side might hold the positions that they do. This in turn might improve the prospects of cooperation when it comes to the difficult matter of making policy about genetic testing for deafness.

Acknowledgements
Thanks are due to Nicole Kouros and Dylan McCulloch for their assistance in preparing this manuscript for publication.

Notes
1. In what follows I will use capital D as in Deaf to refer to this group and those who identify with it and lower case d deaf to refer to a hearing impairment and individuals who have such an impairment.
2. The National Association of the Deaf famously revised its position statement on implants in 2000. The 2000 statement dropped the strong criticism of the implant contained in the 1993 statement and instead emphasised the importance of parents making informed choices about implants after access to information that should include the experiences and perspectives of deaf persons.

References
Adams, D. 1979. *The hitchhiker's guide to the galaxy.* London: Pan Books.
Anstey, K. 2002. Are attempts to have impaired children justifiable? *Journal of Medical Ethics* 28: 286–8.
Balkany, T.J., A.V. Hodges, and K.W. Goodman. 1996. Ethics of cochlear implantation in young children. *Otolaryngology – Head and Neck Surgery* 114: 748–55.
Balkany, T.J., A.V. Hodges, and K.W. Goodman. 1998. Additional comments: Ethics of cochlear implantation in young children. *Otolaryngology – Head and Neck Surgery* 119: 312–3.
Balkany, T.J., A.V. Hodges, R.T. Miyamoto, K. Gibbin, and O. Odabasi. 2001. Cochlear implants in children. *Otolaryngologic Clinics of North America* 34: 455–67.
Barringer, F. 1993. Pride in a soundless world: Deaf oppose a hearing aid. *New York Times,* May 16, A1.
Boorse, C. 1975. On the distinction between disease and illness. *Philosophy and Public Affairs* 5: 49–68.
Boorse, C. 1977. Health as a theoretical concept. *Philosophy of Science* 44: 542–73.

Christiansen, J.B., and I.W. Leigh. 2006. The dilemma of paediatric cochlear implants. In *The deaf way II reader,* ed. H. Goodstein, 363–9. Washington, DC: Gallaudet University Press.

Cochlear Limited. 2006. Cochlear Limited wins gold in New York. Cochlear Limited. http://www.cochlear.com/PDFs/Announcement_MDEA_June_06.pdf.

Cochlear Limited. 2007a. Cochlear wins 2007 DHL Australian Exporter of the Year Award. Cochlear Limited. http://www.cochlear.com/PDFs/Cochlear_Exporter_of_Year_Nov_2007.pdf.

Cochlear Limited. 2007b. Annual Report 2007. Cochlear Limited. http://www.cochlear.com/PDFs/AR07_Editorial_070921.pdf.

Conrad, P., and J.W. Schneider. 1980. *Deviance and medicalization: From badness to sickness.* St Louis, MO: Mosby.

Cooper, R. 2007. Can it be a good thing to be deaf? *Journal of Medicine and Philosophy* 32: 563–83.

Copeland, B.J., and H.C. Pillsbury. 2004. Cochlear implantation for the treatment of deafness. *Annual Review of Medicine* 55: 157–67.

Crouch, R.A. 1997. Letting the deaf be deaf: Reconsidering the use of cochlear implants in prelingually deaf children. *Hastings Center Report* 27, no. 4: 14–21.

Daniels, N. 1985. *Just health care.* New York: Cambridge University Press.

Davis, L.J. 2007. Deafness and the riddle of identity. *The Chronicle of Higher Education* 53, no. 19: B5–B8.

Dillehay, J., and K. Arnos. 2006. The impact of genetics research on the deaf community. In *The deaf way II reader,* ed. H. Goodstein, 370–5. Washington, DC: Gallaudet University Press.

Doe, L. 2007. Cochlear implants: Are they really a threat to the deaf community? *Deaf Worlds* 23: 1–17.

Dolnick, E. 1993. Deafness as culture. *The Atlantic Monthly* 272, no. 3: 37–53.

Edwards, R.A.R. 2005. Sound and fury; or, much ado about nothing? Cochlear implants in historical perspective. *The Journal of American History* 92: 892–920.

Fukuyama, F. 2003. *Our post-human future: Consequences of the biotechnology revolution.* London: Profile Books.

Goodstein, H. 2006. Preface. *The deaf way II reader,* xiii–xxii. Washington, DC: Gallaudet University Press.

Gould, S.J. 1981. *The mismeasure of man.* Harmondsworth, UK: Penguin.

Harris, J. 2001. One principle and three fallacies of disability studies. *Journal of Medical Ethics* 27: 383–7.

Hintermair, M., and J.A. Albertini. 2005. Ethics, deafness, and new medical technologies. *The Journal of Deaf Studies and Deaf Education* 10: 184–92.

Kauppinen, L. 2006. Our inalienable rights: Global realisation of the human rights of deaf people. In *The deaf way II reader,* ed. H. Goodstein, 10–16. Washington, DC: Gallaudet University Press.

Kubo, T., T. Iwaki, and T. Sasaki. 2008. Auditory perception and speech production skills of children with cochlear implant assessed by means of questionnaire batteries. *ORL* 70: 224–8.

Kukathas, C. 2003. *The liberal archipelago.* Oxford, UK: Oxford University Press.

Kymlicka, W. 1992. Liberal individualism and liberal neutrality. In *Communitarianism and Individualism,* ed. S. Avineri and A. De-Shalit, 165–85. Oxford, UK: Oxford University Press.

Ladd, P. 2002. Emboldening the deaf nation. *Deaf Worlds* 18: 88–95.

Ladd, P. 2006. What is deafhood and why is it important? In *The deaf way II reader,* ed. H. Goodstein, 245–50. Washington, DC: Gallaudet University Press.

Lane, H. 1984. *When the mind hears: A history of the deaf.* New York: Random House.

Lane, H. 1992. *The mask of benevolence: Disabling the deaf community.* New York: Alfred Knopf.

Lane, H. 1994. The cochlear implant controversy. *WFD News* 2/3: 22–8.

Lane, H., and B. Bahan. 1998a. Ethics of cochlear implantation in young children: A review and reply from a deaf-world perspective. *Otolaryngology – Head and Neck Surgery* 119: 297–308.

Lane, H., and B. Bahan. 1998b. Reply to the review: Ethics of cochlear implantation in young children. *Otolaryngology – Head and Neck Surgery* 119: 309–12.

Lane, H., and M. Grodin. 1997. Ethical issues in cochlear implant surgery: An exploration into disease, disability, and the best interests of the child. *Kennedy Institute of Ethics Journal* 7: 231–51.

Lane, H., R. Hoffmeister, and B. Bahan. 1996. *A journey into the deaf-world.* San Diego, CA: DawnSign Press.

Levy, N. 2002a. Reconsidering cochlear implants: The lessons of Martha's Vineyard. *Bioethics* 16: 134–53.

Levy, N. 2002b. Deafness, culture, and choice. *Journal of Medical Ethics* 28: 284–5.

Levy, N. 2007. Must publically funded research be culturally neutral? *Virtual Mentor* 9: 140–2.

Mundy, L. 2002. A world of their own. *Washington Post Magazine,* March 31, W22.

Murray, J.J. 2006. Genetics: A future peril facing the global deaf community. In *The deaf way II reader,* ed. H. Goodstein, 351–6. Washington, DC: Gallaudet University Press.

National Association of the Deaf. 1993. *Cochlear implants: A position paper of the National Association of the Deaf.* Silver Spring, MD: The National Association of the Deaf.

National Association of the Deaf. 2000. *Cochlear implants: A position paper of the National Association of the Deaf.* Silver Spring, MD: The National Association of the Deaf.

National Institute on Deafness and Other Communication Disorders. 2008. Cochlear implants. http://www.nidcd. nih.gov/health/hearing/coch.asp.

O'Donoghue, G.M., T.P. Nikolopoulos, and S.M. Archbold. 2000. Determinants of speech perception in children after cochlear implantation. *Lancet* 356: 466–8.

Padden, C., and T. Humphries. 1988. *Deaf in America: Voices from a culture.* Cambridge, MA: Harvard University Press.

Parens, E. 1995. The goodness of fragility: On the prospect of genetic technologies aimed at the enhancement of human capabilities. *Kennedy Institute of Ethics Journal* 5: 141–3.

Sandel, M.J. 2004. The case against perfection: What's wrong with designer children, bionic athletes, and genetic engineering. *The Atlantic Monthly* 293, no. 3: 51–62.

Shannon, R.V. 1998. Review: The ethics of cochlear implantation in young children. *Otolaryngology – Head and Neck Surgery* 119: 308–9.

Silver, A. 1992. Cochlear implants: Sure-fire prescription for long-term disaster. *TBC News* 53: 4–5.

Silver, L.M. 1999. *Remaking Eden: Cloning, genetic engineering and the future of human kind.* London: Phoenix.

Sparrow, R. 2005. Defending deaf culture: The case of cochlear implants. *The Journal of Political Philosophy* 13: 135–52.

Sparrow, R. 2008. Genes, identity, and the expressivist critique. In *The sorting society,* ed. L. Skene and J. Thompson, 111–32. Cambridge, UK: Cambridge University Press.

Taitelbaum-Swead, R., L. Kishon-Rabin, R. Kaplan-Neeman, C. Muchnik, J. Kronenberg, and M. Hildesheimer. 2005. Speech perception of children using Nucleus, Clarion, or Med-El cochlear implants. *International Journal of Pediatric Otorhinolaryngology* 69: 1675–83.

Tucker, B.P. 1998. Deaf culture, cochlear implants, and elective disability. *Hastings Center Report* 28, no. 4: 6–14.

Vermeerbergen, M. 2006. Past and current trends in sign language research. *Language & Communication* 26: 168–92.

Wilson, R. 1997. *Bringing them home: Report of the national inquiry into the separation of Aboriginal and Torres Strait Islander children from their families.* Sydney: Human Rights and Equal Opportunity Commission.

Cyborg anxiety: Oscar Pistorius and the boundaries of what it means to be human

Leslie Swartz and Brian Watermeyer

Department of Psychology, Stellenbosch University Republic of South Africa

Disabled people have a history of being viewed as not entirely human. In the age of spare part surgery and increasing sophistication of drugs, there are increasing concerns about what it means to be human, and, in particular, in what distinguishes people from machines. These concerns have clear resonance with anxieties about disability, and with disabled people being seen as not human. Oscar Pistorius is a disabled athlete whose wish to compete alongside able bodied competitors is causing great concern and worry that his prosthetic legs may give him an unfair – and non-human – advantage. The case of Pistorius breaks entrenched boundaries and lays bare core concerns in society about disability and the body.

At the heart of much discrimination against disabled people is an idea, explicit or implicit, that disabled people do not qualify to be seen as fully human. Similarly, with the advent of spare part surgery, including prosthetics and organ transplants, there are anxieties about what the boundaries of being an individual human being may be. If, for example, I have in my body the heart of another person, to what extent am I still me? If, furthermore, I am dependant on technology, through a pacemaker or a prosthetic limb, for example, to what extent can I be said to have a human body? When biotechnologies and new genetic engineering techniques allow human tissues to be bought and sold the body becomes more porous, and a site of exchange (Rajan 2006).

In the age of new technologies, including computers, the Internet and biotechnologies, fundamental questions arise regarding the nature of humanness and human consciousness. Turkle (1997), for example, has shown that as computer technologies develop and computers break new boundaries in their ability to 'think', lay definitions of what is distinctive about being a human as opposed to being a machine have had to adapt, and humanness has had to be defined more narrowly (Hayles 1999). Similarly, as research on animal behaviour develops,we have had to rethink what is distinctively human – for example, whereas the attribution of emotions to animals was at one time dismissed as anthropomorphism, it is now accepted that animals do in fact experience emotions once thought of as distinctively human (Masson 1997). The domain of 'exclusive humanness' thus seems to be shrinking.

The disabled body then becomes a particularly interesting site for cultural analysis, as well as cultural projections. Once, people with severe impairments were openly deemed not human and even, in the case of severe mental impairment, labelled as 'vegetables'. Although this stigmatizing discourse is still with us, the disabled body now draws renewed attention, by its difference and otherness, to fundamental questions about what it means to be human. Postmodernity and new technologies summon all to question old received ideas of humanness; disabled bodies draw attention to the shifting boundaries of how people define themselves.

As with other forms of segregation (like the racial 'science' of Nazism and apartheid), the policies of keeping disabled people away from others fulfilled a central function of imposing order on chaos and diversity. Once firmly in the category of disabled (or, for example, 'black' in apartheid South Africa), people whose existence might have been perceived as disturbing or dangerous to others could be controlled through the ascriptions that are made about large categories of people. Control is palpable, notwithstanding the apparently benign nature of these ascriptions, as in 'Disabled people are very brave to bear what they have to bear' or 'People with Down's syndrome are happy and friendly'. Policies of inclusion threaten the order of established categories and remove the comfort of clear boundaries.

As an example of processes of inclusion, disabled sport has made substantial progress over the past few decades and it is no mean achievement that now, for example, the Paralympics are held together with the Olympic Games and gain a large degree of media attention. Occasionally disabled athletes compete alongside their able-bodied peers, for example the South African swimmers Natalie du Toit (who has a leg amputation) and Terence Parkin (who is deaf). In the main, though, disabled athletes compete in their own realm against other disabled athletes, in the name of fair play – in order that those who have bodily impairments are ostensibly fairly matched against those with similar impairments.

What happens, though, when the boundary between disabled and non-disabled is challenged in an unexpected way? Oscar Pistorius is a South African sprinter who runs with prosthetic legs and who now wishes to have the opportunity to compete not against disabled athletes, as he has been doing for many years, but against his able-bodied peers. A series of debates about the fairness of the situation has consequently taken shape. Do Pistorius's legs give him an unfair advantage? If, as one commentator warned, he falls when he runs, will he hurt other athletes? The overall question, at a time when there are many worries about the use of technologies (including doping) in sport, is whether it is fair to say that Pistorius can be seen as an athlete to whose body (like the bodies of his able-bodied competitors) his possible success can be attributed.

The investigations launched carry an earnestness which tells of a situation which has called into question something quite fundamental, quite invisible, about the boundaries between disabled and non-disabled groups. The control described above, rooted in bureaucratic categories and physical segregation, must clearly protect and perpetuate much needed modes of construing the world and ourselves. But what, precisely, are these aspects? What does the case of Oscar Pistorius threaten to destabilize?

'Good' people around the world would, if asked, probably align themselves with a form of 'humanitarian' or 'human rights' discourse of 'inclusivity' surrounding the issue of what qualifies one as human. Of course, we all should have access to basic rights, inclusion and respect by virtue of our simple humanness. Whilst this approach is clearly laudable, it sits oddly with the more apparent, yet perhaps less consciously articulated, mechanisms of social closure which surround us, saturate our media and preoccupy our private moments. These processes occupy the cultural turf of real inclusion and exclusion. Inclusivity and legitimacy here are contingent on the approximation of bodily ideals and on performance, status and association; the neo-liberal pecking order of capital accumulation and the economy of power. What Oscar Pistorius threatens to do is move successfully from one discursive meaning system, where he may be seen to belong, to another. His presence in this discourse, based on personal prowess of a bodily nature, serves to shake the very foundations of the attribution system which maintains the separation as meaningful.

Athletics, quite clearly, is about the body and bodily strivings. As such, the meanings associated with the imperative to bodily perfection, with the obsession to perform, are closely linked to broader cultural ideas regarding bodily ideals and what that signifies within the individual. Athletes, like supermodels, shape and sculpt their bodies, for engagement in, in some sense, a pure form of hierarchization through competing. Myths regarding the virtue associated with bodily perfection are as relevant in the athletic world as in the world of tabloid models, rooted as they are in shared discursive foundations. It is in the nature of these worlds of striving that bodily difference or 'abnormality' has no place. The idealized, mythic valuing of the perfect body, with its associations of personal virtue, carries as its counterpoint the denigration of persons with different bodies. The unspoken assumptions about these bodies, and their inhabitants, relate to undesirability, psychological damage, abjection and failure. Oscar Pistorius finds himself, and is found, on the brink of straddling these binary universes. If he is indeed able – allowed – to do so this may lead to the rendering of catastrophic questions regarding what we are striving for in terms of the attendant virtues of culturally designated bodily perfection. He will have encroached on hallowed ideological territory, where deeply entrenched ascriptions of human desirability and value not only buttress our imaginations within the media, but also provide the meaning system which supports daily strivings and aspirations. The imperative to strive for an image of perfection is not only a cultural one, but also carries a moral aspect. Surely, the place of bodily perfection and desirability we are called to reach for is not a place inhabited by disabled people. Or is it?

The 'cyborg' (part human, part machine) aspect of Pistorius' disability deepens the problem, through opening the way to a treacherous debate regarding what technologies are allowed to be 'used' to achieve inclusivity. Irony is not in short supply here; one only has to turn to the ballooning industry in so-called 'technoluxe' medicine. Here we meet New York women who bring the designer shoes they wish to wear to exclusive podiatrists requesting surgery to 'make my feet look good in these'(Frank 2006). The intersection of bodies and technology for the purposes of gaining inclusion seems to shift the goalposts on many fronts. Yet, the ascription of intrinsic virtue rooted in essentialist 'fairness' lives on. No questions regarding the 'humanness' of such surgical fashion devotees are in evidence.

All of this, though, takes us far from the simple issue of a young athlete wishing to participate in his chosen sport. The International Association of Athletics Federations' (IAAF) somewhat tight-lipped, non-committal response to the issue was based on the idea that there is uncertainty regarding whether Pistorius may be 'unfairly advantaged' by his carbon fibre prostheses. This utterance, surely, exposes the official position on the issue of unfair advantage in paralympic competition as disturbingly unthought through. If there is any reason to believe that Pistorius's prostheses afford him some degree of unfair advantage were he to compete in 'mainstream' athletics competitions – and we are informed that there is – then surely there has been a similar, nay greater, risk of unfair advantage in all of his paralympic competing up to the present. What is being shown up here? Is it the sorry reality that, upon closer scrutiny, the IAAF's attitude towards paralympic competition reflects a laissez faire stance not concerned with competitive rigour? The picture of paralympic athletics which, all too readily, springs to mind on consideration of this issue is a bilious one involving 'participation' being 'the most important part' and the question of who wins prizes being of little relevance. Or does the IAAF simply have undisclosed, or unexplored, difficulties with setting limits in competitive regulation for disabled athletes? Whatever the case, such fuzzy boundaries fall away most sharply at the advent of Pistorius's bid for mainstream participation.

A familiar binary stereotype within which disabled people are snared is that which splits disabled people into two opposing, yet somehow inextricably linked, categories. These are the invalid, dependent, incapable, damaged both inside and out, and the so-called 'supercrip' (MacDougall 2006). The latter is that much celebrated media persona of the disabled person who has 'overcome adversity' in a heartwarming manner and not been restricted by his or her 'flaws', but believes that 'everything is possible' for those who work hard. Naturally these ideas of fairness and reward for hard work are cornerstones of the neo-liberal just world tradition. Both poles of the stereotype of course fail to make it possible to see individual lives, much less conceptualize such issues as disablist oppression and exclusion. Further, all disabled people are oppressed by the imperative to 'overcome' in some superhuman fashion in order to be afforded basic acknowledgement.

At the idealizing pole of the stereotype rests an opportunity for the observer to 'rest assured' that those 'less fortunate' can still, albeit in virtually microscopic minorities, find a sort of inclusion, success and 'ability', in the manner of Al Pacino's character in *Scent of a woman*. This discourse, though, is about some hope of a fantasy redemption from the 'horror' of occupying the bottom-most rung of a social power and desirability hierarchy; it is about a sop to those who may be less fortunate but yet are inspiring. It is definitely not part of this script for one such 'inspiring' character to enter the fray on (at least legally) equal terms and prove himself to be stronger, fitter, better than his well-shaped competitors. Consequently, perhaps, the result is a confused flurry of gatekeeping, not only in top flight athletics but in defence against the cascading implications for body culture and othering which emanate from this peculiar situation.

References

Frank, A.W. 2006. Emily's scars: Surgical shaping, technoluxe and bioethics. In *Surgically shaping children: Technology, ethics, and the pursuit of normality,* ed. E. Parens, 68–89. Baltimore, MD: Johns Hopkins University Press.

Hayles, N.K. 1999. *How we became posthuman: Virtual bodies in cybernetics, literature and informatics.* Chicago, IL: University of Chicago Press.

MacDougall, K. 2006. 'Ag shame' and superheroes: Stereotype and the signification of disability. In *Disability and social change: A South African agenda,* ed. B. Watermeyer, L. Swartz, T. Lorenzo, M. Schneider, and M. Priestley. Cape Town: Oxford University Press.

Masson, J.M. 1997. *Dogs never lie about love: Reflections on the emotional world of dogs.* New York: Crown Publications.

Rajan, K.M. 2006. *Biocapital: The constitution of postgenomic life.* Durham, NC: Duke University Press.

Turkle, S. 1997. *Life on the screen: Identity in the age of the internet.* New York: Simon & Schuster.

Conclusion

Alan Roulstone

In many ways the contributions to this *Special Issue on Disability and Technology* for the journal *Disability & Society,* reflect the longer-run global shifts in disability studies itself (Albrecht, Seelman and Bury, 2001; Brechin et al, 1988; Davis, 2010; Watson, Roulstone and Thomas, 2012). The shift in theoretical framing of technology from a fixative, rehabilitation tool to fundamental building blocks of a more enabling society, reflects the shift away from bodily deficits to the mapping of environmental barriers. As with disability studies more generally, academic frames of reference have shifted from positivist, materialist and abstracted empiricism to a rich amalgam of structuralist, post-structuralist and identity politics theory. More proximate theories have emerged from actor network theory and Science and Technology Studies (STS) to enrich disability studies' writing on technology and suggest that disabled people are not simply acted on by technologies, but that disability, technology and opportunity are each 'enacted' and interactive. Overall, there has been a shift away from technology writing emanating from practice contexts in search of technical solutions (Cornes in Oliver, 1991; Hasselbring and Crossland, 1982; Sidler, 1986; Tinker, 1989) to greater emphasis on the political, philosophical, spatial and psycho-emotional role of technologies (Barnartt et al, 1990; Bowker and Tuffin, 2002; Goggin and Newell, 2003).

A reading of technology articles in the journal *Disability & Society* points to the speed of technological change from the mid-1980s. Back then, technology was meaningful for a very small number of disabled people and was likely to be simple domestic sensor alarms for older disabled people, rudimentary DOS-based computing technology, and most commonly medical devices to aid mobility. The internet or more correctly, the Arpanet was still largely a military technology; while social media was the preserve of a small number of Silicon Valley researchers for example with the development of the Internet Relay Service (IRS) in 1988. Only 20 years later the internet was viewed as a necessity not a luxury, as many more services and payments were web-based. Social media, alongside portable and cheap hand-held technologies, provided the scope to subvert distance and time. Disability, becomes a more complex issue, with greater scope to forge many different identities, some embodied, some virtual. Technologies of prosthesis afford not simply practical tools for living, but fundamentally reframe hybrid or cyborg identity in a way that previous binaries of body and technology, natural and 'man-made' cannot comprehend. It is perhaps not surprising that some of the most cited articles in the journal's history focus on prosthetic identity and potential. For others prosthesis can mean alternatives to social interaction. For example, social learning difficulties such as Asperger and autism can be reappraised where interaction is web-based and not of necessity a 'face-to-face' interaction.

By the 1990s technology, both high- and low-tech, began to be linked to the struggle for independent living globally. In the USA, Ed Roberts, a key figure in the US disabled people's movement was earlier supported to have an iron lung in his university accommodation, challenging assumptions as to the boundaries between medical, education, employment and daily living environments. However, not all disabled people attached to the nascent movement were so wedded to the technology. Erving Zola, for example, viewed technology, or to be more precise technology systems, to be a new form of dependency as there was a tendency he felt to over-technologize solutions for disabled people and to make technology the bearer of new normalisations (Moser, 2006; Zola, 1982). As the *Special Issue* articles make clear, by the 2000s, technology was beginning to risk being seen as a panacea for disabled people, while such analyses often overlooked the way technology was shaped by the very forces it was trying to redefine or subvert. In this way, technology has often been seen as simultaneously enabling and disabling (Roulstone, 1998). Indeed, new technological divides have opened up reflecting pre-existing maldistributions of social goods. The design of technology itself can of course create new exclusions. The development of Windows-based icon environments while a clear development for many, was a major setback for those with visual impairments (Kurniawan and Sutcliffe, 2002). The most promising element of the convergence of the disabled people's movement, new models of disability and technological developments has been the shift away from market-driven to user-led design (Newell, 2003). Similarly the ubiquitous nature of social media affords new forms of bullying and hate which some disabled young people are reporting as hate crimes for the twenty-first century (Smith, 2015). However, social media is also being recognised as having real potential in new forms of activism which relies on rapid flows of information and rallying of interest. Certainly we need to be wary of any simple uni-directional theory of social media as 'bad for' disabled people (Youmans et al, 2012).

The scope and enabling reality of new forms of technology are reflected in the articles that make up this *Special Issue* of the journal. We are aware that these articles speak largely to the minority world. It is to be hoped that in another 20 years' time more articles will have been published to reflect the greater dissemination of technologies in the less wealthy nations. We hope that you enjoy the articles and feel that we have chosen judiciously in formulating this *Special Issue*.

References

Albrecht, G., K. Seelman, and M. Bury. (2001). *Handbook of disability studies*. London: Sage.

Barnartt, S. N., K. D. Seelman, and B. Gracer. (1990). Policy issues in communications accessibility. *Journal of disability policy studies*, *1*(2), 47–63.

Bowker, N., and K. Tuffin. (2002). Disability discourses for online identities. *Disability & Society*, *17*(3), 327–344.

Brechin, A., P. Liddiard, and J. Swain, eds. (1988). *Handicap in a social world: a reader*. London: Hodder and Stoughton.

Cornes, P. (1991). Impairment, disability, handicap and new technology. In M. Oliver, *Social work: disabled people and disabling environments*. London: Jessica Kingsley Publishers, 98–115.

Davis, L. (2010). *The disability studies reader*. London: Routledge.

Goggin, G., and C. Newell. (2003). *Digital disability: The social construction of disability in new media*. Rowman & Littlefield.

Hasselbring, T. S., and C. L. Crossland. (1982). Application of microcomputer technology to spelling assessment of learning disabled students. *Learning disability quarterly*, 80–82.

Kurniawan, S. H., and A. Sutcliffe. (2002). Mental models of blind users in the windows environment. In *Computers helping people with special needs* (pp. 568–574). Berlin: Springer.

Moser, I. (2006). Disability and the promises of technology: Technology, subjectivity and embodiment within an order of the normal. *Information, communication & society*, 9(3), 373–395.

Newell, A. (2003). Inclusive design or assistive technology. In *Inclusive design* (pp. 172–181). London: Springer.

Roulstone, A. (1998). *Enabling technology: disabled work and new technology*. Milton Keynes: Open University Press.

Sidler, M. R. (1986). Impact of technology on rehabilitation. *Occupational therapy in health care*, 3(3–4), 55–84.

Smith, M. (2015). Disability hate crime–a call for action. *Tackling disability discrimination and disability hate crime: a multidisciplinary guide*.

Tinker, A. (1989). *The Telecommunications needs of disabled and elderly people: an exploratory study*. Office of Telecommunications.

Watson, N., A. Roulstone, and C. Thomas. (2012). *Routledge handbook of disability studies*. London: Routledge.

Youmans, W. L., and J. C. York. (2012). Social media and the activist toolkit: user agreements, corporate interests, and the information infrastructure of modern social movements. *Journal of communication*, 62(2), 315–329.

Zola, I. K. (1982). *Missing pieces: A chronicle of living with a disability*. Philadelphia: Temple University Press.

Index

Note: Page numbers in *italics* represent figures
Page numbers in **bold** represent tables